The Rise of the Algorithms

How YouTube and TikTok Conquered the World

John M. Jordan

The Pennsylvania State University Press
University Park, Pennsylvania

Library of Congress Cataloging-in-
   Publication Data

Names: Jordan, John M., author.
Title: The rise of the algorithms : how
   YouTube and TikTok conquered the
   world / John M. Jordan.
Description: University Park, Pennsylvania :
   The Pennsylvania State University Press,
   [2024] | Includes bibliographical refer-
   ences and index.
Summary: "Traces the origins and evolution of online video platforms and how
   their algorithms now engineer human
   behavior, discussing present challenges
   and recommendations for reclaiming our
   online futures"—Provided by publisher.
Identifiers: LCCN 2023047088 | ISBN
   9780271096933 (paperback) | ISBN
   9780271096926 (hardback)
Subjects: LCSH: YouTube (Electronic
   resource) | TikTok (Electronic resource)
   | Internet videos—Social aspects. |
   Online social networks—Social aspects. |
   Algorithms—Social aspects.
Classification: LCC HM742 .J673 2024 | DDC
   302.30285—dc23/eng/20231102
LC record available at https://lccn.loc.gov
   /2023047088

Printed in the United States of America

Published by The Pennsylvania State
University Press,
University Park, PA 16802–1003

10 9 8 7 6 5 4 3 2 1

The Pennsylvania State University Press is
a member of the Association of University
Presses.

It is the policy of The Pennsylvania State
University Press to use acid-free paper.
Publications on uncoated stock satisfy
the minimum requirements of American
National Standard for Information
Sciences—Permanence of Paper for Printed
Library Material, ANSI Z39.48–1992.

Contents

Acknowledgments

My thanks go to the following:

For institutional support, the Syracuse University School of Information Studies, particularly Senior Associate Dean Jenny Stromer-Galley.

For providing key ideas and research outside my area of expertise, my students and colleagues Sarah Bolden, Ellen Simpson, Alex Smith, and Qingyi Wang.

For close, critical readings, Rebecca Davis Kelly, Chris LoRusso, and Steve Sawyer, all at the Syracuse School of Information Studies. Four anonymous university press readers also provided thoughtful, informed, and constructive critiques.

For getting these ideas an audience, Patrick Alexander and Archna Patel at Penn State University Press.

For the gifts of perspective and humor, Bill Petersen and Jamie Thompson.

For knowing when I needed encouragement and when I needed to be reminded that anything clever is only clever once, my brilliant children Douglas, Phoebe, and Walker.

Introduction

Tell me to what you pay attention and I will tell you who you are.
—José Ortega y Gasset, *Man and Crisis*, 1962

Pay attention to what you pay attention to.
—Amy Krouse Rosenthal, Twitter, 2013

The transition from mass media to massively personalized Internet platforms is reshaping the competition for human attention. The powerful and insidious algorithmic wayfinding that Facebook and Google pioneered and TikTok's corporate parent, ByteDance, has so successfully exploited has many implications for culture, for what is made, seen, propagated, and imitated. Given how demographically huge and psychologically powerful these platforms are, their effects embody many paradoxes and contradictions. All of them matter.

Celebrity Is Rewarded yet Ephemeral

Online video has helped thousands of people profit from global name recognition, whether by direct monetization of views, endorsement deals, or ancillary businesses. Twenty-four-year-old Jimmy Donaldson, known online as Mr. Beast, earned $54 million in 2021, in part through videos that cost millions to create. One *Squid Game* reenactment, in which the winner took home $456,000, cost $3.5 million to create (compared to an average of $2.4 million per hour for the Netflix original); 142 million people viewed it in eight days. Donaldson also owns a chain of ghost kitchens and sells organic nutrition bars at Walmart. *Forbes* estimates his net worth at $500 million.[1]

At the same time, online video fame can be fleeting. Many creators speak of being "slaves to the algorithm" insofar as view counts may rise or drop dramatically for no apparent reason. More generally, digital media stress the feeling of what the communications scholar Wendy Chun has termed "the enduring ephemeral," and TikTok's manic velocity of memetic spread embodies this tendency: how many people remember Nathan Apodaca?[2] He was the TikTok star of 2020 who drank cranberry juice on a skateboard, now long forgotten. The volume of uploaded material would seem to be unsustainable: if online video is effectively infinite, everything beyond a minuscule slice of the whole will eventually become invisible.

Both Teenage Dance Videos and a Global Political Crisis

TikTok came to prominence by its lightning-fast popularization of teen culture and of instant memes, in particular. During the 2020 lockdown the service surged to prominence in many parts of the world, usurping Facebook and Instagram in key demographics. Music stars including Lizzo have been catapulted to global fame, everyday teens can get their fifteen minutes in the spotlight, and watch times in many countries continue to rise. Such strong performance confounds the local-global distinction that traditionally characterizes media properties.

But TikTok is built in China by parent company ByteDance and is subject to the requirements of the governing Chinese Communist Party. Security concerns soon came to light: How much of the vast sum of data being collected could be accessed by that government for purposes of surveillance, blackmail, or impersonation? And how might the infectious content-matching algorithm be used to advance China-approved messaging under the guise of light entertainment? Then-president Donald Trump ordered the service banned in the fall of 2020, and while his successor, President Joe Biden, did not advance the proposed remedies, the matter remains unsettled at the time of this book's publication. Numerous states and governmental agencies ban the service from workplace-issued devices, and legislation that would effectively ban the service in the United States has been introduced by Senator Marco Rubio of Florida.[3]

The Road from Cat Videos to Live NFL Streams

Although YouTube launched as a person-to-person video repository, and Twitch (now owned by Amazon) was built to livestream players playing video and board games, both have entered the world of big media. Asynchronous streaming of most entertainment has led to fierce competition among Netflix, HBO, Paramount, Hulu, Disney, and others. Sports, meanwhile, still commands live audiences, and in the United States, no sport is more widely watched (and highly valued by advertisers) than football. In September 2022 Amazon began streaming Thursday Night Football, and in December of that year, Google won the out-of-market "Sunday Ticket" contract for NFL games by outbidding Apple and Amazon for a reported price of $2 billion per year. YouTube launched with the tagline "Broadcast Yourself," which was quietly erased in 2019—a reminder that video platforms have outgrown their now-quaint origins.[4]

Transcending Mass Audience Creation with Targeted Content Distribution

The history of online video illustrates a critically important technological and cultural transition. Media businesses traditionally thrived based on how well they could create content that would gather audiences—and how well they could attract advertisers to pay for access to those audiences. (Music and movies operate slightly differently, but in the same vein.) Mass media such as television and newspapers delivered the same message to millions of people. While there could be some customization of the content—the *Chicago Tribune* city edition differed from suburban editions, and the outstate edition was different yet again—the competition for attention was often won with big draws: telegenic stars, widely read columnists, aggressive newsgathering, and the like.

For Internet platforms, content creation is largely outsourced to segments of the audience. TikTok rewards good dancers, popular makeup artists, or funny people who emerge from the billions of viewers, at least initially. (A star system is emerging, and we will discuss that development in due course.) Thus, unlike Netflix, platforms like TikTok, Twitch, and YouTube don't have to try to pick winners. The consolidation of power shifts from content creation and mass distribution to algorithmic distribution, highlighted by deep personalization at planetary scale. Having machine learning determine what we read and watch, distributing what used to be called user-generated content, shifts power from newspapers and television networks to the digital platforms. These platforms are massively profitable, lightly regulated, and to date largely unaccountable. Consequences, including election disruptions, mass shootings, and horrific harassment, are treated largely as externalities of profitability. The fact that YouTube reacts much more effectively to copyright infringement than to child endangerment speaks volumes.

As has always been the case, cultural tastemakers are among the most powerful individuals in a given era—think William Randolph Hearst, Samuel Goldwyn, Rupert Murdoch. In our time, the transition from human gatekeeping performed by editors, publishers, and producers to algorithmic rationing of promotion has reinvented that taste-making process. In light of online video platforms' scale, and because videos are not indexed and searched like the document-centric World Wide Web, most videos are currently watched on the basis of recommendations derived from *behavioral data* rather than the *content of the video*. The way algorithms promote or fail to promote a given piece of content is extremely important, but very poorly understood outside the platforms.

A Dystopia Born from Optimism

Today's problematic attention economy stands in stark contrast to a particular technological optimism. The computing pioneers responsible for the conceptual and technical foundations upon which the web, and later its platforms, were built shared many aspects of this worldview. Stewart Brand migrated from the Whole Earth Catalog's neo-homesteading ethos at the tail end of the 1960s to early online communities and the tellingly named Electronic Frontier Foundation.[5] Tim Berners-Lee and his coauthors in 1992 articulated the positivist ideal of the World Wide Web:

> You would have at your fingertips all you need to know about electronic publishing, high-energy physics, or for that matter, Asian culture. If you are reading this article on paper, you can only dream, but read on. Since Vannevar Bush's article (1945) men have dreamed of extending their intelligence by making their collective knowledge available to each individual by using machines.[6]

Only six years after Berners-Lee, however, James Katz of Rutgers astutely saw the potential for the web to pollute that stream of knowledge rather than nourish it. Acknowledging that "the Internet and the Web allow for the quick dissemination of information, both false and true," he noted that "unlike newspapers and other media outlets, there are often no quality control mechanisms on Web sites that would permit users to know what information is generally recognized fact and what is spurious."[7] Katz predicted large-scale online mis- and disinformation at least fifteen years before they hit mainstream US culture.

The rapid evolution from Berners-Lee's extreme optimism to the many and profound downsides of ubiquitous connectivity—mental and physical health concerns, the monetization of private life via unmonitored behavioral experimentation, the hacking of democratic institutions, trolls and shitposting, swatting, aggressively nasty harassment of women and ethnic populations—is part of a much more complex story we cannot probe here. The short version, as per the cultural critic Kurt Andersen, is that the Internet age combined with an older distrust of authority (academic, religious, scientific, journalistic) to create what he calls America as Fantasyland.

The first contributing factor "was a profound shift in thinking that swelled up in the '60s. . . . *Do your own thing, find your own reality, it's all relative.*"[8] The second ingredient was the dawn of the information age:

> Among the web's 1 billion sites, believers in anything and everything can find thousands of fellow fantasists, with collages of facts and "facts" to support them. Before the internet, crackpots were mostly isolated, and surely had a harder time remaining convinced of their alternate realities. Now their devoutly believed opinions are all over the airwaves and the web, just like actual news. Now all of the fantasies look real.[9]

Summary

These, then, are the ultimate tensions embodied in the World Wide Web, and in online video. The promises of instantly accessible knowledge, of global connectivity, and of truth shining light on ignorance have been proved to be null and void. Any open Internet discussion turns disgustingly toxic if left unmoderated. Extremists want to post not wedding videos or dating profiles (two early YouTube use cases) but beheadings and mass murder. The increased availability of facts has led to the rise of bold anti-intellectualism and the denial of even basic scientific literacy. Exactly as print did in its early years, online video fuels the wider dissemination of both dogma and heresy. Unprecedented scale has led us to this juncture—10 percent, or even 1 percent, of 3 billion people is a lot of extremists, misogynists, trolls, and foreign agents—and algorithms will have to be a big factor in finding a way out given that human moderation cannot scale to the demand. At the same time, as Tarleton Gillespie of Microsoft Research notes, the platforms have been promoting "the promise of AI" for years. Users, regulators, and investors are presented with an as yet unrealized technological solution to a much more complex and nuanced challenge.[10]

Those algorithms are themselves problematic, however. As humans have uploaded, one at a time, billions of videos to repositories of huge scale, machines are watching us humans watch the videos. Unlike when conducting a Google search, users don't leave the YouTube site or the TikTok app. Accordingly, the computational models are designed to and effective in getting us to stay on the site longer, to "like, comment, and subscribe," and to come back later today and again tomorrow. TikTok usage is evolving rapidly, but one report stated that 90 percent of users checked the app daily, that US users spent thirty-three minutes per day on the service, and that that average US user opened the app eight times every day.[11] We have in our midst not only a powerful new way to communicate but also unseen, unspoken rules of the game manipulating our attention to it. ByteDance, Facebook, and Google are the early leaders in collecting our contributions and making those rules to adjust our behaviors. Amazon, Apple, Baidu, Netflix, and others are near neighbors.

Machine learning about users quickly fuels machine direction of them. As this tendency is more widely realized, familiar questions emerge, as they do with the rise of any new regime. What will people tolerate and when might they rebel? What platform practices will cross some legal, cultural, or emotional line? How will we each individually justify the costs of these platforms related to their benefits? These are the questions the book ultimately attempts to engage.

Chapter Overview

We begin the book with a discussion of the origins of online video. One precondition is intellectual: the emergence of a technical and cultural vocabulary in "Web 2.0" discourse to describe services that became the megaplatforms. Chapter 2 examines the technical challenges that have been posed and solved with varying degrees of success. These challenges include search and recommendation, ad serving, storage, streaming, content moderation, protection of copyrighted material, and the upload process.

Chapter 3 looks at the years of functional evolution that have defined online video. The commercial, legislative, jurisprudential, and computational evolution of content moderation (defining, finding, and removing forbidden material) is one strand. Curation (discovering and elevating the material the service wants viewers to watch) is the other. Together, these processes have in many ways defined the emergence of online video platforms. We also pose some issues for the future, including accountability, regulatory oversight, accuracy, and transparency.

After talking about the emergence and history of the major platforms, we look at what's on offer in chapter 4, which is about learning. Because we learn by imitation, online video is a terrific teacher, whether of ballroom dancing, home appliance repair, makeup technique, or new languages. Teaching is done under a surprising number of auspices, and traditional education providers are lagging at video. At the same time, evolving gatekeeping mechanisms and misinformation campaigns compromise online video's ability to inform and teach.

Entertainment, the topic of chapter 5, is a big part of the story of online video. YouTube, Vimeo, and their kin act as a repository for everything from political speeches to movie clips. They serve as a sort of attic for many cultural artifacts, both widely popular and deeply personal to an individual or small group. Simultaneously, online video defines great swaths of current culture. As of 2021, YouTube was the most popular music streaming service in the United States, India, and France. For every Justin Bieber, who was propelled to global stardom by Usher using YouTube, or Lil Nas X, who built his career on TikTok making "Old Town Road" a sixteen-time platinum seller, there are many millions of amateur entertainers. One finds both Hollywood hits and anonymous piano practices. Self-made stars have emerged in areas from high school sports to fashion to online gaming to social commentary. Meanwhile, millions of videos get views in the single digits. The paradoxical story here is as old as celebrity. The downsides of Internet fame, including parasocial relationships, derive from the mismatch of the human psyche as it confronts the vast scale of the Internet platforms: television invited a person in a studio into a given living room at a given time, whereas TikTok brings a famous influencer into their bedroom and into a viewer's life any time they want.

In chapter 6, we briefly discuss three examples of how changes in technology reshape artistic expression. These examples are Adobe Flash as used in Homestar Runner, the mashup, and the reaction video.

Chapter 7 scratches the surface of the many issues raised by cross-platform migration, coordination, and dissonance. Scholarship knows little of what people do on any given platform, but almost nothing of how people operate across and among multiple ones. Men's rights activists, drill rappers, and beauty vloggers, not to mention the 2012 effort to urge the capture of

African guerrilla leader Joseph Kony using an Internet movie, all illustrate how online video exists within a complex ecosystem. Backchannel communications, memes, noise, cross-promotion, competition, and infrastructure (including payment platforms like Square) all come into play. The biggest issue related to cross-platform behavior is trying to understand how online actions both derive from and influence the offline world. Very little scholarship has even attempted to define or measure what might be called platform ecosystems, the particular and evolving combinations of Facebook, Snapchat, YouTube, LinkedIn, Line, TikTok, Pinterest, and Reddit or some other service that a given user might construct.

Chapter 8 attempts to situate online video. At the end of the day, what do we call it? How do we define it, conceptualize it, regulate it, tax it, subsidize it? In line with this set of cultural functions, another theme of the book relates to how we currently, and might in the future, understand online video as a medium that brings massive value but also puts new demands on regulators, viewers, uploaders, algorithm designers, advertisers, content owners, and others in the vast ecosystem.

Online video is a different kind of text compared to either print or broadcast TV, and new forms of literacy and illiteracy are emerging. Unlike television, where a linear schedule was the organizing principle[12] until the dawn of the streaming era, asynchronous online video is governed by search and, primarily, recommendation, both human and algorithmic. The role of online video in a wider trend toward nostalgia in digital platforms must be noted, particularly in a few of its global variants. The use of online video by displaced populations and in nations recovering from authoritarian rule bears mention. Concluding by investigating the early history of print to look for parallels helps frame online video as a new kind of cultural resource with side effects we should anticipate.

In the conclusion, we begin by looking at 2020 as a marked inflection point in the history of online video. YouTube increased its production of branded content, cracked down on misinformation, and embraced a social change movement more assertively than at any previous time. TikTok, meanwhile, exploded in US popularity among those under thirty, breaking new ground both in algorithmic effectiveness and in the success of a Chinese Internet company outside China. That success, however, spurred a new stage of involvement by the Chinese government in its consumer tech sector, potentially depriving these companies of capital, engineering talent, audience access, payment gateways, and other critical elements in their previous rise to prominence. In mid-2021, the picture suddenly grew blurry for Ant

Group, Tencent, Baidu, ByteDance, and others. Later developments continued these trends, as we will note.

As the opening epigraphs illustrate, we are living in a time when old ideas can be conveyed in new ways. However it is expressed, the newly redefined fight for our attention changes who we are. The lack of human gatekeepers means that any viewpoint can find an audience. A whole discipline known as "brand safety" has emerged as some advertisers seek assurance that their messaging will not appear in proximity to objectionable content. Millions of people are sucked into such content with the promise that "this is what the mainstream media won't tell you." Even the premise of fact-checking has been challenged by the promise of a media landscape in which one consumes only what agrees with their preconceptions, white supremacy and vaccine-induced autism included.

This state of affairs—unprecedented scale created by billions of independent individuals who both upload and watch, managed by generally invisible algorithms—is too huge to plumb, catalog, or otherwise digest. Nonetheless, we need somehow to come to terms with this new chapter in the human condition. As people among us *create* more of what we watch, and algorithms *determine* more of what we watch, the choices that platform companies, regulators, investors, creators, and viewers make both shape and reveal macro social priorities, economics, and cultural tendencies. The book attempts to explore a series of polarities and contradictions. Online video is both inclusive and toxic, global and personal, enduring and ephemeral, mindless and mindful, vast and intimate. That's a heavy agenda, so let's get to work.

1

The Big Picture

On April 23, 2005, a high school friend of former PayPal developer Jawed Karim used Karim's video camera to capture a nineteen-second video of him at the San Diego Zoo. The website Karim cobuilt and to which he uploaded the video—YouTube—started growing at an extraordinary rate shortly thereafter. Bear in mind that neither Facebook nor the iPhone were generally available in 2005. YouTube began life in a now-unrecognizable technology startup environment. There was no cloud computing or app store, and there was little appetite for distributed workforces connected virtually. As a result, YouTube's operating assumptions are important to unearth and to consider.

First, digital video was still new in the consumer market. The technology had only recently become affordable and sufficiently easy to use. Second, YouTube was built as a website, to be viewed on laptop or desktop personal computers via Internet browsers. Computer video windows were new, and they were oriented horizontally to mimic television and movies. Third, the idea of "Web 2.0," Tim O'Reilly's buzzword of the era, was steering innovation toward the notion of the web as a platform, in a computational sense. This phrasing resonated heavily among a reasonably small percentage of the general population but mattered little elsewhere (see charts 1 and 2).

Fourth, rights holders successfully defused the utopian and libertarian components of 1990s Internet politics. Information may have wanted to be free, as the rhetoric went, but property rights dictated that it couldn't be. As a result, automated detection of copyrighted material immediately became a high corporate priority at parent company Google after it acquired YouTube. Hollywood companies threatened to shut down YouTube, in the same way Napster had been shut down, for illegal use of music files, movie clips, or

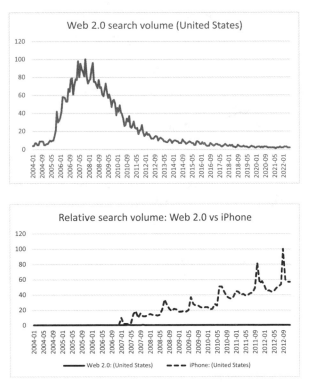

Chart 1 Google Trends data showing relative interest in Web 2.0 as measured by searches over time (June 2007 = 100). Source: Google Trends.

Chart 2 Google Trends data comparing search volume for "Web 2.0" (black) to "iPhone" queries (dashed) (September 2012 = 100). Source: Google Trends.

television recordings, so removing them automatically was imperative. Fifth, social media sharing of videos happened by accident after YouTube's launch; email links were initially the main path for word of mouth. Finally, globalization of online video was evolutionary, with new national sites added slowly under corporate leadership governed by US regulation and equities market expectations. These six themes constituted a design debt, a conceptual inheritance that complicated efforts to innovate after 2005.[1]

Thirteen years later, a Chinese consumer Internet company called ByteDance launched a US version of its short-video service. Brilliantly branded TikTok (the name works in many languages), the app quickly became the world's most downloaded nongame title on the Apple app store. By 2021, the service was watched by 100 million US users per month; total downloads surpassed 2 billion. Contrast TikTok's conceptual and strategic DNA with YouTube's:

- High-resolution digital video capture is a feature of every modern smartphone, of which there are currently about 4 billion worldwide. Video long ago stopped being the province of wealthy Western consumers, particularly among teens all over the world who use it routinely.

- TikTok was built as a mobile app, with vertical full-screen video overlaid with controls. The website is a secondary consideration.
- ByteDance functions as an "attention factory," in the analyst Matthew Brennan's words, rather than a content repository. Like YouTube, Facebook, and similar services, TikTok is a global platform, in a business and social rather than computational sense.
- While automated content moderation to spot copyright and other violations is important, ByteDance's core capability is understanding and manipulating human behavior using machine learning techniques.
- Sharing of videos, via TikTok and other social platforms, is an integral aspect of the service's design.
- ByteDance was conceived of and operates as a global company in a gray area between Silicon Valley libertarianism and the privately conveyed expectations of the Chinese Communist Party.

That journey—from technically complex and topically random video uploads intended for family and friends to an age of five hundred hours of YouTube uploads per minute and social media "influencers" earning $50 million a year—is our concern here. There is no single master arc to this book; the changes we witnessed are wide-ranging and rapid, and they defy a conventional narrative structure. Here are a few of the storylines that emerged.

Unprecedented Scale

YouTube and TikTok are huge by any measure, joining Facebook properties as megascale Internet platforms. Even though TikTok and YouTube historically *create* very little video (though this is changing at YouTube), their *curation* processes for attracting, organizing, promoting, and distributing user-generated content are extremely important. In contrast to print media that is characterized by high costs and resultant gatekeepers who ration scarce production and distribution capacity, online video is a big tent. The volume of contributed video that is available is simply staggering, unfathomable—not to mention uncatalogable—at human scale. The extreme scale of the Internet platforms increases diversity of viewpoints but raises powerful questions about truth, fact, and accuracy. No person could ever read every book in the Library of Congress, but the collection is of a known size and cataloged along consistent and recognizable principles. The vastness of Internet platforms precludes similar comprehension or navigation.

Unlike Facebook, Instagram, and Twitter, neither YouTube nor TikTok is built on a digitized version of an individual's friendship and other connections. While there are ways that each service can tap into a person's "social graph," both rely heavily on recommendation algorithms to put content in front of viewers. The fact that said video might have been created by someone they know or follow is incidental. As TikTok soars to new heights of user enthusiasm and engagement, Facebook's and Twitter's follower-based models lose their competitive advantage, and those companies then move to algorithmic content recommendations that overrule or ignore the social graph. Facebook's market power was based on its status as a giant social network, and TikTok's algorithmic expertise essentially did an end-run around that supposed competitive "moat."[2] TikTok, in short, achieved massive scale without asking or (initially) monitoring who your real-life friends might happen to be.

Let's dig into that extreme scale for a moment. The Pew Research Center analyzed the behavior of select YouTube channels with high subscriber counts during the first week of 2019. Each of these more than 43,000 channels had at least 250,000 subscribers. Roughly half of these channels posted at least one new video in the week under examination. Collectively, the high-subscriber channels' new videos were viewed 14 billion times in their first seven days after posting. Significantly, only 17 percent of the videos were in English; YouTube is truly a global phenomenon.[3] Pew Research Center measured one week of traffic at the fat-tail end of the statistical distribution. Trying to do a more inclusive and comprehensive longitudinal study in multiple languages at this scale is a daunting task for anyone outside the platforms' research and development organizations.

TikTok is much younger and faster growing than any service in history. According to *Financial Times*, it reached a billion users in about two years, less than half as long as it took WeChat and a quarter of the time it took Facebook. Even before the 2020 pandemic, when it reached mass adoption in the United States, TikTok increased in-app spending by 500 percent between May 2018 and April 2019. As a company that is privately held as of 2023, TikTok parent ByteDance does not release detailed financial, usage, or geographic statistics. TikTok is only one aspect of ByteDance, which offers a variety of short-video and other consumer-facing apps across the world. To take only one example, one of these services, Helo, was temporarily banned in India but surprisingly (to Western analysts anyway) found traction in

Indonesia, the world's fourth most populous nation. The interrelationships of ByteDance's various global franchises are unclear. TikTok, meanwhile, was accused of removing prodemocracy content from the service in countries outside of China after pressure from the Chinese government. There is much we cannot measure and much we do not know about the video platforms that operate globally yet beyond national oversight.

The New History of Computing

Writing this book challenged decades of my training and experience as a student of technology. That journey began with a PhD in history focused on the engineering ethos in 1920s US politics, led to work as a subject-matter specialist at several consulting firms during the Internet boom, and ended as a professor of business and later information studies. I've worked in and around the global tech sector for nearly thirty years. During that time, I've taught and written about it from many different angles, including supply chains, online marketing, digital strategy, robotics and machine learning, and innovation and entrepreneurship. An eclectic intellectual portfolio plus heavy use of online video in teaching between 2008 and 2016 (when my kids nicknamed me "Professor YouTube") have prepared me well for this project.

For years, I accepted the wisdom of those who asserted that our technologies shape us as much as we shape them. Examples can be found among Japanese sword-makers, Latino car customizers, and French users of Minitel terminals. In part, I treated the information technologies I studied as tools, evaluating them using the logic of affordances. In shorthand, what are the action possibilities provided (afforded) to the human user? How well did web browsers, text messaging, or smartphone apps allow people to accomplish a task?

Over the decade of the 2010s, computing changed. At many of the large-scale online platform companies—Amazon, Facebook, Google, Netflix—computing is now only partly assessed on how well people can use it to perform tasks. The big money, meanwhile, depends on how well algorithms can direct people to complete actions in the interest of the platform company: sign in, click, watch, like, subscribe, follow, share. That is, the desires of the system's user now compete with the needs of commercial entities that trade in human attention, emotion, and belief.

Those who argued that "if you're using the service for free, *you* are the product" spotted the beginnings of this trend. More recently, the retired Harvard Business School professor Shoshana Zuboff connects modern computing to the behaviorist psychology of B. F. Skinner, famous for his theory of operant conditioning. As Zuboff put it in her book *The Age of Surveillance Capitalism*, "machine processes not only *know* our behavior but also *shape* our behavior at scale." It is a short hop to our current state: "It is no longer enough to automate information flows *about us*; the goal now is to *automate us*."[4] Not only have we (the users of Facebook and Google) become factors of production whose attention is traded on massive and often real-time online adtech markets but, lately, we have also become subjects in invisible aggregations where our essential properties—religious belief, sexual orientation, fears and insecurities, networks of blood and kinship—are mined and exploited.

Contemporary debates about "ethical AI" (artificial intelligence) often focus on issues of demographic representation and exclusion, algorithmic transparency, and futuristic scenarios involving autonomous vehicles or military robots. Many productive discussions are underway, with significant policy implications. Privacy is an important example. The behavioral turn in machine learning, meanwhile, is still emerging as a scholarly area.[5] There are many reasons for this situation. Data is difficult to obtain given both the platforms' scale and the intense personalization applied to each user. The relevant algorithms for filtering and recommending videos change rapidly and remain "black boxes" given their competitive importance combined with the lack of regulatory oversight. Finally, cultural trends emerge and decay with such speed and magnitude that longitudinal studies are difficult to conceive and conduct before the winds shift as something new catches on.

The New Context for Computing

The transition in online video from 2005 until 2020 did not occur in isolation from larger trends in the socioeconomic context of computing. It's straightforward to identify seven stages in a history of computing's relation to its political, social, and economic setting that has transpired since World War II. The operative questions relate less to how computing works and more to its side effects. Who could buy and operate computers in a given era? What could computers accomplish to further these parties' objectives? What were the wider implications of a given stage in the technical development of digital technologies?

Stage one was experimental, in which computing was the province of government and advanced academia. At Bletchley Park, Alan Turing helped crack the German Enigma code. In the United States, the ENIAC at the

University of Pennsylvania calculated artillery firing tables to aid the war effort. Rear Admiral Grace Hopper helped develop the notion of computer programming as a language rather than mere instruction sets. In stage two, companies like IBM and Remington Rand (later Sperry, then Unisys) commercialized computing in the 1950s and sold large systems to governments. To this day, the public sector remains a major consumer of computational capability for everything from GPS satellites to tax receipts to immigration and passport record-keeping to continued projects involving warfare, surveillance, and espionage.

Stage three began in the 1960s as large commercial enterprises deployed systems similar to the ones used by governments. Mainframe systems fed by magnetic tape or paper punch-cards maintained hotel and airline reservations, financial statements, and other transactional details. In the 1970s, the boxes got smaller and the uses to which the systems were put evolved. The focus was still on enterprise users, but individuals could now interact with word processors or engineering workstations in something closer to real time rather than waiting for an overnight batch run.

In the early 1980s, stage four began to take shape as IBM responded to the Apple computer aimed at students and hobbyists with a workplace-ready "personal computer." After Apple introduced the graphical WIMP interface (pioneered at Xerox PARC) that utilized windows, icons, a handheld mouse, and an on-screen pointer, Microsoft responded by bringing a similar interface to the IBM PC. Computers now automated word processing outside typing pools, and the newly invented spreadsheet was used extensively in financial applications. Games were available, but not widely adopted. Computing was still complex and expensive, and few devices were networked, most of these only locally. The industry was still a niche. Microsoft's 1990 revenues totaled $1.2 billion while General Motors's were almost $127 billion.

The Internet age is closely associated with stage five, in which desktop and laptop computers emerged as a mass market. Dial-up and then cable modems provided internet in Western Europe, the United States, and Japan. Websites were easy to build, largely devoid of video, and quickly ubiquitous. Web-based businesses launched by the thousands, among them both Amazon and Charles Schwab, as well as Pets.com and Excite. My 1995 self would be astonished to learn that in 2023, Craigslist looked exactly the same and was more valuable than either Yahoo or AOL, which were merged by corporate parent Verizon in 2017 before being sold.

Computing moved from desktops to pockets with the launch of the smartphone in 2007, launching stage six. Cameras, color displays, and microphones became invisibly commonplace almost overnight after a few years of "multimedia PCs" being a cumbersome and rapidly obsolete product category. Wireless networking—via Bluetooth, Wi-Fi, and cellular—made hardwired connections a rarity in consumer markets. Uses moved from office suites to include entertainment and personal connection. App stores made mobile software development for everything from horoscopes to highway navigation accessible and lucrative.

In recognition of these changes, Apple dropped "Computer" from its name in 2007 as firms like HP and Dell became substantially less relevant. Software as a service, whether delivered by Google, Facebook, or Salesforce, and computing as a service, delivered initially by Amazon Web Services, displaced previous industry leaders selling physical software or hardware. Revenues and profit margins surged, as did equity valuations: Apple, Microsoft, and Amazon all eclipsed $1 trillion in aggregate stock-market valuation in 2020. During this transition, the energy cost of cloud computing became significant. The fact that Bitcoin mining grew by 2021 to require as much electricity as the entire nation of Malaysia hinted that computing was becoming a massive economic sector with significant spillover effects.

Also in stage six, the shift from software as product to software as service, especially ad-funded models, includes much more than online video. Nevertheless, the plastic discs sold in "computer stores" migrated to software embedded in everything from refrigerators to televisions and computers counterintuitively called phones. This transition coincides perfectly with the time frame of the book. The change in the funding stream makes user attention the new currency for many technology companies. In response, ad-funded software and content drives a behavioral turn on megaplatforms. To oversimplify, the best way to predict a behavior is to motivate it, so it's now people as much as systems that are the object of programming. YouTube's video recommendation algorithms are based far less on the content of the video than on other viewers' responses to it. It's a far cry from Google's original search technology based on the words contained in a web document combined with the hyperlink structures associated with it. But even those hyperlink analyses presaged behavioral engineering, as search engine optimization made clear in the 2000s.

Stage seven is only beginning, and the online video pioneers are central to this segment of the narrative. Given the sophistication of these platforms' manipulation of human attention, the ubiquity and intimacy of smartphone use, and the massive user bases, firms like Google, Facebook, and ByteDance have become important players in geopolitics.

For example, the Arab Spring of the early 2010s was inextricably intertwined with the rise of social media and mobile computing in the region. Facebook *is* the Internet in many places, including Cambodia and Indonesia; billions of users have never experienced websites. Facebook was also a key locus of foreign intervention in the 2016 US election. The rules of content moderation (essentially a term of art for censorship) are political. Coups are one example. How do the platforms follow law and custom when a junta sets out its agenda? YouTube, meanwhile, is a tool of many terror groups. Some post beheadings of opponents and martyrdom of adherents for recruitment and hortatory purposes. Others call for violent overthrow of democratic institutions from within.

Google Maps has for years struggled with how to represent Kashmir, an Asian territory with disputed boundaries. TikTok is the first Chinese app to go global, and the Chinese government is not clear on how it will be regulated or even tolerated. As I write in 2023, ByteDance is part of a group of consumer Internet companies whose financial success has led to their being recategorized by that government. Initial public stock offerings have been canceled or negated by rule changes, private businesspeople such as Jack Ma have for a time disappeared from public view, and the alignment of entertainment and profit with government industrial and cultural policy is being reset. To speak of Microsoft Word as a factor in foreign policy in 1999 would have been puzzling, but given the events of 2005 and after, online video is very much a factor in both domestic and global politics.

Reinventing Television

Online video is also part of a much bigger transition in what we used to call television. YouTube, in certain of its formats, blurs into the Internet television delivered by Netflix, HBO, Amazon Prime Video, Hulu, Disney+, and the like. All of these competitors are driving a transition away from broadcast's time-scheduled model to Internet on-demand distribution. Many of the effects of this transition are still playing out. For its part, YouTube creates effectively infinite video inventory, frees up content from the conventions of thirty- or sixty-minute multiples, and, like Internet television, time-shifts consumption from distribution. At TikTok, meanwhile, highly engaged users plus short-format clips equals viewers who can watch (and skip) hundreds of unique videos at one sitting.

Most importantly, television is moving from something people *watch* to a range of things people *do*. I can capture my dances or rants, learn boomerang-throwing or the Japanese language, remix existing content, or watch other people play video games. (The role of TikTok in the spread of "challenges" will be addressed in chapter 2.) On Amazon's Twitch livestreaming service, yet another facet of online video, people can interact with both game players and other watchers, either synchronously or in a variety of time-shifted ways. The fact that personal expression has moved from text to include video, in a very short moment of historical time, should also be stressed.

We also need to pay attention to the *content* of online video, independent of its hosting and delivery. To begin with, changes in distribution implied new forms of video discourse. The short-lived Vine service trafficked in six-second clips and is much missed within a particular demographic. Netflix, meanwhile, dropped entire seasons of its dramas and comedies, each of which could escape the thirty-minute multiples of network programming, in a single release. Some of the strengths and weaknesses of online video date to a more innocent time; a lot changed in only fifteen years as the focus shifted from casual cat clips to calculated clickbait. Regardless of how we find videos (or they find us), nostalgia, persuasion, education, and participation matter for the viewers. Online video embodies countless tensions and frank contradictions.

While new and more diverse content creators get access to distribution, online video also allows conspiracy and hate-speech theories to thrive. For a few years, TED talks undertook to elevate public discourse, with mixed results in a brief window of time. Despite all the page views, many of the TED critiques—such as a lack of cultural inclusion, too-easy answers, and techno-utopianism—were well deserved. Musical artists from nearly anywhere in the world no longer need the infrastructure of recording studios, CD pressing plants, radio stations, or retailers to enjoy global fame. But music economics have changed as streaming fails to pay many bills, and as always, fame comes with personal challenges. Online video can teach people to cook, to repair, or to dance—but also to hate, to distrust, and to injure.

Online video is also a story about the recent availability of new tools for video creation. Here, TikTok and Twitch are in the vanguard. The services both create and nourish new content types and genres. TikTok's video editing tools are so good that other online platforms recommend them openly. The TikTok app environment is particularly effective at creating powerful economic incentives to remix, comment on, or parody existing content. This tendency toward layers of inside jokes means that irony is a dominant motif inside the TikTok universe. TikTok and Twitch are also highly specific to certain age demographics as facility with a toolset helps define one's generation. At the same time, conventions pioneered in the gaming world (video narration over an inset of gameplay) have expanded into wider usage as reaction videos apply the same recipe to many kinds of video: comedy routines, musical performances, movie clips, kitchen demonstrations. It's a textbook example of a wider group unconsciously adopting the behaviors of a subculture without knowing the referent.

New Global Public Spaces

In contrast to television and movies, the cultural ethos of online video is markedly more diverse. As I write, Wikipedia's list of the seventeen historically most viewed YouTube videos includes Brazilian soccer legend Ronaldinho, US-based amateur dancer Judson Laipply, the finger-biting English baby Charlie, and Luis Fonsi, a Puerto Rican singer singing in Spanish. The longest-tenured artist on the list is the Korean singer-songwriter, record producer, and rapper Psy; "Gangnam Style" was the most-watched YouTube video in history for 1,689 days—more than four and a half years. Such cultural reach and range bring a multitude of opportunities and side effects.

This diversity is in itself both unprecedented and extremely complex. I lack the scholarly and technical apparatus to analyze a service that operates in one hundred countries and eighty languages but promotes US baseball to French audiences and Vancouver lifestyle content in Japanese (see figs. 1 and 2). Why is the YouTube banner presented in French but the video titles in English? Why are these titles suggested in the United States? How do the one hundred national sites' promotional algorithms run compared to those in other countries? TikTok, meanwhile, moves memes so fast that even teens with ample leisure time can spend well over an hour a day on the service trying to keep up with the extreme cultural velocity, much of which ignores national boundaries.

The age of planet-wide online platforms, of which YouTube is the largest by some metrics and TikTok the fastest-growing by others, creates new public spheres with unanswered policy questions. What responsibility do platforms have for fairness, privacy, or accuracy? Who enforces which social norms, where? What rules apply to algorithmic management of user bases measured in billions? Humanity has never created or managed institutions of this scale. The "attention factory" metaphor draws the useful parallel of cognitive automation to mechanical automation. How can human regulators

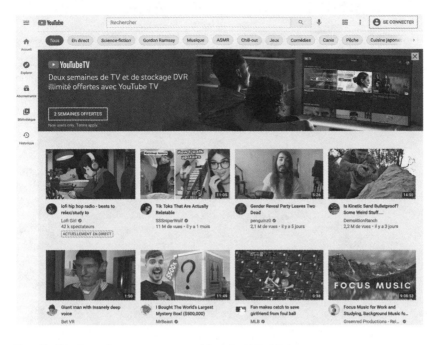

Fig. 1 YouTube France homepage as accessed from the United States, 2021.

police algorithms, which themselves interact unpredictably within and across platforms, deployed at unprecedentedly large scale? A 2021 paper published in *Proceedings of the National Academy of Science* called for more disciplined scientific investigation of these platforms, arguing that understanding them is as important as climate science or medicine: "The digital age and the rise of social media have accelerated changes to our social systems, with poorly understood functional consequences. This gap in our knowledge represents a principal challenge to scientific progress, democracy, and actions to address global crises."[6]

Online video also takes many other things people do and makes them more widely accessible. The process of learning is far easier, especially for physical tasks, when we can see them demonstrated. E-sports are only one outgrowth of a redefinition of play. Reminiscing in the age of online video is an entirely new process, and we will spend some time discussing nostalgia as an aspect of these platforms. If learning is enhanced, meanwhile, so is deceiving. The platforms' complex relationships with fact-checking and content moderation are a major issue in the age of widespread, complex, and well-funded dis- and misinformation.

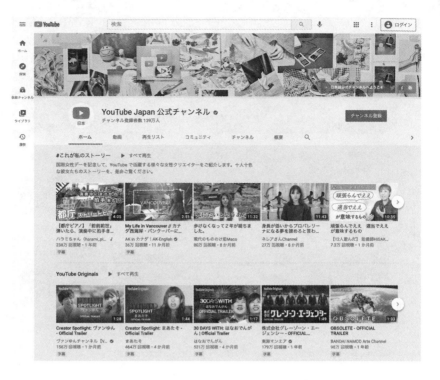

Fig. 2 YouTube Japan homepage as accessed from the United States, 2021.

Follow the Money

It's difficult to draw a definitional fence around online video. As I noted, we are leaving aside Hulu, Netflix, and their kin even as we note that lines get very blurry. For example, Amazon owns television rights to Thursday American football games and it's possible Twitch will be part of the streaming distribution model.

When we consider online video—YouTube, Twitch, and TikTok primarily, with more to come—there's a big economic footprint. Television is the biggest global entertainment sector, at roughly $230 billion in a pandemic-dampened 2020. Video gaming is a $180 billion industry worldwide, earning almost double the movie industry revenues, which come in at about $100 billion. Music revenue for 2020, meanwhile, barely exceeded $20 billion worldwide. That's more than half a trillion dollars of entertainment spending potentially affected by online video.

But the footprint is even bigger. Social networking, a competitor for the ad spend devoted to television, is a market growing from more than

$100 billion a year. A huge market primed to be upended by online video is education, as the rapid 2020 transition to Zoom illustrated. Any global market summary will be an approximation, but UNESCO (United Nations Educational, Scientific and Cultural Organization) estimated that number at $4.7 trillion for 2019. As we will see, online video is bringing significant changes to entertainment and instructional markets, so it's a conservative assertion to say that hundreds of billions of dollars in existing practice are in play.

Given the stakes, it's important to acknowledge the roles of video creators and rights holders in the online ecosystem. Their interests in being discovered and promoted by the relevant algorithms both align with and diverge from those of the other constituencies: platforms and viewers. In addition, protection from copyright litigation was addressed early in online video's history, posing as it did an existential threat to the platforms. Note that child endangerment, hate speech, and extreme violence were still live issues nearly twenty years after YouTube's founding. Developing algorithms to detect these abuses was never as important as protecting the rights of copyright holders.

We will see that algorithmic content moderation continues to be both technically difficult and politically controversial, especially in the age of well-orchestrated misogyny, racism, and antiscience sentiment. For example, YouTube found that training video-based machine learning and natural-language processing algorithms to detect hate speech and disinformation was unusually challenging.

The original tagline at YouTube's launch was "Broadcast Yourself." That tagline has been removed from all facets of the service as of 2019. The reality is that Alphabet (along with ByteDance and Amazon and the rest) makes its profits from those who watch, not those who upload. Consider a few data points in advance of meeting these people later in the book. TikTok star Charli D'Amelio has roughly 100 million followers but collects most of her more than $10 million a year in third-party endorsements, not direct payments per stream for her dance clips. Still, it wasn't bad money for a sixteen-year-old. Ryan Kaji is a preteen who, with his parents, makes more than $29 million a year by opening toys on YouTube. Over at Twitch, meanwhile, the top streamers Ninja and PewDiePie both exceeded $20 million in annual earnings in 2021 (some of which came from YouTube). The scale of online video services comes into sharper focus in light of so much money. They are now massive microtargeted ad-delivery vehicles, the rhetoric of amateur content creation standing to the contrary. Online video profits and thus the platforms' priorities revolve around what you watch, not what you upload.

How big is the online video economy? Automating behavioral conditioning follows essentially the same logic as that of the industrial assembly line. With only about eighteen waking hours in the day, every minute on one service generally means that another is neglected. In 2019, Netflix acknowledged this competition across platforms when the company stated in a shareholder communication that "We compete with (and lose to) Fortnite more than HBO." Unlike television or the movies, most online video consists of short bursts on a small device, with the individual viewer well-known to the service delivering the content. The value of this resource to advertisers is obvious. Here are the stakes of the fight for attention: Google earned about $30 billion from YouTube in 2022, but Amazon's ad business—which includes Twitch—in that same year surpassed $30 billion after growing about 25 percent year over year. Even Apple, for all its talk of user privacy, generated $31 billion in ad revenue in 2022. For scale, the *New York Times* reported about $500 million in 2022 ad revenue; in the TV business, ESPN reported about $9 billion.

This, then, is why online video matters. YouTube out-earning the *New York Times* by a factor of sixty reveals that every minute of human attention has a price. Algorithmic optimization of that attention becomes a new competitive advantage, subject to the laws of capital and driving ever more intense competition to innovate. Tellingly, nobody outside ByteDance knows how much TikTok and its stars earned, raising another set of important questions.

Some Notes on the Book's Limitations

Given that Facebook, Baidu, Google, and the rest of the major platform companies are highly secretive, much of what we know about them is either derived from third-party analysis (of limited accuracy) or carefully filtered before dissemination by the platforms themselves. As opaque as any given service or company might be taken on its own, meanwhile, we will see in chapter 7 that it is even more difficult from a logistical standpoint to study cross-platform behavior, and theory has been slow to emerge for this reason. Although we live in the golden age of the Internet platform, there remains much to be learned about this new type of locus of—and actor in—human affairs.

TikTok is an important example. Absent a burner smart phone or a sandboxed computer in a lab, I did not sign up for the app because of the uncertainty around its privacy and security. Facebook has already been shown to track nonusers across non-Facebook properties.[7] TikTok could well do the same, or worse—some reports suggest a keystroke logger is embedded[8]—and I chose not to accept the risk. Not using the app complicated analyzing it, and there are undoubtedly things I missed.

This book's case study, rather than encyclopedic, approach has the benefit of not attempting to come to terms with online video's sheer vastness. Humanity has never created, confronted, or managed anything this large. That five hundred hours of video uploads to YouTube per minute translates to more than eighty years every day, a sum of video so enormous that it cannot be cataloged, monitored, or curated with any significant human input. Instead, online video is a creation of algorithms, some clever, others legally necessary, all operating at a remove from the control of viewers and to a degree too complex to be completely the creature of their programmers. The so-called Flash Crash on Wall Street in 2010 remains a telling example of what can happen when independent algorithms can interact unpredictably to generate emergent effects on a shared computational platform. A trillion dollars of market value was wiped out, then restored, in a span of thirty-six minutes, and it took years to uncover the many root causes of both the crash and the recovery.

Considering the computational power and complexity involved, any attempt to study online video must transcend disciplinary approaches that might have been adequate to the histories of computer networking, television, human-scale social networks, or cultural transmissions such as memes. Given that I am one observer and not a research team, my approach here is to suggest some lines of inquiry. Touching on such areas as computer science, business strategy, media studies, social psychology, and European history, the book attempts to ask more questions than it answers as one of numerous voices in an ongoing discussion. I am aware that using a five-hundred-year-old literary form to analyze twenty-first-century communications and social interactions is an anachronism. But I'm convinced that the long-wave nature of book creation and readership is appropriate to a medium that is rewriting culture and resetting economics on a much shorter time frame. We'll begin that project by examining the intellectual and technical origins of this new medium.

2

The Time Was Right

Online video has become so commonplace—pervasive—that it's difficult to remember life before its ubiquity. YouTube launched in 2005, when the World Wide Web of text and static images was only fifteen years old. A confluence of technical and social developments made video easy to upload and uneventful to view. In this chapter, we will explore the conceptual origins of YouTube compared to TikTok, explain how online video works, and consider why it surged in popularity when it did.

The Evolution of Platform Thinking

The emergence of TikTok helps illuminate the evolution of platform thinking between 2005 and 2015; YouTube began with a very different set of assumptions. After a brief run as an upload site for video dating profiles, YouTube pivoted to become a much more open-ended hosting venture. A common phrasing at the startup held that the service was going to be "Flickr [a photo upload site] for video." One voice in the mix belonged to one of the startup's venture capitalists, who thought there might be utility in the site hosting wedding and honeymoon videos.[1] Another unmet need: being unable to post video of a house party. A soft launch in spring 2005 as a general-purpose upload repository included a short clip of one of the founders at the San Diego Zoo. In September, the first viral video—a Nike soccer ad featuring Ronaldinho—launched a rocket of growth that hasn't ever stopped.

It's important to consider the context of technical thinking in 2005. Facebook was tiny, exclusive to Ivy League email addresses. The 2000–2001 bursting of the Internet financial bubble was still sufficiently fresh that many Internet startups had a hard time getting funding. Investors still talked of finding "the next Microsoft." Google had staged its initial public offering in August 2004. Because the stock did not break $100 a share until eight months later, it was not yet an investor success story. 2004 also saw such companies as Salesforce and Tencent go public after three very lean years followed the tech-stock meltdown.

Into this environment strode Tim O'Reilly, a Harvard-educated publisher of technical books, including well-regarded programming guides. His company was in the process of branching out into events, and he struck a nerve with the notion of "Web 2.0" in 2004. The concept is worth examining in some detail insofar as it turns out to have provided a detailed blueprint for YouTube.

In "What is Web 2.0: Design Patterns and Business Models for the Next Generation of Software,"[2] O'Reilly began by noting that 2001 led to many skeptics mistakenly writing off the web. Instead, he argued, the bursting of the financial bubble provided the catalyst for a new wave of thinking. The group's whiteboard list at the original brainstorming session of "from . . . to" is instructive:

Web 1.0		Web 2.0
DoubleClick	→	Google AdSense
Ofoto	→	Flickr
Akamai	→	BitTorrent
mp3.com	→	Napster
Britannica Online	→	Wikipedia
personal websites	→	blogging
evite	→	upcoming.org and EVDB
domain name speculation	→	search engine optimization
page views	→	cost per click
screen scraping	→	web services
publishing	→	participation
content management systems	→	wikis
directories (taxonomy)	→	tagging ("folksonomy")
stickiness	→	syndication

What do the terms in the right column have in common? O'Reilly and his colleagues developed seven principles that have proven durable, embodied as they are in YouTube, Facebook, Uber, and the other large-scale digital platforms that have come to replace the original notion of entities conceived of as websites. This transition explains why Facebook eclipsed

GeoCities, why Google surpassed Yahoo so decisively, and why both Google's acquisition of YouTube and Facebook's purchase of Instagram were so consequential. Not only did O'Reilly introduce the age of the Internet platform with his mental model, he also wrote the epitaph for the original vision of the World Wide Web.[3]

1. *The Web as Platform.* The contrast between Netscape—a near neighbor to desktop-software pioneer Microsoft—and Google highlights this concept, a core of O'Reilly's worldview:

> Google, by contrast, began its life as a native web application, never sold or packaged, but delivered as a service, with customers paying, directly or indirectly, for the use of that service. *None of the trappings of the old software industry are present.* No scheduled software releases, just continuous improvement. No licensing or sale, just usage. No porting to different platforms so that customers can run the software on their own equipment, just a massively scalable collection of commodity PCs running open source operating systems plus homegrown applications and utilities that no one outside the company ever gets to see.[4]

Implicit in this assertion is the platforms' reliance on ad revenue and user attention rather than license fees, a shift with far-reaching implications. It also highlights how far we have come from the 1990s software industry that featured physical distribution at stores like Computer City and physical loads (and patching). Now, software is generally built, priced, and delivered as a service rather than a product. Tablets and most laptops lack any form of disk or CD drive. Most people can't remember the last time they loaded computer software from physical media.

2. *Harnessing Collective Intelligence.* Platforms rely on crowdsourcing. O'Reilly seized on the up-and-coming startups del.icio.us and Flickr, along with Wikipedia and the open-source software movement his company quite profitably enabled, to show the way forward. The article prophetically proclaimed "the lesson: *Network effects from user contributions are the key to market dominance in the Web 2.0 era.*"[5] The unprecedented scale of today's platforms is a product of the leverage gained from user-generated content, multiplied by advances in machine learning that today's platform leaders—Amazon (AWS launched in 2006), Apple, Facebook, Google, Netflix, and others—have both driven and exploited. TikTok took crowdsourcing a step further than YouTube by directing users as they created videos via

suggestions to use this music, wear these colors, connect to this celebrity, acknowledge this meme.

3. Data Is the Next Intel Inside. Put aside the now-dated reference to the iconic business-to-business branding campaign that launched in 1991. O'Reilly was prescient in seeing data as, to use later phrasing, "the new oil." What he missed was the automation of data manipulation: seeing Google as a "database company" after 2012 feels anachronistic. Even though application software companies are no longer the dominant forces in tech markets, O'Reilly was more correct than he could have known in spotting a nascent land grab taking shape: "We expect to see battles between data suppliers and application vendors in the next few years, as both realize just how important certain classes of data will become as building blocks for Web 2.0 applications. *The race is on to own certain classes of core data*: location, identity, calendaring of public events, product identifiers and namespaces."[6] He could have added users' social networks, credit data, Internet usage, purchasing data, exercise history, and others.

4. End of the Software Release Cycle. O'Reilly's insight builds on the Netscape-Google difference, and here, he may have been limited by his hacker orientation. The first of his insights—"*Operations must become a core competency*"—is spot-on: the big platforms have become operationally extraordinary to handle the extremity of their scale and complexity. Insight number two—"*Users must be treated as co-developers*"—is a nod to open-source practices that instead gave way to the behavioral experimentalism that characterizes Facebook, Netflix, Google, and Amazon.[7] User interfaces are shiny objects, sleek and inviting, rather than "perpetual betas" serving as testbeds for collaborative innovation.

To his credit, O'Reilly did foreshadow the behavioral turn in computing when he noted that "Real time monitoring of user behavior to see just which new features are used, and how they are used, thus becomes another required core competency." A/B testing, just one category of such monitoring, is by itself a billion-dollar industry; 77 percent of companies use the technique on their websites while 93 percent A/B test email campaigns.[8] As of 2017 Google and Microsoft were reported to run more than 10,000 A/B tests apiece.[9]

5. Lightweight Programming Models. Twenty years is a long time in software engineering, and the incredible scale of the Web 2.0 platforms ended up demanding a different kind of software—and hardware—landscape than O'Reilly could have envisioned in 2004. His "significant lessons" don't really apply to the Google, Facebook, and Amazon software factories attached to planet-scale computing infrastructure.

29

The first of O'Reilly's lessons advises: "*Support lightweight programming models that allow for loosely coupled systems.*"[10] As the platforms continue to integrate more and more web services (Facebook, Messenger, Instagram, and WhatsApp, for example), it's hard to understand how the adjective "lightweight" might be interpreted. Is a programming model undemanding of compute resources? of developer time? of developer expertise? of developer scaffolding such as libraries, test environments, documentation, or training data? YouTube is written consistently with other Google products in C, C++, Go, and Python, some lightweight and others not. If you look at the history of job postings at TikTok, meanwhile, C, C++, and Python were in demand, among many other languages, including Java and Javascript (including Google's Angular and Facebook's React variants), and Objective C (heavily used in MacOS and iOS for many years).[11] Given this heterogeneity, it's likely loose coupling is an architectural priority at both ByteDance and Alphabet, sometimes in public ways as with the releases of Hadoop, Bigtable, and Chubby to the wider computing market.

Second, he advises: "*Think syndication, not coordination.*"[12] O'Reilly noted that web services such as RSS (Really Simple Syndication, a web-based data feed often used for news and other frequently updated content) were worth emulating as an instantiation of the end-to-end principle underlying the Internet. The platforms that have emerged since 2005 have been more proprietary, less interoperable—try moving a Facebook comment into Twitch—and less "lightweight" in the syndication sense of the term.

Third, "*Design for 'hackability' and remixability.*"[13] While there are some examples where this lesson has taken hold, such as the wide adoption of the Google Maps API, YouTube in particular is extremely cautious of being attacked by copyright holders. As with the second lesson, YouTube is built to maximize viewer engagement in a relatively passive stance, one where remixes are not a high priority. TikTok, meanwhile, explicitly encourages remixes, but it's far from being hackable.

6. Software Above the Level of a Single Device. Here, O'Reilly was positively far-sighted in ways he could not have appreciated. Given the migration to cloud computing and the global adoption of smartphones, tablets, fitness trackers, and the like, "Web 2.0 is not limited to the PC platform" is an understatement of the highest magnitude.[14]

7. Rich User Experiences. Applications like webmail or static browser display of text and images ran on PCs in O'Reilly's time. Later, the widespread availability of multimedia—gaming and various types of video—via online platforms proved the importance of the continued migration away from the computer and toward the mobile app. Despite Facebook's heavy investment in virtual reality and TikTok's popularity as a meme mover, YouTube's web service that both replicates and transcends television appears to be the current ceiling for mass use of computational multimedia. "Rich" in 2024 means something very different from what it did in 2005.

Overall, YouTube began as a service that bet on compression software, improved broadband connections, and cheap storage in the bid to make online video easy to upload, tolerable to watch, and accessible from anywhere. What might be termed the behavioral turn came later, after Google and Facebook (along with Amazon along different lines) realized the imperative to keep users on the platform, and TikTok perfected the execution of the model in a delimited market segment. Three forces powered YouTube's transcendence of the Web 2.0 framework: (1) how easy humans are to hack; (2) the massive scale of these platforms; and (3) the convergence of bigger-than-ever bodies of training data, bigger-than-ever compute clouds, and better-than-ever algorithms. In light of these forces, the 2010s saw great strides in and wide adoption of machine learning for the purposes of behavioral tracking and manipulation. What began as Web 2.0 ended with a few powerful players controlling walled gardens of proprietary (even though it was user-generated) content in which user behavior was tightly constrained.

While there is no equivalent of O'Reilly's document for ByteDance's founder Zhang Yiming, he clearly understood industry dynamics when the company launched its Toutiao news aggregator in the Chinese market in 2012. Toutiao, or "Headlines," began as a recommendation system but pivoted to delivering content in various formats, such as texts, images, question-and-answer posts, microblogs, and videos. Significantly, the firm's research division was headed until 2020 by Wei-Ying Ma, who was formerly a senior executive at Microsoft Research Asia. Downloads totaled well over a billion by 2019. By 2020, ByteDance was operating more than twenty apps in many global markets. The firm is unusual in attempting to balance its relations to New York-based private equity firms including General Atlantic, Silicon Valley venture capital firms including Sequoia Capital, the Japanese SoftBank Group, and the Chinese Communist Party.

TikTok (formerly Musical.ly) is a version of the Douyin site that is used outside of China, launched in 2017, at which time users could upload music and lip-sync videos of three to fifteen seconds or looping videos that could initially run up to a minute. In 2021, the time limit was increased to three minutes, then, in 2022, to ten. The service skews toward female users worldwide (57 percent, compared to 43 percent male), with 43 percent of the audience between eighteen and twenty-four.[15] Children use the site heavily but are not counted in official statistics for a variety of reasons. In 2020, at the peak of TikTok's growth spurt during the pandemic, internal company documents were reported to have measured one-third of the US user base as being under fourteen years old.[16]

The parent company, ByteDance, remains in China, leading to concerns about user privacy. For its part, the company states that as of 2019, all TikTok data is stored outside of China and no longer subject to Chinese government requests for access to biometrics, metadata, and other potentially revealing details.[17] In 2021, however, the Chinese government took a board seat on a Chinese ByteDance company, complicating those claims of independence. (ByteDance and TikTok are incorporated in the Cayman Islands, but key technology operations are performed in China.) In 2022, BuzzFeed reported that China-based ByteDance employees had ready access to US user data, including birthdays and phone numbers. These both are prized UIDs (unique identifiers) that can be used to disambiguate people with the same name.[18]

TikTok is repeatedly characterized as "addicting," in part because behind-the-scenes machine learning algorithms optimize content for a viewer's revealed preferences. Andreas Schellewald of the University of London makes an important point: these users were not mindless zombies. Rather, they sought to be entertained, and the service did an effective job of doing so. Similar behaviors on other apps did not produce the same reaction. Thus, the app's capabilities and the users' state of being combined to produce the sensation. Schellewald draws a useful comparison to prior technologies—soap operas and magazines—that performed a similar function, in this case, of escape from the boredom and claustrophobia of life during the COVID-19 pandemic.[19]

Three billion downloads have been reported worldwide, excluding China. US users total 100 million per month, only 10 percent of ByteDance's total user base. Despite US government concern about user privacy (it is banned on US military–issued devices), the NFL followed the NBA's lead and announced a TikTok partnership in September 2019, both aimed in part at non-US fans. (Major League Baseball tried a different approach, enlisting creators in a contest designed to increase the sport's appeal to people under thirty.) TikTok also helps promote new music, but concerns remain about the lack of royalty payments to artists. A new program called SoundOn, launched in 2022, was designed to address these concerns, but its impact is not yet clear. TikTok is still sufficiently new and different from past online services that businesses have yet to settle on a standardized approach to the medium. As of 2022, a highly unscientific survey of "the best [US] brands on TikTok" was headed by the NBA but included no major consumer brands in the tier of Nike, Apple, and Coke.[20]

As the analyst firm CB Insights stated, ByteDance's product portfolio builds on its three core strengths:

1. The user base is consistently young and highly engaged, regardless of national markets that span northern and southern hemispheres. 60 percent of US TikTok users, for example, are between 16 and 24. Worldwide, about 70 percent of TikTok users are under 30.
2. ByteDance has apparently cracked the code for understanding virality of online content, whether news, music, social recommendations, or GIFs.
3. ByteDance's core competency appears to be its application of machine learning to a particular young demographic, regardless of the content domain or geography.[21]

In summary, today's two primary video-sharing platforms started from very different origins. YouTube is an aggregation and storage play that morphed into a recommendation (for the viewer) and retention (for the platform) service within a portfolio of other similar businesses. Google's published mission remains "to organize the world's information and make it universally accessible and useful." YouTube falls in line with this objective and has become one of many interrelated machine learning plays at the company.

TikTok, YouTube's younger and less transparent competitor, is engineered from day one to be an AI-powered behavioral manipulator. YouTube was built to serve horizontal video windows to people who chose from a selection on a computer. TikTok serves one vertical video at a time on a smartphone or tablet. ByteDance founder Zhang Yiming has stated his objective is to eliminate the need for search across all corporate properties, a stark contrast to Google's approach.[22]

Other Aspects of Platform Thinking

Depending on where one looks, the word "platform" can mean many different things. Being aware of this lack of linguistic and conceptual consistency leads to several insights into the current debates over the role of the big machine learning companies. It also suggests that efforts to regulate these entities will require more precision and most likely transparency in the debates. Online video can at once be a social network, a broadcast medium, a streaming music service, an instructional repository, and a commercial gold mine attracting thousands of would-be stars looking to become "influencers" or "creators."

Online video cannot be analyzed outside the framework of an online platform: it is part of an ecosystem that includes Facebook and Wikipedia, LinkedIn and eBay, Reddit and Tinder, and dozens more. For expediency, I will use the definition offered by Tarleton Gillespie, now at Microsoft Research, who contrasts these online platforms to the more conventionally defined computing platforms that constitute various forms of programmable infrastructure. "Platforms," Gillespie writes,

> are online sites and services that
> a. host, organize, and circulate users' shared content or social interactions for them,
> b. without having produced or commissioned (the bulk of) that content,
> c. built on an infrastructure, beneath that circulation of information, for processing data for customer service, advertising, and profit.[23]

As Gillespie wrote back in 2010 when he was at Cornell, the word "platform" is at once "specific enough to mean something, and vague enough to work across multiple venues for multiple audiences." He cites other words that function similarly—"network," "broadcast," or "channel"—and notes that platforms in the social media sense are a leap removed from the original computational use of the term to denote an operating environment such as Linux or Windows.[24]

Hard-core computer scientists such as Marc Andreesen, by 2007 a venture capitalist, objected to the O'Reilly Web 2.0 characterization for precisely this reason. Citing a "swirling vortex of confusion," Andreesen asserted a litmus test: "whenever anyone uses the word 'platform,' ask 'can it be programmed?' ... If not, it's not a platform, and you can safely ignore whoever's talking."[25] This of course proved to be a rearguard action, and the "web as platform" school won the day.

Gillespie notes that "platform" has many traditional definitions that preceded the computer science usage; architectural, figurative, and political platforms all have long histories. Today, a decade after Gillespie, even Internet platforms are conceived of differently by different constituencies.

The master metaphor has great appeal. As he wrote, "In any of platform's senses, being raised, level, and accessible are ideological features as much as physical ones."[26] In YouTube's case, this is particularly true. Google can at once claim to be the future of television (when addressing advertisers especially), a repository for user-generated content (when claiming immunity from broadcast regulation), and an open medium without gatekeepers (when attracting users).

YouTube is of course all of these things, but it is also many more. In particular, the substitution of algorithmic takedowns and recommendations for human producers and network executives does not imply a level playing field. In addition, after quietly retiring the "Broadcast Yourself" tagline in 2019, YouTube has serious designs on the production side of online video, given its formidable presence in distribution. All the company has disclosed, however, is that creators were paid $30 billion over three years ending in 2021.[27] (For scale, YouTube is estimated to make slightly less than $30 billion per year; precise figures are not broken out in the company's financials. That $10 billion per year is in the same league as Netflix spends on more traditional shows and movies.)

Media Studies

In a different vein, Nick Montfort of MIT and Ian Bogost of Georgia Tech introduced the term "platform studies" at a 2007 academic conference and expanded on the concept two years later in *Racing the Beam*, their book about the Atari video game. Montfort and Bogost define platforms as "the hardware and software design of standardized computing systems" and as one of five layers of technology present in all media, with code, form and function, interface, and reception and operation being the other four. In this view, culture and computing are coevolutionary, much like traditional science, technology, and society thinking (see chapter 8). Cultural context shapes platform development, and platforms' affordances and internal cultures enable multiple means of creating, sharing, and discussing creative content.[28]

Business Strategy

If one ventures into the business school literature, "platform" operates very differently. Marshall Van Alstyne (Boston University), Geoffrey Parker (Dartmouth), and Sangeet Paul Choudary (INSEAD) wrote an influential 2016 article in the *Harvard Business Review* based on their collaboration on a book. In "Pipelines, Platforms, and the New Rules of Strategy," they contrast Alibaba, Apple, and Google to conventional manufacturing businesses, and encapsulate a key competitive advantage of capturing value from the user base: by gaining demand-side economies of scale. US Steel or General Motors gained power by consolidating *supply-side* economies of scale: factories, distribution networks, bulk purchasing of raw materials.

In contrast, as their book put it, platforms scale with external relationships rather than internal assets: "A platform is a business based on enabling value-creating interactions between external producers and consumers. The platform provides an open, participatory infrastructure for these interactions and sets governance conditions for them. The platform's overarching purpose: to consummate matches among users and facilitate the exchange of goods, services, or social currency, thereby enabling value creation for all participants."[29] The authors' framing is useful insofar as it does not focus on the traditional economic inputs of land, labor, and capital. Instead, attention is centered on interactions facilitated by a network of computational resources; on standards, norms, and processes (including what they call "governance conditions"); and on relationships to people who fall somewhere between conventional definitions of viewers and users.

This view, however, makes "social currency" sound benign when it shouldn't be. To take only one example, fear of missing out (FOMO) can motivate a range of unhealthy emotions and behaviors, and people have died from participating in TikTok challenges. The perspective also centers on the user experience rather than on the behavioral manipulation behind the walls of the platform companies: it's not clear that the algorithms that generate user views are either "open" or "participatory." They certainly do constitute "infrastructure," however.

For adherents of the business-strategy perspective, a key idea that factors less prominently in the media studies world is the notion of network externalities, or network effects. In its popular variant, AT&T president Theodore Vail understood in the early twentieth century how control over a collection of local telephone companies could increase the value of each independent company taken separately. Many years later, Robert Metcalfe cofounded 3Com to commercialize the Ethernet computer networking technology. According to Metcalfe, the rationale behind the sale of networking cards was that the *cost* of the network was directly proportional to the number of cards installed, but the *value* of the network was proportional to the square of the number of users.[30]

"Metcalfe's law" was never formally proven, but the thinking is directionally sound.[31] The first fax machine or Facebook profile is worthless, but every subsequent fax machine or Facebook profile increases the option value of all previous units without their owners having to do anything. Shortly after Metcalfe's prominence, coinciding with the early days of the public Internet, economists Carl Shapiro, Garth Saloner, and Joseph Farrell formalized the theoretical foundations of network effects.[32] Significantly, one of Shapiro's primary coauthors was Hal Varian, who went on to play a key role at Google in turning academic theory into highly profitable strategy.[33]

Critical Studies

Critical perspectives on platforms come from a wide variety of disciplines, but several core themes emerge. The first is platforms' invisibility. As we have seen, Facebook is understood to be the Internet in several countries. Few regulations govern the creation and management of tools used by billions of people and that collect (or can derive) highly personal information—religious affiliation, sexual orientation, medical queries, social network maps, travels to physical locations such as abortion clinics or gay bars—without overt notification of doing so. According to David Berry of the University of Sussex, "these new digital technologies form path dependencies that can become strengthened and naturalized as platforms, therefore becoming self-reinforcing, creating a circle of technological leaps and accelerations. These new forms of knowledge platforms are built to structure our reading in particular ways, opening the possibility of distracted and fragmentary reading habits in contrast to deep reading, which may make it difficult to develop critical reflection or offer space for contemplation."[34] Technologies that change how we take in knowledge are powerful indeed, but the privacy intrusions seem a more pressing issue than a decline in reflective reading.

A second critique concerns the economic power accumulated at the big platforms, whether through monetization of user-generated data, low wages for the psychically traumatic work of content moderation, or the oligopoly of online ad providers. There is also a type of alienation that occurs when we become the sum of the platforms' interactions with our digital breadcrumbs. What John Cheney-Lippold of the University of Michigan calls our "datafied self" is not us, and it's also seldom subject to verification or correction.[35] If we use smartphones near Kendall Square on a summer night, we become Boston Red Sox fans to the algorithm. If we search for jewelry for a teenaged niece, we become a Forever 21 shopper. If we buy a bag of potting soil, we become aspiring master gardeners. Most of the examples are far more complex than this, but the associational logic can be both blunt-instrument inaccurate and invidiously self-reinforcing, as Berry noted above.

The key impact of platform thinking, however one defines it, lies in its implications for scalability. The flagship platforms—Amazon, Google, ByteDance, Baidu, Tencent, and Facebook—all claim massive user bases: in the billions for the pure digital plays, and in the hundreds of millions for Amazon, a company that faces the challenge of fulfilling physical orders. No human entity, whether the Chinese army, AT&T at its peak, or any nation-state, has ever built let alone maintained infrastructure to manage multiple billions of users. Nudged forward by sophisticated psychological tactics, the crowdsourced content-generation, referral, and commenting functions make possible web and app-centric businesses that no previous structure could generate or support.

How Does It Work?

How does online video work? Speaking of the original and still-predominant model—in this context, YouTube is a particular and widespread example as well as being the first of the breed—users upload video created by them, Google hosts the content and provides curation, and other users watch the video, sometimes with advertising appended.

Such a process implies several problems being solved. First, there must be sufficient bandwidth for both upload and download to complete smoothly and quickly. The early days of video on the Internet were full of frozen frames, audio-video sync failures, and absurdly long download times. Multiple minutes could be required over phone lines for a low-resolution twenty-second clip to make its way to the destination computer. One underappreciated aspect of Internet architecture is the content delivery network or CDN, which helps YouTube and other services, including Netflix, move bulky video files much less painfully than used to be the case. Akamai, Rackspace, and Cloudflare—companies most users have never heard of—cache content close to users to reduce network latency and balance the load on both the host servers and the overall network infrastructure.

Second, a device sits at the edge of the network from whence uploads commence or upon which content is viewed. These devices must have sufficient computing capacity to run compression and decompression algorithms. The regular doubling after 1965 of computational performance every eighteen to twenty-four months, known colloquially as Moore's law, ensured that desktop PCs were generally capable of such tasks by the mid-2000s, and mobile architectures from Apple, Samsung, and other providers delivered impressive video processing shortly after the first generations of smart-phones were launched.

Third, digital video cameras must be readily accessible. Early smart-phones on both Apple and Android platforms lacked any video capability; today's 4K smartphone cameras are impressive, and historically recent. Even broadcast networks use consumer-grade video cameras for certain shots.[36]

Fourth, once the video is uploaded the hosting service needs to store it. Google's data centers are (and have been for some time) among the largest in the world. The company has the financial and engineering capital to host the vast amounts of data involved in a crowdsourced video service. TikTok, meanwhile, is rapidly building infrastructure but the exact ownership and structure of its data centers in various countries are not fully public. As of June 2022, ByteDance announced that its data centers in Singapore and Virginia would be reassigned as backup and that US TikTok Internet traffic from henceforth would be handled on Oracle Cloud Infrastructure.[37]

Why Now?

Why did YouTube emerge when it did? The service has become so familiar so quickly that it's worth examining its preconditions, the building blocks that founders Jawed Karim, Steve Chen, and Chad Hurley so successfully assembled. All three had experience at PayPal, so were accustomed to the explosive growth of Internet startups. Indeed, in addition to the three people named above, the so-called PayPal Mafia includes such powerful tech figures as Elon Musk, LinkedIn cofounder and serial investor Reid Hoffman, Yelp cofounder Jeremy Stoppelman, and megainvestor Peter Thiel. It's difficult to envision a richer training ground (and network of invaluable contacts) for a group of aspiring entrepreneurs.

The facts of the launch are remarkable, particularly the speed. The domain name was registered on Valentine's Day 2005, and the first video—starring cofounder Karim—was entitled "Me at the zoo." Nineteen seconds in length, it was uploaded to the site on April 23, 2005. After angel funding got things started, Sequoia Capital invested $3.5 million that November. A subsequent round of $8 million from Sequoia and Artis Capital Management followed in April 2006. Given the rapid growth of the site, it's likely that much of the capital was allocated to infrastructure: the service was report-edly delivering up to 100 million videos per day barely a year after launch.

On October 9, 2006, Google acquired YouTube for $1.65 billion in stock. The startup was spending considerable time and effort defending against copyright infringement litigation that could have shut down the site in Napster-like fashion. The acquisition turned the issue over to a larger and more experienced legal department. Similarly, managing the infrastructure required to service the growth in both uploads and downloads likely stretched the startup's sixty-five-person team to its limits. Google pretty much left the site alone, wisely postponing monetization. A few months later *Time* magazine called YouTube its "person of the year."

In 2007, a team from Simon Fraser University crawled YouTube's early videos and found familiar power-law distributions that recur in Internet phenomena. (The Pareto 80/20 rule familiar to many readers is a type of power-law distribution.) That is, unconstrained social systems often have a tiny "fat" tail of extreme outcomes—wealth, fame, customer profitability— and the long tail of potentially millions of individual entities. Power-law distributions occur in nature (earthquakes as measured by intensity), at winner-take-all survivors like Google, and wherever inclusive communities like eBay sellers or Wikipedia contributors can be convened. YouTube exhibits power-law behavior in many regards, as we will see; for now, chart 3 shows the Simon Fraser team's findings with regard to video uploads after the site's launch.

Ten years later, Professor Mathias Bärtl published a statistical analysis of YouTube uploads and downloads, and the same power law held true: 3 percent of all channels uploaded 28 percent of all content and received 85 percent of all views.[38]

The growth is truly staggering. Though it is comparing apples to oranges, in a sense, it's still interesting to see Facebook—launched at almost exactly the same time—follow a similar growth pattern (see chart 4), albeit in users rather than uploaded videos.

For comparison, TikTok was "born global" rather than expanding off a US user base, and so tapped into a much larger market to achieve unprecedented growth (see chart 5).

What made it possible for YouTube to experience this kind of success? Bearing in mind the notion of "combinatorial" innovation discussed by Eric Brynjolfsson and Andrew McAfee in *The Second Machine Age*, YouTube stands as a textbook example of recombining existing technological resources in a new way.[39] That is, YouTube's success came not in inventing something new (such as NCSA Mosaic/Netscape Navigator or Google search) but in applying a novel software-driven combination of existing technologies and trends.

Chart 3 YouTube growth as extrapolated from crawling the site in 2007. Source: Cheng, Dale, and Liu, "Statistics and Social Network."

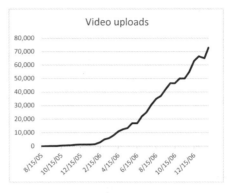

Video uploads

Chart 4 Facebook subscriber growth occurred simultaneously with YouTube's immediate popularity. Source: Facebook reported data, https://www.statista.com/chart/870/facebooks-user-growth-since-2004/.

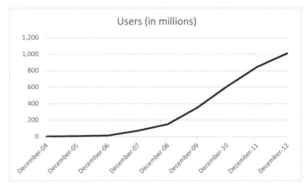

Users (in millions)

Chart 5 TikTok was the fastest app to reach one billion users. Source: Sensortower, https://sensortower.com/blog/tiktok-downloads-2-billion/.

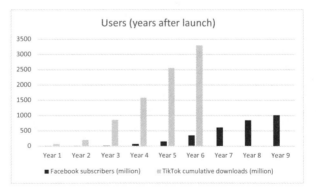

Users (years after launch)

■ Facebook subscribers (million)   ■ TikTok cumulative downloads (million)

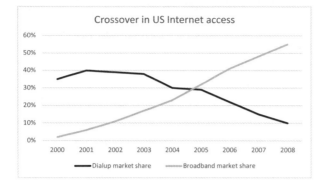

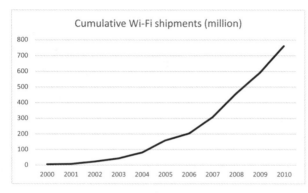

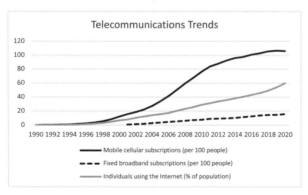

Chart 6 US dial-up versus wired broadband access, 2000–2008. Source: Pew Internet.

Chart 7 Global Wi-Fi chip shipments. Source: ABI research.

Chart 8 Worldwide broadband deployment is led by mobile phones. Source: World Bank.

These technologies are bandwidth, video, digital social networks, and storage. Notably absent from the list is search, which we will discuss separately later in the book.

Bandwidth

As of 2001, US dial-up Internet access peaked at about 40 percent of households. From there, it plunged as cable modems and DSL services rapidly climbed to reach more than half of US households.[40] It's uncanny that YouTube launched at precisely the crossover from predominantly dial-up to broadband home access (see chart 6).

Further, Wi-Fi shipments were rapidly increasing at exactly the same time (see chart 7), bringing mobile broadband to schools, coffee shops, and fast-food restaurants across the world. Outside the United States and parts of Europe and Japan, most of the world connected to broadband in more public venues, such as in Internet cafés, parks, and libraries, in the 2000 to 2010 decade.

For those of a certain age, the tiny windows and painfully slow downloads for even a few seconds of video in the dial-up era made YouTube feel like a revolution. These access trends were accelerating, especially with mobile broadband, all over the globe as the data in chart 8 make clear.

In summary, video on the Internet was rare, clumsy, slow, and low-resolution before YouTube. After its launch, the service harnessed the rapid growth of broadband connections to make online video as easy as text for many users.

Video

Even before the launch of smartphones led by the iPhone in 2007 and its Android counterparts slightly later, digital video was getting cheaper and easier to produce as YouTube was preparing to launch. It came from sources as diverse as VHS or DVD rips on a PC, Flip and GoPro video cameras (launched in 2006), and video features could increasingly be found on stand-alone cameras from Nikon, Canon, and the like. Miniaturization and economies of scale brought high-quality digital video production capacity to the masses. After the smartphone took hold, most other digital camera formats, including video cameras, plummeted in popularity. For YouTubers in search of high production value, dedicated HD cameras are available for well under $1,000. Apart from capture, addressing the large number of video formats and players in the market in 2005—Windows, Apple, and Real Networks for starters—was simplified by using Adobe's Flash as a common denominator. This practice stopped in 2015 as HTML 5 (an open standard as compared to Adobe's proprietary player, one with lower system overhead) supported video playback across all major browsers.

As chart 9 shows, video-capable smartphone availability preceded two noticeable changes to YouTube videos. First, after 2009, when both Apple and Samsung launched smartphones with video cameras, YouTube videos got longer. Then, after 2013, uploads surged toward the five hundred hours

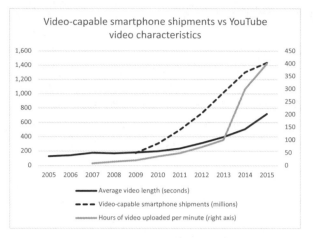

Chart 9 After Apple and Samsung added video functionality to smartphones in 2009 and other vendors followed, YouTube uploads got longer and proliferated. Source: Hours per minute from Tubular Insights (https://tubularinsights.com/hours-minute -uploaded-youtube/); smartphone shipments from Statista; and average video length courtesy of Pex (https://pex.com).

per minute level reported in 2019. As channel creators started to realize the amounts of money involved in a successful YouTube franchise, a small number of uploaders got extremely busy, as Pew Internet reported in the introduction. It's important to note that these full-time workers did not, by and large, shoot video on their smartphones, but at the global scale, those billions of smartphones now in the market appear to have some impact on what got uploaded.

Storage

One reason video was slow to be adopted in the early Internet years was its huge file sizes. Relative to available bandwidth, it was a recipe for frustration. In addition to the broadband buildout noted above, computing continued to follow Moore's law, and in the early 2000s, hardware was good enough that many computers could compress and decompress video relatively painlessly. Much as the MP3 format facilitated digital audio file sharing, Advanced Video Coding (also known as H.264 or MPEG-4 AVC) helped make video streaming possible at YouTube as well as at Netflix, Hulu, and iTunes. (In the early days, YouTube used a variant of H.263: the video window was 320×240 pixels with mono MP3 audio.) As with broadband deployment, YouTube benefited from excellent timing in relation to the H.264 codec, which was launched in 2003. As of 2019, the pool of more than 4,000 patents related to the codec was dominated by Panasonic, LG, the Japanese sovereign patent pool, and

Dolby. YouTube, or even Google, could never have developed that complex an algorithm independently.

Google is very quiet with any numbers relating to YouTube, but as we have seen, five hundred hours of video have been uploaded every minute since 2015. At 1080p resolution (not the highest resolution, nor the lowest), that's 1.5 GB per hour per video. At this rate and size of upload, which occurs twenty-four hours a day, more than a million gigabytes of video is uploaded per day—close to four hundred thousand petabytes per year. Very few companies on the planet have the ability and capacity to design and manage a distributed storage environment at that scale, including crawling videos to look for illegal material, possible copyright infringement, and other signs of trouble. TikTok states that its servers are not collocated with those of parent company ByteDance in China, but employees report that the two data streams have in fact commingled, as has algorithm development.[41]

Consumer Readiness

YouTube launched in the right place at the right time. In part, this was a matter of technological preconditions, as we have just seen. Equally, if not more, important were customer expectations. A familiar narrative in tech circles holds that technological capability rises over time. Look at how black-and-white TV was followed by color TV, which was followed by HDTV then 4K TV. But in practice, this generalization turns out to be complicated. The LP record was succeeded in sales dominance not by the compact disc but by the cassette, a medium of arguably lower fidelity but higher convenience. Very few car-mounted record players were ever delivered, for example, nor did Sony ever produce a pocket-sized "LP-man."

In the case of YouTube, online music sharing via MP3 files similarly conditioned listeners to accept lower fidelity as the tradeoff for greater convenience and lower cost. When online video came around after MP3, it objectively wasn't very clean and the audio, especially in early years, was notably poor. With an audience accustomed to and comfortable with highly compressed sound, "good enough" video lowered the barrier to entry; imagine if people had insisted on DVD-level video quality over the Internet in the early years. It also helped that YouTube was a simple browser-based application, requiring a very short learning curve. Had it launched only six years earlier, YouTube would likely have come on plastic discs to be installed on PCs. Growth would have been substantially slower. Instead, under the software as a service model, in 2007, Google was able to announce localization of YouTube with 102 variations of the front page of the website.

Another factor in consumer acceptance of YouTube was dissatisfaction with network television. Indeed, the original tagline "Broadcast Yourself" implicitly attacks the cable TV world and worldview. Again, "good enough" was sufficient. Even today, audio and video quality on YouTube are marginal in many cases, subservient to the sufficient attraction of the material. Whether it was music (like Napster, available free), creative artistry, entertainment, or nostalgia, the novelty and variety of on-demand video carried the day, compression artifacts notwithstanding.

On the supply side, YouTube succeeded because enough people were ready, willing, and able to upload content that the phenomenal growth rate noted earlier was possible. Put slightly differently, YouTube works because of crowdsourcing, just as Wikipedia, Linux, and Kickstarter do. In the early years, many videos were responses to other videos, making them small-world social networks of a sort.[42] The notion of virality had not yet become widely available as a conceptual framework. Instead, in the early days most videos were said to be intended for an audience of fewer than one hundred people.

None of these factors in user sentiment and behavior would matter if there weren't a path to corporate profitability. Adding ads in 2007 gave Google the beginnings of a monetization mechanism that continues to evolve through such efforts as paid subscription to YouTube Red (now called YouTube Premium), an ad-free version currently serving about 50 million subscribers that also includes original programming and downloadable videos. While financials were not reported for many years, in 2022, Google revealed that YouTube brought in $29 billion in 2021, or about a sixth of overall corporate revenues.

Algorithmic Content Filtering

At the time of its origination, YouTube acted in a manner that suggested the history of Napster was very much front of mind. Copyrighted material was present almost from the outset, and Google's initial stance was to force copyright holders to report improper uses of their material. The Digital Millennium Copyright Act (passed in 1998) simultaneously expanded the coverage of copyright law while limiting the liability of Internet service providers and other intermediaries from prosecution. Google invoked this so-called safe harbor provision (that originated in earlier 1996 legislation) after it bought YouTube, but that position was quickly challenged.

NBC was displeased with the handling of a *Saturday Night Live* clip and sent a letter demanding removal of the clip in 2006. Viacom (at the time, the parent company of MTV, Comedy Central, and other television networks, along with Paramount Pictures) sued Google in 2007. In conjunction with the litigation, the media company had submitted more than 100,000 takedown notices, some of them for material it did not own. The case made its way through multiple courts, with complex judgments giving neither side a clear-cut victory. In the end, the parties settled in 2014, reportedly with no money changing hands.[43]

The case made both sides look bad. Viacom was proved to have uploaded some of the clips they demanded be removed (sometimes using one of eighteen different external marketing companies). Google executives, meanwhile, were quoted in emails saying that the service needed to grow as fast as possible, by whatever means necessary. Notably, Viacom did not pursue any damages from copyright infringement after Google launched its Content ID filtering system (initially called Video Identification[44]) in 2008. (One source suggests Google was working on Content ID before the YouTube purchase was announced.[45]) After all the litigation, Viacom realized it needed YouTube's reach and demographics to promote its shows and movies. Google had successfully shown it could identify copyright infringement proactively. Violations are now referred to the rights holder who can determine the subsequent course of action. Some videos are taken down while others are monetized with the rights holders' interests protected; and for still others, the video's ad revenue is permitted to flow to the YouTube creator.

The prospect of being sued out of existence (as Grokster was in 2005) motivated Google to apply machine learning to the copyright issue. As of 2018, the parent company revealed it had spent $100 million on developing Content ID, which led to $3 billion in payments to rights holders. It's important to note the changing role of machine learning at the major platform companies. Here, it was initially deployed to defend against litigation before later being mobilized to increase watch time, view counts, and other drivers of profitability.

Beyond copyrighted material, other forms of objectionable content still find their way onto the platforms. Once again, US federal law drove change. Dartmouth professor Hany Farid's PhotoDNA technology (developed in conjunction with Microsoft and now freely available to many service providers) is now used to compare uploads to known existing child pornography, with mandatory reporting to the National Center for Missing & Exploited Children. But PhotoDNA only works on copies of existing images. Furthermore, many people who exploit children connect to others who do so via the YouTube comments section rather than direct uploads. Google was embarrassed in 2017 and again 2019 by revelations that predators and pornography buffs were exchanging information in the comments. They congregated around presumably innocent videos of gymnastics and other activities that the predators sexualized. Here, the threat of Federal Trade Commission investigation into insufficient protection of user data was concerning,[46] but the more imminent spur to action was an advertiser boycott. In February 2019 AT&T, Disney, and Fortnite creator Epic Games all announced they were leaving the YouTube ad platform because of Google's ongoing failure to police comments.[47]

While copyright infringement is ably handled with machine-learning-driven comparisons, and pedophilia is universally abhorrent, there remain millions of videos (and comment sections) where ideology, custom, and user cleverness make detection of objectionable or forbidden content more difficult. Terrorism recruitment and glorification videos are an obvious example. Machine learning cannot reliably pick out beheadings or shootings. Racism, misogyny, and gun-training are usually not illegal, and are often addressed in coded language. The material can include text and audio not in English. For these and similar edge cases, platforms must rely on human moderators.

In addition to protecting the interests of the platform, algorithmic curation also shapes the behavior of millions of uploaders and billions of viewers. Being a "slave to the algorithm," as multiple YouTubers have called their status, is perhaps *the* defining characteristic of the people for whom online video is a livelihood. (The phrase has become a mantra among content creators, to the point that it is available on mugs and T-shirts.) The rules are opaque to viewers more than to uploaders, who themselves learn what works through trial and error. After that discovery, however, what worked in February might not work in March. Algorithmic curation presents a moving target that is never fully visible. What scholars call "digital traces" represent a huge part of creator feedback: changing viewership patterns and numbers, telling comments from users, and chance encounters with other video creators—often on other platforms such as Facebook, LinkedIn, or Instagram. We will have much more to say of curation in chapter 3.

2020: The TikTok Moment

A number of cultural weather systems converged in 2020 to create a massive storm that affected millions of viewers in many nations across the world. First, ByteDance, a Chinese tech firm, had by that time built considerable algorithmic expertise, finding success in short-video services in both the United States (Musical.ly) and China (Douyin) as well as a profit-able advertising business on a news site running under a different Chinese brand (Toutiao). Even so, US market penetration was primarily limited to teenage girls sharing lip-sync videos. Second, the pandemic locked up billions of people who grew hungry for distractions from both quarantine and polarized political discourse. Finally, ByteDance controlled the algorithmic landscape around the renamed TikTok service and exploited a combination of purpose-built training data and viral sharing on other social media services to grow at a stunning rate.

Numbers tell only a part of the story, but they make for compelling headlines:

- As of May 2020, the TikTok app had been downloaded 2 billion times.
- In the first quarter of 2020 alone, TikTok accumulated 315 million new downloads according to the media analyst firm Sensor Tower. That appeared to be a world record.
- Users behaved as though they were addicted to TikTok, watching nearly an hour of the less than one-minute clips a day.

TikTok's Chinese ownership at ByteDance raised security concerns that were not eased by early (2018) versions of the user agreement that stated that "we will also share your information with any member or affiliate of our group, in China, for the purposes set out above, to assist in the improvement and optimization of the Platform, in order to prevent illegal [under what jurisdiction?] uses, increase user numbers, development, engineering and analysis of information or for our internal business purposes."[48] The US military banned the app from government devices beginning in late 2019 and several firms, including Amazon and Wells Fargo, followed suit, at least temporarily.

President Donald Trump took dramatic action against TikTok later in 2020 as he threatened to shut it down in the United States unless ownership and data centers were transferred out of Chinese hands. There were likely many causes for his concern, not least of them the perception that teenagers had spread the word via this social medium to register for a Trump campaign rally in Tulsa, Oklahoma, to inflate crowd expectations before essentially nobody showed up. Whether or not TikTok and K-pop fans were actually responsible (as we will see, TikTok is not really a social network), the perception may well have provided sufficient motivation for the threatened ban.[49]

For our purposes, TikTok matters for several reasons: its cultural migration, its subject matter, and, primarily, its algorithm. Prior to TikTok, big

US tech firms had often tried and failed to succeed in Chinese markets. Apple stood as something of an exception, but the fact of counterfeit Apple *stores* suggests that success was relative. Conversely, it's difficult to think of a Chinese brand that has succeeded globally. Haier appliances and Lenovo PCs are moderately successful, but Haier still largely sells under purchased US nameplates and Lenovo used IBM product names after buying that business. TikTok is the first consumer tech brand to originate in China and succeed worldwide. Some analysts suggest the reason for this success is the power of an app designed to support its algorithms and, in the process, leap over all manner of cultural barriers.[50]

TikTok's content format—initially, the fifteen- to sixty-second video—has proven to be amenable to many subjects. These range from teen culture and fashion to sports highlights to unselfconsciously goofy dancing and lip-syncing. The genre of the "challenge video," while not original to TikTok (think of ice buckets), flourished there. Originally focusing on dance moves, the genre has expanded to beauty, sports, and fashion, all of which are attractive to advertisers.[51] Other challenges involve vandalism, humiliation, bullying, and physical harm. Water bead gels are shot out of pellet guns at delivery drivers, Hyundai and Kia automobiles are hotwired and taken for joyrides, Tide Pods are eaten, Super Glue is used as hair gel—all on camera. Multiple deaths have occurred, for instance, after a "blackout challenge" led to suffocations.[52] Pediatricians now get regular updates on the stupid things large numbers of kids will be doing to themselves.[53] Importantly, the algorithm can feed these videos to kids who don't search for them, spreading the fad faster than it might otherwise have caught on.

For all the power of the For You algorithm, marginalized ethnic groups face a conundrum. TikTok at once supports diversity of ethnicity and sexual orientation and also has actively directed content moderators to block videos of overweight, disabled, and queer people. The explanation was ostensibly to prevent bullying, but in the end, the decision further homogenized the environment at the cost of people who looked or acted differently.[54] A study by my colleagues Ellen Simpson and Bryan Semaan performed during the COVID-19 lockdown tracked the use of TikTok by LGBTQ people and came to a complex conclusion. The tool both helped people find stories they could relate to and reinforced feelings of exclusion from predominant norms. When the algorithm was particularly successful, the feelings could be paradoxical. One respondent stated that "TikTok . . . just continually knows what content you want and gives it to you. And you're like, that's a little scary. But also, I really like . . . seeing all this content and not having to search it out. . . .

It's nice, but it's a little bit scary." The paradoxical feelings of the individual echoed the overall conclusion: "We found," the authors write, "that TikTok's For You Page algorithm constructs contradictory identity spaces that are both supportive and also exclusionary."[55]

It is to this For You algorithm that we will direct our attention in chapter 3, for it has proven to be the engine that powers the rapid adoption, viral memetic spread, and high degree of user engagement. The Musical.ly app focused initially on teenaged girls, so did not need to be concerned with mass audiences. The constraints on time and types of content similarly narrowed the technical scope of the effort. Finally, the app made feedback easy to offer, and users could see the app evolve rapidly in response to feedback—fueling further feedback. At that point (2018), ByteDance's acquisition of TikTok introduced a new factor into the growth curve: massive advertising. According to the *Wall Street Journal*, ByteDance spent $1 billion on advertising in the United States alone in 2018.[56] Three years later, much of that advertising was placed on Snapchat, which makes complete demographic sense. All the new users, from many parts of the world, would not have been worth the investment had it not been for the success of the For You algorithm in keeping many of the new users stuck to the app.

Conclusion

Before looking at what online video has become since 2005, it's worth acknowledging how hard it is to do what the platforms do at the scale they must manage. To get some sense of the machinery behind the curtain, we now turn our attention to how online video's functional operations have evolved.

3

How Do Video Platforms Work?

After looking at the basic technical elements of online video in chapter 2, we will assume that such matters as storage, compression, bandwidth, and the like will be addressed by highly competent teams at the platform companies. Apart from video compression—the switch from Adobe Flash to HTML 5—there have been few publicly visible shifts in the technical landscape of video production, transmission, and storage since 2010. Viewership is much more heavily mobile, and ByteDance gears all its many properties to a smartphone-first paradigm. The technologies of curation, however, have evolved dramatically: how forbidden material is detected, how questionable material is addressed, and how novel material is introduced to users who didn't search for it. All of these tasks have proven to be technically difficult, managerially contentious, and politically loaded.

Tarleton Gillespie, the former Cornell professor now at Microsoft Research, argues persuasively that content moderation is a core attribute of a digital platform when he writes that "moderation is, in many ways, *the* commodity that platforms offer."[1] Given that YouTube, Facebook, Twitter, and other such platforms create very little, if any, content on their own, how these companies recruit and retain users who create the business is of the highest importance. At the same time, the scale of participation combined with the Internet's tendency to flatten nuance and drive trolling and other incivilities means that the problem is hard.

Moderation

As we have seen, Google invoked the "safe harbor" provision that originated in the Communications Decency Act (CDA) of 1996 to exempt itself from responsibility for much of the content that YouTube's users uploaded. Even though the CDA was ruled unconstitutional by the US Supreme Court in 1997, the "safe harbor" concept remained in force. Eventually, it fell under section 230 of the United States Code, which is the legal underpinning of the Federal Communications Commission and related matters such as penalties for damage to underwater communications cables. Section 230 does two things. First, it protects providers of Internet services from liability for the speech exercised by users of that infrastructure. Second, when those providers do choose to police some speech or behavior, it does not imply that they must police *all* behavior.[2]

Gillespie points out a crucial distinction: section 230 was meant to apply to Internet service providers like AOL or Comcast, although it was quickly invoked by social media companies a few years later.[3] Because Facebook and YouTube are exempted from responsibility for what their users post, except in a few extreme cases of child endangerment and terrorism, these companies have been slow to regulate other troubling behavior. In late 2020, Facebook finally reversed course and decided to ban Holocaust deniers, for example. Because the law in the United States, where the companies are headquartered, is so favorable, those companies act to moderate content primarily for economic reasons rather than legal ones. Google has repeatedly failed to pay fines levied on it by the European Union. For its part, eBay first tried to block sales of Nazi-related memorabilia in only France and Germany but, finding that nearly impossible, pulled such items from the site entirely. The point here is that US economic logic is dictating what billions of non-US citizens see and don't see.

For their parts, Facebook and YouTube both consciously defined themselves as communications conduits rather than broadcasters; the precedent is that AT&T isn't responsible for any horrible things an individual might speak over its wires. As both services grew, however, and functioned more as amplifier than as conduit, issues of what broadcasters called "standards and practices" came to the fore. What value judgments must we make as a company distributes calls to action, ideas, and attacks of others? Facebook long resisted content moderation to take down (or affix warnings to) hate speech, claiming a high-minded commitment to freedom of speech. But repeated episodes of bullying politicians (in many parts of the world) clearly violating the standards led to advertiser boycotts and other public relations disasters. External pressure appeared to be the only kind that mattered. Internal concerns from content moderators, often contractors who work under strict nondisclosure agreements, reportedly were ignored since the politicians' feeds drew viewership and the all-important "engagement."[4]

As of 2020, YouTube and its kin in the United States were (lightly) regulated by laws related to the phone companies. YouTube is of course heavily reliant on telecommunications, but it is also a near neighbor to the movie industry. Movies are governed largely not by federal law but by self-regulation: movie ratings derive from the Motion Picture Association, a trade group. In other ways, online video resembles newspapers, which in the United States fall under the umbrella of the First Amendment related to freedom of the press, and so are regulated by court cases. Further, Google, as a major actor in the advertising ecosystem, is subject to oversight by the Federal Trade Commission. Predictably, any entity that spans so many jurisdictions—in only one country representing a minority of its total traffic—will often escape close scrutiny by claiming exemption from any given mandate.

For the platforms, section 230 is a great gift. Facebook and others can profit from content they neither produce nor must police. Inaccuracy, whether random and inadvertent or aggressive and programmatic, is rampant, and profitable. Digital literacy is troublingly low—especially when sites that could be used for fact-checking, namely Google, often surface results that have been cleverly promoted by peddlers of falsehoods.[5] Anti-Semitic, misogynist, and racist stereotypes, as well as new additions such as anti-vaccination ideas, only begin the list.

When accounts do get banned, how do users respond? Sarah Myers West of the University of Southern California contacted more than five hundred individuals who reported having been the subject of content moderation. Her study is instructive with regard to both persons and bots that remove objectionable content. First, many respondents reported that the exact offense was never specified on the takedown notice nor via customer service channels. Second, most personalized the action, typically attributing the ban to an unnamed "they" who are unjustly targeting "me." Contrast this attitude to the receipt of an IRS audit or parking ticket: both are bureaucratic functions of a functioning civil order, and while nobody likes either penalty, the response is not usually to attribute malice to a person. Third, mistakes happen: one person's surname was Pizza and Facebook repeatedly suspended the account. Recourse was slow and frustrating. The study implies that if content moderation were represented differently, perhaps more users would adopt an "if you did the crime you do the time" perspective rather than leap to conspiracy and other paranoid fantasies.[6]

This is not for a moment to suggest the problems of accuracy on and abuses of online platforms are simple to address. Twitter's vice president of trust and safety Del Harvey used simple statistics to drive home the scale of the moderation issue in a TED talk in 2014. "Given the scale Twitter is at, a one-in-a million chance happens 500 times a day," she stated. That changes operating assumptions. "For us, edge cases, those rare situations that are unlikely to occur, are more like norms." If you assume 99.999 percent of tweets pose no threat whatsoever, "that tiny percentage of tweets remaining works out to roughly 150,000 per month. The sheer scale of what we're dealing with makes for a challenge."[7] Bear in mind that Harvey was speaking in 2014, when YouTube uploads were probably half of 2020 levels, and that YouTube sees three times the monthly active users Twitter has; the scale of the moderation problem gets tangibly staggering.

It's important here to look at the issue of scale carefully: scale is not merely a question of size. In food preparation or pharmaceutical manufacturing, merely multiplying a small batch to larger quantities will not always yield consistent (or safe) results. Scale is the ability of actions taken in small contexts to behave predictably in much larger contexts. If a hate-speech detection algorithm finds offensive content in ten out of every hundred posts in, say, an American football fan site of 1,000 members, it will likely not scale to the discussion boards related to, say, world football on Eurosport, not to mention Asian meme stocks on Reddit. Content moderation for the platforms is only partially a technical problem, involving as it does (relatively) expensive human moderators and, more importantly, public perception.

The moderation problem is made harder yet by the platforms' need to maintain the illusion of civility and neighborliness (treatment of the banned to the contrary).[8] Few platforms publicize their moderation teams; in 2013, an *NPR* reporter was denied access to moderators at both Google and Microsoft, though a spokeswoman at the latter said moderation was "a yucky job."[9] Much of the work is outsourced. One moderator told a reporter in the fall of 2019 he was paid $18.50 an hour (about $37,000 a year). For that salary, he watched "VE"—violent extremism, primarily in Arabic—videos all day as an employee of Accenture, the tech services firm Google contracts with for some of its moderation.[10] In October 2019, Google reported that it had removed 160,000 pieces of violent extremism material from various of the company's properties over the previous year. That's about 450 per day, every day—a big number, but far from sufficient.[11]

The stress of watching violence and degradation for an entire shift—YouTube publicly promised that its moderators would work only four-hour shifts but had not followed through a year later[12]—is borne by a relatively small number of people for the benefit of billions of users. Some of these moderators have sued Microsoft and Facebook, claiming damaged health in the workplace, compounded by insufficient training and resources.[13] On-shore contract moderators, for example, do not qualify for the benefits (including employee perks like climbing walls and access to internal job postings) granted to full-time Google employees. These full-timers, meanwhile, themselves report severe psychological ramifications of their job.[14] Off-shore, contract workers in the Philippines and elsewhere enforce Silicon Valley cultural norms the world over. The exhausting and challenging job of content moderation is an entry-level opening as they aspire to move up inside their services firms to the more prestigious job of call center representative as their spoken English improves.[15]

In the realm of sexualized images of people of legal age, the situation is much more complex and culturally contingent. Tumblr, for example, had allowed many subcommunities made up of body-positive, queer, and gender nonconforming individuals to post nude images over the decade-plus after the service's launch in 2007. Labeling the images as pornographic would ignore many of the subculture-specific messages (often relayed or implied in hashtags) that were conveyed. When a 2018 ban on NSFW (not safe/suitable for work) images was suddenly announced as a response to possible episodes involving child endangerment, algorithms were implemented that essentially destroyed much of the previously legitimate discourse.[16]

Censorship of sexualized images, anywhere but especially on the Internet platforms, encodes human attitudes into either machine learning or policy documents. This process, not surprisingly, is predominantly performed by males. Two episodes are instructive. In the first, three scholars at the University of Utah reverse engineered computer-vision pornography filtering (CVPF) based on the academic articles that supported its commercialization. CVPF was born in the late 1990s in response to the porn panic of the early Internet period and continues to be deployed. Pornography, for the machine seeking it, consists of rules generating the classification of human heads, nipples, and pubic hair. All the training data was of females, and "the word 'penis' does not appear in the 102 articles." When images were included in the scholarly articles under review, 78 percent of the pornographic images depicted females compared to 17 percent with men; 5 percent were not able to be classified. Breast detection is always of the female variety: heads are detected, sometimes using facial recognition, in order for them to be used to triangulate the chest and thus the decisively important nipples.[17]

More recently, a former TikTok employee encapsulated the content moderation issue there as binary: "B*obs, or no b*obs?" Note the very nonbinary policy challenges the author enumerates:

In a way, TikTok is like a mini society (albeit a lot less complex lol) because they need to create rules and governance systems for:

- Who should have decision power? How do we choose these people and what training do they need?
- How do we enforce "laws"?
- When is the law negotiable? Under what circumstances do they make exceptions?
- Who goes to prison (*which accounts do we remove*)?
- How do we classify risk and harm on a scale of 1–10? Are drugs worse than guns? If users are allowed to post violence during the war and it leads to more misinformation and fraud, is it still worth it?
- How do we tackle information/content around biased news, climate change, human rights, hate speech, free speech, safety, etc.[18]

Then comes the reality of billions of users uploading millions of hours of content per day. Such gray areas as feminist nudity, artistic nudity, and women's health nudity stand little chance of surviving the yes-or-no logic necessary to power the content moderation algorithms. As the former TikTok employee concludes: "Moderating content is very hard, and I have deep admiration for the work moderators are doing for us to enjoy this amazing platform. Without them, you would not want to spend much time on the platform; I can tell you that. Policies and moderation exist to protect users against the worst-case scenarios. Unfortunately, this also means a cost of business to the platform in the form of unnecessary removals and bans."[19]

How might things be different? The technical challenge is not trivial, as Facebook found out in 2017. In that year, video of a random gunshot killing by a man upset with his girlfriend was posted to his page and not taken down for more than two hours. Two years later, a terrorist livestreamed his attack on a mosque in Christchurch, New Zealand, during which he killed fifty-one people; 1.5 million reposted copies of the video were subsequently taken down, and Facebook worked with law enforcement to better train its detection algorithms.[20] Global video sharing without human gatekeepers so far exceeds human scale that machine learning must be employed, and in both of these incidents, there was simply insufficient training data to teach the algorithms what to block.[21] Meanwhile, the fact that millions of people and bots apparently wanted to praise a terrorist for murdering worshippers raises its own set of troubling questions.

After the Christchurch attack, YouTube, like Facebook, was deluged—seeing "an unprecedented number of attempts"—with reposts of the shooter's video. His seventy-four-page "manifesto" featuring explicit calls for violence was also excerpted and redistributed on other Google properties. An internal email directed moderators to mark anything questionable as "terrorist content," with exemptions for legitimate news sites. A statement to *Vice* explained:

> Since Friday's horrific tragedy, we've removed tens of thousands of videos and terminated hundreds of accounts created to promote or glorify the shooter. The volume of related videos uploaded to YouTube in the 24 hours after the attack was unprecedented both in scale and speed, at times as fast as a new upload every second. In response, we took a number of steps, including automatically rejecting any footage of the violence, temporarily suspending the ability to sort or filter searches by upload date, and making sure searches on this event pulled up results from authoritative news sources like *The New Zealand Herald* or *USA Today*.[22]

Because of the immense volume, Google automated the takedown process by using machine learning to perform the work of the human moderators who were essentially overrun. The platform risked some false positives in which videos were removed that shouldn't have been in the service of a more pressing need.[23]

Mass shootings tend to focus corporate attention. Meanwhile, it took BBC reporting for Google to fix YouTube's type-ahead search feature which had completed the query "how to have" with the phrase "s*x with your kids."[24] Dropbox told the *New York Times* scanning uploaded videos was "not a priority" as of July 2019 even though the service was known to be used by predators.[25] What else is lurking in the eighty years of video uploaded every day—to YouTube alone?

Again, human screeners are already overtaxed and stressed: watching a steady diet of horrible images and videos in a sick game of cat and mouse is not sustainable. Neither is fact-checking. Those who called for Facebook to have spotted the Christchurch video faster have no sense of what it takes for a two-billion-member social network to operate, much less be policed. YouTube had announced in 2017 that it was hiring more screeners and other content graders to bring "the total number of people across Google working to address content that might violate our policies to over 10,000 in 2018," according to a blog post by YouTube's CEO.[26] Even if those people were in fact hired and deployed, significant abuses persisted into the 2020s.

How many screeners are needed? Here is a back-of-the-envelope guess given that the platforms don't say much, except to promise that algorithmic detection will improve. Five hundred hours of uploaded video per minute, at an average of 6 minutes per video, would be 5,000 videos per minute, times 60 minutes per hour, times 24 hours per day. That's 7.2 million videos per day at YouTube alone, in a wide range of languages and with a wide range of cultural norms and laws. Let's assume 5 percent are problematic. That's 360,000 videos per day, or about 2.5 million judgment calls per week. Let's assume a screener can process 15 videos per hour (4 minutes apiece) and that screeners work 4-hour shifts as promised, 5 days per week. That's 300 videos per week, per screener. 300 into 2.5 million is 8,000, roughly in line with the YouTube CEO's promise.

What meaningful action can be taken to address the issue of content moderation? Clearly automation is not catching the "bad actors." At least 100,000 content screeners work across the tech industry addressing flagged content. As one might expect, the job can alternate between drudgery and horror. Burnout is common. According to Sarah T. Roberts of UCLA, who interviewed dozens of such workers: "One woman used to work for MySpace, which used to be a big thing, and she told me that she's now a bookkeeper. She got as far away from dealing with humans as she could and got into the dealing-with-numbers business. She told me that she wouldn't shake people's hands for about three years after she quit her job. I asked her why, and she said it's because she knew people were disgusting."[27]

Because many of these people work as contractors, mental health care is not included as part of the employment. Given nondisclosure agreements, arms-length employment, and the taboo nature of much of what they see, this work occurs outside public view or even awareness. The scale of the problem underlines a consistent theme with regard to social media platforms: computation and crowdsourcing have built something too big to understand, manage, or police. It's impossible to find enough people to volunteer for such duty, even if the content platforms were committed to cleaning up their operations. Assuming 100,000 people are insufficient to the task of finding all abuse, prohibited violence, criminal conduct, and hate speech, how many people would it take to filter out the sewage? Where would they work, how would they be paid, what workplace safety provisions would be necessary?

Follow the Money: Moderation Is for Advertisers

If one follows the money, the content platforms are feeling pressure—from advertisers. The public outcry (particularly on social media) that can snowball against a brand when it is associated with something deemed "unacceptable" in a moment's notice typically caroms back to the platform owner. If the platforms are going to allow advertisers to capitalize on video creators' fame to get in front of millions of eyeballs, the reasoning goes, then they must provide assurance that said creators will abide by some version of "standards and practices" or what YouTube calls "Community Guidelines."

A year of reckoning came in 2018 as Google tried both to assure advertisers and to retain talent who were tempted by Amazon's Twitch or Facebook's Instagram. The population that suffered was the small creators who were big enough to have tasted ad revenue. Google seemed to realize that policing and providing incentive to the top of the long tail eliminated many of its problems. By the end of 2018, each video posted on the top 5 percent of channels, the Google Preferred monetization tier, was viewed by human content moderators. According to the audience insight firm Nielsen, the top sixty-five media brands on YouTube account for half of the views, so ignoring small content producers makes financial sense, albeit at the cost of new voices.[28]

After the mishaps of 2018, advertisers are also turning to third-party solutions that promote what's called "brand safety.[29]" That is, a tool like Grapeshot (owned by Oracle since 2018) will screen content for messages, images, and language that would harm a brand advertising in the context of said content. Adobe and other software companies offer similar tools. Interactive agencies and other players in the ad-placement industry have also announced offerings: an example is the European demand-side platform Targetoo.[30] Other third parties serve as rating agencies: the Media Rating Council, a longtime television ratings watchdog, attested that YouTube had a suitably low advertiser safety error rate in both 2020 and 2021.[31]

Beyond Search and Recommendation: The TikTok Video Presentation Algorithm

Eschewing Google's longtime emphasis on search and recommendation, ByteDance instead automatically launches videos, full screen, on the viewer's device (see fig. 3). For all the hype around the mysterious brilliance, verging on premonition, of TikTok's algorithmic "secret sauce," close examination shows there is little brilliance, just extreme coherence and focus. That is, the recommendation engine in the For You algorithm breaks little new ground, instead applying existing techniques consistently, pervasively, and within

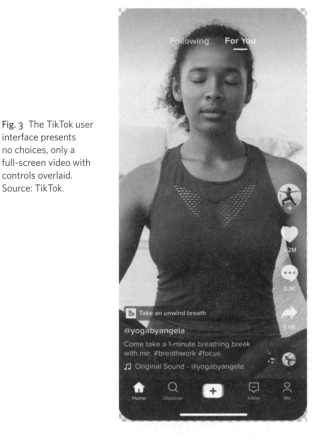

Fig. 3 The TikTok user interface presents no choices, only a full-screen video with controls overlaid. Source: TikTok.

tight constraints. TikTok doesn't pretend to compete with other services that deliver rants or lectures, long-form music videos, or television content.

As TikTok states on its website,

> Recommendations are based on a number of factors, including things like:
> - *User interactions* such as the videos you like or share, accounts you follow, comments you post, and content you create.
> - *Video information*, which might include details like captions, sounds, and hashtags.
> - *Device and account settings* like your language preference, country setting, and device type. These factors are included to make sure the system is optimized for performance, but they receive lower weight in the recommendation system relative to other data points we measure since users don't actively express these as preferences.[32]

TikTok is careful to collect a lot of basic information, such as what device(s) are used, which videos a user shares and how they are shared, beats per minute of the song used as a soundtrack of favorite clips, and geotagging of the user in motion in their locality, region, and country.[33]

TikTok also benefits from gathering data during video creation. If a video is made inside the app environment, matching that video to user preferences is easier given this knowledge of the creator and the content, some of which may have been performed at the request of the algorithm ("wave your hand" or "jump up and down"). As one analyst said of Netflix years earlier, the recommendation algorithm is much like a dating app "except that the movie doesn't have to like you back."[34] In TikTok, the video can in fact sometimes be classified in terms of the users it will potentially seek or attract.

TikTok's format provides it with algorithmic and other advantages. Given their previous cap at one-minute duration, a user will often watch many videos during a viewing session. In contrast to YouTube, whose algorithm has of late emphasized watch time (in doing do, increasing average video length), TikTok extracts a lot of user insight every minute. The video player presents no other competing content, so all user reactions are known to be in response to what is playing. In contrast, within the scrolling-based apps at Facebook or Twitter, algorithms cannot assume to know what a viewer is actually looking at relative to what they are hearing. Importantly, over twenty minutes, TikTok gets more data and more *specific* data about what the viewer likes than Google does, given the way it built YouTube.[35]

TikTok is not and does not pretend to be a social graph. One is not required to create an account to use the service. Users are matched only with content, not people (even if those people are content creators). This design has the effect of allowing people to be individuals. I might like sushi-making videos, sunsets, and wallabies. TikTok retains a tight focus on those interests, not abstracting out to say I like cooking, meteorology, and animals. By recording my preferences with a specificity lacking in other services, TikTok builds my unique feed that is more likely to surprise and delight than cruder "people like you" assumptions found on Facebook and YouTube.

This focus on the video also avoids a problem found on social networks. To oversimplify, TikTok disaggregates people's identities. I might like Jane Doe's wallaby videos but not her vegemite recipes or racism toward Indigenous peoples. By isolating my contact to Jane's wallaby videos, TikTok avoids my having to deal with other people's complete makeups—and they mine. This contrast to the effort required by social media—Do I unfriend? Do I like? Do I reply?—is a large part of TikTok's appeal. The algorithms are trained to detect precisely what people like so they can just lean back and enjoy rather than have to engage at a meta level.

The success TikTok has found (among many different kinds of users) depends on the service having solved a difficult technical problem: machine learning requires training data. In a nifty bit of technical judo, TikTok got its user base to create vast quantities of training data, using reactions to short videos (built to some extent on demand) to rapidly get better at predicting user reactions to short videos. TikTok appears to both track and generate a lot of metadata about the video the viewer is seeing. For example, given that there is only one video on the page (the nonscrolling model), the algorithm can learn from a quick exit what a viewer does *not* like. The algorithm is also focused only on the viewer's interaction with the video content, not the video's creator. Finally, the navigation to the next video tells a lot. Does the user watch a video more than once? Do they choose another video featuring the same music? Or one by the same creator? Finally, TikTok can determine memetic spread so can determine whether I like wallabies or simply favor ironic Australian stereotype commentary.

For movies, this task is considerably more difficult. As of 2014, Netflix built a categorization system that was found to have 76,897 specific genres built on tags denoting "their sexually suggestive content, goriness, romance levels, and even narrative elements like plot conclusiveness."[36] Once the *Atlantic*'s Alexis Madrigal and Georgia Tech's Ian Bogost cracked the code, they generated categories that Netflix hadn't named yet, including:

- Deep Sea Father-and-Son Period Pieces Based on Real Life Set in the Middle East For Kids.
- Assassination Bounty-Hunter Secret Society Dramas Based on Books Set in Europe About Fame For Ages 8 to 10.
- Post-Apocalyptic Comedies About Friendship.[37]

Returning to TikTok, the service faces the same content moderation challenges as its older platform peers. One of these challenges is the take-down. As of September 2020, TikTok had more than 700 million users. In the first six months of that year, parent company ByteDance—in addition to fighting generally uphill battles for government approvals all over the globe—removed just over 100 million videos (or about 1 percent of total uploads). Given that 96.4 million of those 100 million takedowns came before a complaint was filed, and 90 percent were removed before they received any views, algorithms are doing a lot of heavy lifting. Another 10 million videos were automatically removed for violating COVID-specific content guidelines, again suggesting that human moderators are being augmented with effective application of machine learning.

India was by far the worst offender among nations, representing more than one-third of all takedowns. The country's 37.6 million removals amounted to about four times the United States total, not unreasonable given both the relative population of the two nations and the later climb up the adoption curve in the United States relative to many Asian markets. India also had far more requests from law enforcement than any other TikTok market (note that TikTok does not operate in China despite being head-quartered there) as well as also leading the world's countries in government requests for content takedown.[38] Eventually the situation deteriorated to the point where the Indian government banned the app in late 2020.

From "Broadcast Yourself" to Competing with Disney and Netflix

As we will see in chapter 5, discussing the price of fame, by 2018 YouTube's content producers were burning out, flaming out, or opting out. Even so, Google had even bigger problems than poor taste by twenty-something bro vloggers (video bloggers). Netflix was continuing to spend more than $10 billion a year on original video content. Meanwhile, advertisers and regulators were restive given Google's poor record of oversight and slow takedowns of terrorist and child abuse videos. Both Facebook and Instagram were supporting video formats. 2018 marked the escalation of the fight for the soul of YouTube. How much was it to be the continuing home of the long tail of amateur cat videos or cute things a child did? How much was it a new kind of entertainment network, competing with Disney (including ABC and ESPN), Hulu, and Netflix? How much of that soul belonged to innovative creators and how much to algorithmic optimizers?

The fact that YouTube promoted ongoing bad behavior by boorish white males did not go unnoticed. Punishment, often in the form of the amorphous term "demonetization," was never remotely consistent. In numerous examples, YouTube flipped, then flopped, then sometimes flipped back again. In the video game Red Dead Redemption 2, suffragettes can be attacked and killed within gameplay. Videos of said gameplay were posted, taken down (with the poster banned), then reposted (with an under-age-eighteen prohibition), for example.[39] Countless observers have noted the discrepancy between what is allowed at high-profile channels and what is formal policy. Former moderators have confirmed the wide latitude given to big draws. In a story in the *Washington Post*, anonymous former YouTube employees stated that "their recommendations to strip advertising from videos that violate the site's rules were frequently overruled by higher-ups within YouTube when the videos involved higher-profile content creators who draw more advertising." More fundamentally, they asserted that "many of the rules are ineffective and contradictory to start with."[40]

In its efforts to reduce reliance on copyrighted material from others, YouTube quickly found itself in a conundrum. On one side, Google can claim it is a platform for other people's content; it is merely a hosting service. On the other, it derives substantial revenue from that content, and it clearly promotes some content to the marginalization of others. The lack of transparency with regard to this promotion is convenient, but the claimed lack of responsibility opens a much more complex debate about all modern hosting platforms, as we saw in the study of banned individuals earlier in this chapter.

The Responsibilities of a Platform

As we saw in the introduction, TikTok has been downloaded more than 3 billion times worldwide and was built by a Chinese startup but is not available in China as of 2022. The app aggressively collects user data under Western-style agreements and under at least one version of its privacy policy can share that data with Chinese governmental agencies.[41] That government took a board seat on a ByteDance company in 2021, further muddying the user privacy waters. Meanwhile, stateside, the *New York Times* found that many tech hosting platforms—including Microsoft, Amazon Web Services, Apple, Google, and Facebook—vary considerably in how they monitor hosted material to seek out images of children in danger.[42] Facebook, to date more aggressive than the other firms in seeking out and reporting abusers, will soon be tested by its previously announced decision to encrypt Facebook Messenger, in part to counter Apple's positioning of its services as more protective of consumer privacy. The same *New York Times* report also stated that livestreaming of abuse was becoming increasingly frequent, including on the Zoom teleconferencing platform.

Balancing digital privacy with the needs of governments has involved online video providers in a range of thorny legal issues. These involve state surveillance that includes DNA and facial recognition data (including of ethnic minorities in several countries) and life-altering abuse of defenseless children—far from a victimless crime. The future of personal privacy in multiple jurisdictions will be tested by long-term "drip irrigation" of data breadcrumbs. Each one is seemingly innocuous, but in aggregate, they are hugely revealing of everything from medical conditions to sexual preference and behavior to financial details. Many (most?) banks have custom scoring algorithms for creditworthiness and other decision criteria, rendering public credit-ratings agencies less useful as a predictor of what rates and products a given consumer might be offered. Data-driven profiling algorithms are used in more companies and agencies every year. One example is automated employment screening using machine learning analysis on an applicant's video interview.[43]

Online video falls squarely into this conundrum. Google, Facebook, TikTok, and other hosting services claim both legal and commercial immunity from what users might post. With the numbers of uploads and streams involved, lots can and does fall between the cracks. Given the size of the ad revenues, many algorithms are designed as a defense against litigation from content owners, while others serve the advertisers. The video watcher's stated search queries are lowest in priority, it would appear, as video search remains far less precise than its text-based cousins. The privacy of that watcher, meanwhile, is only minimally protected given Google's and Facebook's web-wide behavioral tracking along with TikTok's innovations in this area, such as asking for Facebook and phone book contacts.

Looking ahead, online video will have to contend with a further category of deception: deep fakes. These videos are the equivalent of Photoshopped still images, generated in video by machine learning algorithms that are getting better by the month and more accessible every year. What used to be an expensive, complex lab project for AI researchers is getting closer to consumer grade. Hany Farid, a leading academic in the field now at UC Berkeley, told the *Washington Post* in 2019 that "we are outgunned. The number of people working on the video-synthesis side, as opposed to the detector side, is 100 to 1."[44]

So far, the fakes can be seen in Hollywood movies (*Forrest Gump* is an example), porn videos with celebrities' heads appended to nude bodies, and a video of Nancy Pelosi appearing to be drunk. The latter was achieved merely by slowing the frame rate of the original video during playback, but it still convinced millions of its reality. Facebook announced in 2020 that it would ban AI-generated fake videos but not content where words were edited out or other types of deceptions—the Pelosi video was not subject to the new rules.[45] As of early 2023, YouTube had no published policy on fake videos, AI-generated or otherwise, apart from rules pertaining to election-related video.

A 2019 document entitled "How Google Fights Disinformation" made no commitments but was fully buzzword compliant as it stayed "ahead of the curve" and defended against "threat vectors" while not prohibiting anything:

> To stay ahead of the curve, we continuously invest resources to stay abreast of the next tools, tactics, or technologies that creators of disinformation may attempt to use. We convene with experts all around the world to understand what concerns them. We also invest in research, product, and policy developments to anticipate threat vectors that we might not be equipped to tackle at this point.
>
> One example is the rise of new forms of AI-generated, photo-realistic, synthetic audio or video content known as "synthetic media" (often referred to as "deep fakes"). While this technology has useful applications (for instance, by opening new possibilities to those affected by speech or reading impairments, or new creative grounds for artists and movie studios around the world), it raises concerns when used in disinformation campaigns and for other malicious purposes.
>
> The field of synthetic media is fast-moving and it is hard to predict what might happen in the near future. To help prepare for this issue, Google and YouTube are investing in research to understand how AI might help detect such synthetic content as it emerges, working with leading experts in this field from around the world.[46]

By 2020, the US presidential election spurred Google to ban a variety of postings related to political candidates, the mechanics of voting or the census, and the like. Neither deep fakes nor "synthetic media" are mentioned or prohibited, only "deceptive practices." According to Leslie Miller, YouTube's vice president of government affairs and public policy, "content that has been technically manipulated or doctored in a way that misleads users (beyond clips taken out of context) and may pose a serious risk of egregious harm; for example, a video that has been technically manipulated to make it appear that a government official is dead" was expressly prohibited.[47]

Rules of the Game

Moving from macro-level policy to day-to-day operations reveals the complexities of running these global user-powered platforms. Every platform has rules. Examining them can tell us about what people have done that the platforms want to prevent, and what incentives are provided for other kinds of behavior. As Tarleton Gillespie persuasively argues, when YouTube or Facebook write of "our community," the massive scale of these winner-take-most online platforms means that moderation and rulemaking occur at industrial scale; norms that might work in a physical town hall or online forum for eco-travel buffs cannot be relied on. Whether it's the child pornographers, the trolls, or the bots, populations that in the real world either don't exist or are socially marginalized emerge and make unmoderated user-generated content unusable. As Whitney Phillips puts it in the title of her study of online trolling, "this is why we can't have nice things."[48]

As video-driven platforms, YouTube, Twitch, and TikTok are possibly less ruined by trolling than Facebook or comment forums on media websites. These are huge properties, though, and I'm not going to generalize too assertively. Sports fans, one would think, would be passionate about teams and players but ESPN had to dismantle their comments pages in 2018 as the vitriol became routinely predictable. Within the first five posts on almost any story somebody called somebody else an idiot or worse. Content moderation on Facebook, meanwhile, involves its own laundry list of abuses and creative workarounds as the site continues to try to tweak its tools. [49] On Twitch, the language of the terms of service is formal legalese; there is little pretext of "our community" and more emphasis on "you will comply and not do any of the seventeen categories of prohibited behavior." Elsewhere, "community guidelines" underline Twitch's formal prohibitions by telling users not to break laws, do or portray self-destructive behavior, exhibit hateful behavior, or commit or encourage physical violence.[50]

While trolls may not be the death of YouTube, it's clear that pedophiles could be. In 2019, YouTube banned all comments on all videos aimed at children, prompted by advertisers that were boycotting the site. In January 2020, in part because of a $170 million fine for getting caught collecting information related to child viewers, Google broadened its changes to YouTube's children's content. After that date, to comply with Children's Online Privacy Protection Act (COPPA), all videos marked "made for kids" did not serve personalized ads, did not enable comments (continuing the 2019 ban), did not support merchandise sales, and could not be saved to a playlist, among other changes.[51] While these changes do restrict Google's information collection of children's viewing habits, they also hit content creators in the wallet, restricting monetization options.

Comparing 2010 and 2020 versions of YouTube's Community Guidelines pages tells many stories, many of them of interest primarily to lawyers. In

2010, the site listed "common-sense rules," paraphrased and numbered for convenience here:

1. Don't post pornography and we will alert authorities if you post child pornography.
2. Don't post videos involving "negative activities such as animal abuse, drug use or bomb manufacturing."
3. "Explicit or free violence is not allowed." No attacks or humiliation.
4. No shocking images: "Don't post creepy videos of accidents, dead bodies and the like."
5. Respect copyright. There is explicit prohibition of things that might reasonably be considered fair use.
6. No hate speech.
7. No threats, harassment, invasions of privacy, or disclosures of other people's personal information.
8. No spam. This includes misleading titles, thumbnails, or "abundant repetitive, unwanted or unoriented content" (including private messages and contents).[52]

Ten more years of experience added some items to the list and removed some explicit prohibitions: no longer is "bomb manufacturing" singled out. Items 1, 4, 5, 6, 7, and 8 carry over, sometimes almost verbatim but also with a "Learn more" link that was not present earlier after every bullet. Item 2 ("negative activities") is now framed as "don't post videos that encourage others to do things that might cause them to get badly hurt, especially kids"; drug use is no longer called out. The previous item 3, focusing on violence and humiliation, is now broken into two items, one containing the "violent or gory" clause, and an item now simply called "threats."

One new item in 2020 elaborates on item 7's focus on threats and harassment with a separate section on "Harassment and cyberbullying," now distinct from "Threats," which also prohibits harassment. In a second new item, personal privacy is spelled out: one can request removal of content if someone uploads a video of you or other personal information without your consent. Third, child safety is its own set of rules, breaking out child endangerment from its previous position in item 1. Finally, impersonation of other channels or individuals is expressly prohibited.[53]

In addition to the list of prohibitions changing, so too do the sanctions. The old version stated that "your account may be canceled" if Google found a violation of the Terms of Use. Further, in bold print, the user was warned "If we cancel your account, you will not be able to get a new one."[54] By 2020, the amount of money involved for content creators changed that blunt instrument to something much more nuanced: "If a YouTube creator's on- and/or off-platform behavior harms our users, community, employees or ecosystem, we may respond based on a number of factors including, but not limited to, the egregiousness of their actions and whether a pattern of harmful behavior exists. Our response will range from suspending a creator's privileges to account termination."[55] Those suspensions could be perceived as arbitrary in both their application and duration. The formal legal Terms of Service, interestingly, actually got *shorter* between 2010 and December 10, 2019, dropping from 3,566 words down to 3,369.

Note what is *not* prohibited. There is no guarantee of accuracy, including of faked words or actions. There is no recognition that what is blasphemy in a theocracy might be parody somewhere else. As long as it's not overtly sexual, violent, or threatening in US terms, a given video will probably stay up. "Hate speech" is in the eye of the beholder in the offline realm as well. Native North American populations are told to "just live with" professional sports team names that are patently derogatory. The situation gets worse in a global context. Deciding what to call the Islamist militants in the Middle East is entirely political and, especially across linguistic divides, some names might be perceived or declared hateful. Whose opinion counts? Right now, those of a few employees of a global machine-learning-powered ad-serving giant.

This brings us to a crucial insight, one well argued by Gillespie among others.[56] The rules of content moderation reflect value judgments, and in Google's case, primary among those values is monetization of user behavior. At the same time, billions of site visitors will hold millions of moral positions, and the flagging mechanism for "offensive" content is highly ambiguous. Flagging a given video for any reason doesn't start a "community" discussion so much as pour a small amount of sand into the gears of ad serving.

TikTok's terms of service, meanwhile, vary by geography. The European Union, United Kingdom, and Switzerland get one set of rules, India another (caste is mentioned for example), the United States a third set, and everyone else, still another. Twenty-three bullets in the US version enumerate what is forbidden: using the service at too young an age (though it's not stated that way), copying and redistributing TikTok content, spam and other commercial uses, trying to interfere with the service's operation (including by malicious code), screen scraping, impersonation, bullying and harassment, fraud, gambling, racism and other hate speech, inclusion of personally identifiable information of a third party, promotion of harm (self and otherwise),

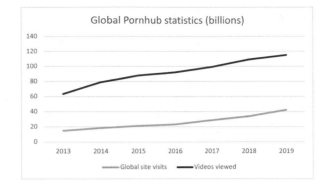

Chart 10 Global online video pornography continues to grow by any measure. Source: Pornhub.

Global Pornhub statistics (billions)

Global site visits — Videos viewed

directions for illegal or dangerous activities, threats, sexual content, and so on. A whole set of rules pertains to the sale of virtual items, something more common on Twitch than on YouTube. Overall, the rules of the road feel much more thorough on TikTok, possibly because of the comparatively young age of the demographic.[57]

Online video's powerful emotional and instructional capability is currently governed not by the *New York Times* editorial board as it functioned in either 1900 or 2000, case or statutory law, agency regulation, or even the Motion Picture Association. "Community" standards of decency, propriety, or legality vanish at global scale. YouTube and TikTok are neither "common carriers" like AT&T nor media outlets. They fly between external regulatory regimes. So while we struggle to grasp the size of the platforms' reach, we should also pause to wonder if such behemoths should lack any real accountability.

Along the lines of rules and prohibitions, it is impossible to discuss online video without mentioning pornography. Numerous commentators are noting that children are seeing porn earlier than ever before, and the video porn they are seeing is far more psychologically problematic than the airbrushed nudes of the *Playboy* magazine era.[58] Insofar as such research is ongoing, and far from my expertise, I will simply note that one network of sites under the Pornhub umbrella released annual statistics through 2019, and they give an extremely rough insight into the scale of the phenomenon (see chart 10).[59] For comparison, Pornhub says it reached 115 million daily hours viewed in 2018; YouTube reported a billion hours a day in 2017. (Pornhub's Canadian parent company MindGeek owns twenty-four porn sites so it's unclear how much the Pornhub numbers reflect just one site versus an aggregation.)

Conclusion

Disembodied algorithms most certainly place a disturbingly high priority on sensationalism and other crude proxies for "engagement." Even so, moving away from demonization of the algorithms and toward an instrumental view of online video is a first step in understanding these platforms. Yes, some algorithms are written by humans (but in unsupervised learning, the algorithm teaches itself), and yes, the platforms have deployed algorithms that exhibit troubling cultural assumptions, but once again we must recognize something that is not comprehendible. YouTube serves a billion-plus hours of video a day and copes with eighty years of uploads in the same period. TikTok has yet to release comparable statistics, but they are sure to be staggering. The platforms are being called upon to fact-check these videos (or at least some of them), screen them for sex and violence, prevent pedophiles from sexualizing children's innocent uploads, screen for copyrighted content, and satisfy both advertisers' desire for audiences and audiences' desire for education, instruction, and entertainment.

No army of human programmers, contractors, and crowdsourced volunteers can ever remotely approximate an adequate labor force to accomplish all the aforementioned goals. We humans have built a number of systems with direct human implications that exist on a scale vastly larger than anything anyone can comprehend, much less regulate. Online video is perhaps foremost among them.

The speed and scale of adoption of online video for everything from electronic babysitting—81 percent of US parents surveyed by Pew Research Center in 2018 reported letting kids watch YouTube—to vicarious electronic gaming to the world's biggest music streaming service mean that new uses are being discovered every year and new abuses are emerging just as quickly. Given how many smartphones are in circulation and how popular online video has become, those uses and abuses get to be very big very fast. The dark side of online video has no easy answer. It's too big for human moderators and too complicated and rapidly evolving for machine learning to keep pace. We will discuss the implications of this arms race in the remaining chapters.

Learning

When people hear that you are researching online video, there's a universal reaction: "Oh, I learned how to _____ by watching YouTube. It was great!"[1] For all the music videos, nostalgic clips, and political rants, the how-to component of online video can be refreshingly free of ideology, trolling, and flame wars. (It is important to note, however, that one can also get steered very wrong by online video. Simple misinformation—misquoted song lyrics or folklore that isn't actually so—and active, sophisticated disinformation campaigns all ride the same wave of popularity.) The shift from text on paper to vocal instructions accompanied by color video makes for a powerful instructional environment. Conveniently for Google and other providers, including Microsoft (which owns the Lynda video tutorial library), instruction continues to attract large audiences. Google framed a 2019 ad campaign around the power of its learning platform, and advertisers flock to the medium because seeking instruction can be a strong indicator a viewer is in buying mode.

Statistics from Pew Research Center bear out anecdotal intuition. A survey from 2018 found that of those surveyed, more people use YouTube for "figuring out how to do things they haven't done before" than for any other purpose. Eighty-six percent of respondents were "very" or "somewhat" likely to do this, and learning far outpaced "just passing the time" and "deciding whether to buy a new product or not."[2]

The range of skills a person needs to survive in their particular milieu is staggering. The philosopher Michael Polanyi famously wrote, "We know more than we can tell," but very little is innate. We had to learn how to cook a meal, fix a flat tire, or fill out financial aid forms *someplace*. In an era when more households have two working parents and more households are headed

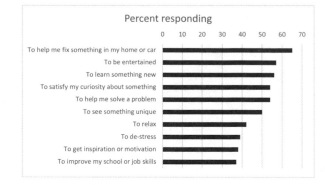

Percent responding

	0	10	20	30	40	50	60	70

To help me fix something in my home or car
To be entertained
To learn something new
To satisfy my curiosity about something
To help me solve a problem
To see something unique
To relax
To de-stress
To get inspiration or motivation
To improve my school or job skills

Chart 11 Google's internal 2017 survey findings regarding why people use the platform.

by single parents, that tribal knowledge is increasingly coming from online video. One *Atlantic Monthly* author asserted that "YouTube Is My Father." His hard-working single mother didn't know "how to tie a tie, nor pick out a suit. It was not my father who taught me how to change the oil in my car, drive a six-speed, build a fire, or shave with a straight razor. All that I owe to one website: YouTube."[3]

Google of course recognizes this. A 2017 internal survey revealed that nearly two-thirds of respondents had been motivated by a home or automotive repair issue. If the survey is in fact representative (it only asked 1,000 people; the site serves a billion people a month), most people on YouTube at some point want to fix something (see chart 11). This is a stunning finding.

When we actually look at the how-to content, however, the line between "help me fix my home or car" and "be entertained" blurs pretty quickly, as the success of house-flipping cable TV programming demonstrates. Power-tool reviews, for example, can fall into both categories. Similarly, "being entertained" and "learning something new" also overlap. Google's in-house research reports that people are drawn to the reviews given by everyday people more than established outlets in many cases. A person test-flying a drone, for example, might show it exhibiting stability in a high wind, something magazine reviews can't standardize for. In addition, nonprofessional videos can give people confidence to try a new hobby. Canning fresh fruits and vegetables during the COVID-19 pandemic was one telling example.

Unboxing videos are extremely popular, and a big unboxing is buying a new car. "First ride" videos follow a person through their initial day with a new vehicle, providing everything from vicarious enjoyment to product knowledge to "I wouldn't have thought to ask about that" moments.[4] Other related genres include "haul" videos in which shoppers unload a shopping trip's purchases for the audience or review toys. It is here that Ryan Kaji established his dominance of a kid-related genre to become, for a time, the best-paid YouTuber of all, with earnings of about $30 million a year at nine years of age.[5]

Shifting back to more conventional types of learning, the range of skills one can learn is truly mind-boggling. Almost every sport and its ancillary activities is covered, from boomerang-throwing to unicycling to field-dressing a wild boar. Crafts and hobbies are well represented. A search for "how to knit a cap" in Google returns 34 million video results. Cooking and kitchen videos are popular, whether for knife skills, first-time Thanksgiving chefs, or advanced esoteric techniques. These include brewing kombucha or, more questionably, identifying poisonous mushrooms. Clothing and fabrics occupy their own category, where one can learn everything from stain removal to T-shirt folding. Overall life skills—starting a wood fire, whistling through your fingers, dancing, ordering wine at a restaurant, playing pool, performing CPR, or making paper airplanes (7 million Google results for videos on this last topic alone)—are amply represented. Even the most basic skills such as riding a bike, speaking a foreign language, or learning to swim are well taught, for free, via online video.

In all of these instances, video triggers human learning in ways print (either text or still images) cannot. Like our mammalian kin, human brains are keen observers and mimics. Anyone who has watched babies learn can recall seeing the process in action. Apparently seeing something performed triggers the same neurons that will be required when we perform it ourselves.[6] The scale of the video platforms has fueled rapid progress in select endeavors. For example, Rubik's cube solving times have dropped close to the theoretical minimum (current record: 3.47 seconds). Everyone can learn from the best practitioners, and many skills lend themselves to video tutorials.

It's difficult to overstate the importance of this phenomenon. Compared to libraries and universities that have evolved over thousands of years based largely on print, most online video repositories charge no tuition, confer neither degrees to learners nor tenure to teachers, and cover every aspect of human existence that can be taught. (Some of those aspects—relating to self-harm for example—have proven problematic.) Formal educational institutions have struggled to adapt, which is not surprising considering how rapidly this change has occurred. Even so, one could approximate an amazing college education just culling great lectures from the millions of hours of video available.

Here are just a few examples of the educational power of video:

- Alice Waters explains how she rethought the relation of food to diner and in so doing helped launch the "farm to table" movement that affected all of US cuisine.[7]
- Before Alice Waters there was Julia Child, teaching omelet technique by using beans.[8] (It's just as important to watch Dan Ackroyd's parody of Child's TV show, which she loved showing her dinner guests.[9])
- Yale art historian Vincent Scully's lecture on Frank Lloyd Wright, complete with dual slide projectors, shows a master teacher in his element.[10]
- In response to the question, "How do we teach everyone to code?" Carnegie Mellon professor Jeanette Wing introduced the concept of teaching "computational thinking" instead, and in so doing reshaped her field.[11]
- Harvard professor Latanya Sweeney has done foundational research into online privacy, served in government, and stood as a powerful mentor.[12]
- At the frontiers of basic science, Richard Feynman's epoch-defining Messenger Lectures at Cornell are available to anyone.[13]
- Indiana University political science professor Elinor Ostrom made history by winning a Nobel Prize in economics, and this lecture showed her innovative clarity of thought relative to the idea of social commons.[14]
- Speaking of Nobel lectures, Toni Morrison's 1993 address still stands as an important document about art, race, and craft.[15]
- Hearing David Foster Wallace give the graduation address later published as "This Is Water" is at once inspirational and deeply sorrowful.[16]

This list is mere cherry-picking. MIT's OpenCourseWare is much more systematic and very well taught, and it includes many of the university's departments.[17] As just one example, the computer scientist Erik Demaine is featured in many of these videos. He was the youngest faculty member ever hired at MIT and won a MacArthur Fellowship (the "Genius Grant")—a pretty compelling resume for the instructor of a free course. That free course does not lead to anything, however—no certificate of completion or grade, much less a degree. Such certifications were possible elsewhere online, such as at the joint Harvard-MIT venture called EdX. For all the great content EdX hosted, however, the economics of video learning remained challenging to traditional institutions and the joint venture was sold to the for-profit 2U company in 2021.

If we look at education outside the walls of academia, we find two particular institutions that embraced online video early in its availability. Each has made an impact on the practice of learning, broadly conceived: Khan Academy and TED talks.

Khan Academy

Salman Khan utilized the infrastructure of YouTube in its early days to launch what became a global education revolution. Khan Academy has grown to serve millions of learners per month in 190 countries via multiple native-language sites and translations into forty languages. Individual videos currently number more than 10,000. The site and videos remain not-for-profit, and Khan's longtime dream of "an integrated global classroom" has, to some degree, come to fruition. According to YouTube, the videos had been viewed more than 2 billion times as of 2023; the Khan Academy site also streams the content directly, adding to the aggregate view count.

Khan was born in Louisiana and raised by a single mother near the poverty line. He notes that he ate free school lunches, a fact that appears to have shaped some of his later decisions. Khan made his way through MIT in unconventional fashion, earning two bachelor's degrees (electrical engineering and computer science, and math) and a master's in electrical engineering and computer science in four years. After working at Oracle, Khan attended Harvard for his MBA, during which he interned at Xerox's famed Palo Alto Research Center (PARC), then moved to working at two hedge funds while living in Boston as his wife completed Harvard Medical School.

By now it was 2004 and the Khan Academy story begins. His niece lived in New Orleans and Sal tutored her by phone in math. After two years, he was tutoring more than a dozen relatives via remote technologies (he wrote software lessons for them in addition to his lectures) and after YouTube launched in 2005, he began uploading the lessons in November 2006. As he recalled in his autobiographical TED talk, Khan was emotionally moved by the testimonials from kids and parents who benefited from his tutorials. "I was an analyst at a hedge fund. I wasn't used to doing anything of social benefit," he explained.[18] One email came from a young man who, like Khan, came from a tough family circumstance. He was admitted to college but was struggling. At that juncture Khan's videos changed the narrative: "Spent the entire summer on your YouTube page . . . and I just wanted to thank you for everything you are doing," he wrote. "Last week I tested for a math placement exam and am now in Honors Math 200. . . . I can say without any doubt that you have changed my life and the lives of everyone in my family."[19]

Inspired in large part by that email, in 2009, Khan quit his job to work full time on the videos. He had an infant son and his wife was still in medical training. They agreed to take one year to test the model. Ten months in, the venture was still self-funded and the future looked uncertain. Despite wide public visibility, there was no funding model, a fact that shocked Ann Doerr, whose husband, John, is a leading Silicon Valley venture capitalist. She wrote a moderate check, then over lunch learned of the desperate straits in which the couple found themselves. She then contributed $100,000 and institutional gifts snowballed. Google, AT&T, and the Carlos Slim Foundation all eventually contributed. Early and visible support came from Bill Gates, who shouted out the videos at the Aspen Ideas Festival and later introduced Khan to the TED stage. The sight of the world's richest person leading a standing ovation for the clearly stage-struck Khan, not yet thirty years old at the time, is memorable.[20] Significantly, Ann Doerr now chairs Khan Academy's board of directors.

Soon after the cash infusion, the videos became more widely available and addressed more topics. The team grew to the point where Khan Academy now employs an estimated seven hundred people across four countries. Coupled with quality content, YouTube then helped change the structure of an existing institution. As Khan's cousins showed, people liked watching lectures at their own speed, at a convenient time of day, with the ability to speed up or slow down the content delivery. In a practice now known as "flipping the classroom," teachers assign the lectures as homework then do practice problems and other former homework assignments in the classroom. Freed from one-size-fits-all lectures, teachers can now circulate and deploy faster learners to help those students who may be struggling. Because the format demands mastery of a concept before the next chunk of material is unlocked, everyone is building on a shared, solid foundation rather than what Khan called the "Swiss cheese" model. Many of us have some concepts we never really "got," and the holes in our knowledge hampered our later learning.

As Khan experienced firsthand, social capital is a key factor in academic success, especially for first-generation students at elite institutions. Khan Academy is addressing this dimension of education as well with free SAT, LSAT, and Praxis Core coaching. Being able to learn privately, without peer pressure or embarrassment at not knowing the unwritten rules of the game, changes education dramatically, and Khan Academy has played a key role in first-generation college students' success. Score increases from the PSAT to the SAT for students using free Khan resources are 50 percent higher than students who don't use such tools. In a 2015 survey, 64 percent of first-generation college students reported using Khan Academy. One Stanford student said that "it was the private tutor my family could not afford."[21]

Khan Academy has its critics. Some lectures have been found to include erroneous statements, but in the tradition of peer review, the site has corrected the errors. Early skeptics compared the videos to colleges' attempts to use radio for course credit in the 1920s or to CBS television's twenty-five-year collaboration with NYU called Sunrise Semester that launched in 1957. Khan himself is adamant that the online videos are not meant to stand alone as a complete education. The scale of YouTube, meanwhile, overshadows any previous print- or other media-based education reform.

Furthermore, Khan shook up not only US public education—a monumental achievement on its own—but schools all over the world. As he noted in his book, *One World Schoolhouse*, in 2012, the mission that has guided Khan Academy since its inception is "to provide a free, world-class education for anyone, anywhere."[22] He notes that he has seen the world as a child of immigrants and has traveled to Bangladesh, India, and Pakistan as well as having attended MIT and worked in Silicon Valley and Boston's financial sector. The breadth of this exposure is rare, but a perfect match for YouTube's vast reach, infinite capacity, and intimate connection of learner to material.

Khan Academy creates ideal content for what the Internet does well: distribute digital video at zero cost. Furthermore, the "special sauce" added by the nonprofit is structure. Rather than hunting in vain for the lecture that follows polynomials on the YouTube search bar, learners get a well-conceived and consistently executed taxonomy of knowledge. In one tiny corner of online video, rather than chaos and algorithmically gamed playlists, we find order, organization, logic, and motivation. Economic mobility is but one consequence that will never be fully measured, in part because Khan spurred countless imitators to launch their own tutoring services.

TED Talks

It's impossible to discuss the impact of online video on education without noting the evolution of the TED conference. As of 2019, TED talk videos had been watched more than 3 billion times. It's an extraordinary count given that the talks can center on such cognitively challenging topics as astrophysics, clinical depression, and redesigning education. The origins go back to 1984, when the first conference on the convergence of technology, entertainment, and design was held. It was cohosted by graphic designer Harry

Marks and architect Richard Saul Wurman. Demos of the Apple Macintosh and Sony-Philips compact disc along with talks from early digerati Stewart Brand and Nicholas Negroponte (along with the mathematician Benoit Mandelbrot) set the tone for later meetings. The event was financially unsuccessful, and six years passed until TED2.

From 1990 until 2009, the conference was held annually in Monterey, California, and quickly became an exclusive event with celebrity attendees from many fields. Speakers have included Samantha Power and Bill Clinton, Bono and Richard Dawkins, Sergey Brin and Jane Goodall. Intellectual eclecticism combined with A-list star power to make TED a coveted invitation. Wurman sold the event in 2000 to the British magazine publisher Chris Anderson (no relation to the *Wired* editor Chris Anderson of "Long Tail" fame).

Anderson changed TED's direction. Ownership was transferred to the non-profit Sapling foundation. The conference venue moved from Monterey to Long Beach and then to Vancouver. Speaker talks were posted for free viewing in 2006. By January 2007, forty-four talks had been posted, amassing 3 million views. In April of that year, TED.com was relaunched to highlight video talks. By 2011, TED was licensing the conference format (including its rigidly timed and tightly rehearsed eighteen-minute format for speakers, regardless of their pedigree) to hundreds of TEDx spinoffs held all over the world as a locally focused, bottom-up counterweight to the star-driven main event. What Anderson called "radical openness" paradoxically made the physical conferences even more desirable and the admission price soared from $4,400 in 2006 to $10,000 in 2018. Other TED events have narrower foci, including TEDMED, TEDWomen, TEDGlobal, and TEDYouth.

As Anderson said in 2012, "It used to be 800 people getting together once a year; now it's about a million people a day watching TED talks online. When we first put up a few of the talks as an experiment, we got such impassioned responses that we decided to flip the organization on its head and think of ourselves not so much as a conference but as 'ideas worth spreading,' building a big website around it. The conference is still the engine, but the website is the amplifier that takes the ideas to the world."[23] TED talks have evolved as a distinct genre. Although the coaching and time clock impose a certain homogeneity on the talks, global intellectual superstars have emerged from unexpected directions.

Chimamanda Ngozi Adichie

Adichie was born in Nigeria, studied medicine and pharmacy in her native country, then began college at Drexel. She then moved to be closer to her older sister and complete a bachelor's degree at Eastern Connecticut State University. Master's degrees at Johns Hopkins and Yale followed soon thereafter. She was awarded a MacArthur Fellowship the same year she earned her Yale masters in African studies. A year later she delivered her TED talk, "The Danger of a Single Story," which has been viewed 30 million times as of 2021. A later TEDx talk, "We Should All Be Feminists," was sampled in a Beyoncé song.

Brenè Brown

Brown was born in San Antonio, Texas, raised for a time in New Orleans, and has spent her adult life in Houston as a practitioner and later professor of social work. Her work focuses on leadership, particularly the role of vulnerability. She has written five number one *New York Times* bestsellers and her 2010 TED talk, "The Power of Vulnerability," is one of the five most-viewed TED videos of all time.

Ken Robinson

Robinson was born in Liverpool, England, and, in contrast to his brother (a professional soccer player) had to attend special schools on account of aftereffects of polio. His PhD from the University of London focused on the uses of drama and theater in education, and this degree led to a career in arts education. Before his death in 2020, he developed into a sharp critic of many educational practices. His TED talks, viewed tens of millions of times, stress the role of schools in encouraging—or more often killing—creativity in students.

Hans Rosling

Rosling was born in Uppsala, Sweden, in 1948, the same town where he died sixty-eight years later. In between, however, he lived in India, Mozambique, and the Democratic Republic of the Congo, working as a physician and public health investigator. His TED fame comes from his many talks on global health and economic development. His compelling use of attention-getting devices in the service of helping attack ignorance made his talks exemplary. In one video, he launches the Trendalyzer software built by his son Ola, which presents United Nations data in compelling visuals.[24] Google bought the software and now makes it publicly available at Gapminder.org, the website devoted to the foundation launched by Rosling and his children.[25] In a different video, Rosling exhibits his skill as a sword-swallower, and in another, he deploys plastic Ikea bins to illustrate potential paths to a nine-billion-person planet.

These four individuals illustrate several aspects of the TED universe. Previously unknown experts in a particular geographic or intellectual area could transcend boundaries with global exposure that crosses traditional disciplinary lines. Note that traditional US academics don't attract massive viewership, except in a few cases (positive psychology as researched by Martin Seligman, Dan Gilbert, and Shawn Achor being one).

There are many critiques, and most hit the mark. Even including some of the superstars listed above, the talks can feel massively over-rehearsed. The staging can make even minor insights and anecdotes come across as profound. The British political activist Julie Bindel notes that "the talks are so rehearsed that even the well-placed pauses and casual hair flicks look hideously false. TED-bots strut around the stage, posing, delivering well-crafted smiles and frowns. It's like amateur dramatics for would-be intellectuals."[26] The cognitive authority of the speakers varies. Some are the genuine article, a truly original and rigorous thinker. Often, however, the featured points of view come courtesy of self-described "thought leaders" who convey a large portion of form and little substance. Houman Harouni, writing in *The American Reader*, succinctly nailed this point: "TED's is the language and tone of the *pitch*."[27] Finally, the TED stage became a kind of church, one where Ideas are Good and can make Good Things happen. *The New Statesman*'s Martin Robbins noted in 2012 that "'Ideas worth spreading' sounds more like the slogan of the Jehovah's Witnesses."[28]

Statistically, the speakers (as of 2017[29]) skew heavily white and heavily male. The expected power law applies. Despite there being more than 2,000 talks, the top twenty-five accounted for more than a quarter of all views. The most viewed profession is author, lending credibility to the critique of TED as a book-flogging exercise. Among nationalities, the United States dominates with 467 talks between 2001 and 2017. That's four times as many as the UK in second with 113, which in turn is three times as many as India, with 41, in third. Canada, Israel, Australia, and France follow in low double digits, with Switzerland, the Netherlands, and Italy rounding out the top ten, all in single digits. The average female speaker is about forty-five years of age, whereas men are typically about forty-nine. The top ten topics, as measured by views, are as follows (numbers are rounded to the nearest million):

1. Communication (224)
2. Technology (197)
3. Health (147)
4. Art (119)

5. Happiness (109)
6. Education (98)
7. Creativity (97)
8. Motivation (86)
9. Design (62)
10. Politics (58)

Equally enlightening are the bottom ten categories (again with views rounded to the nearest million):

1. Film (0.3)
2. Anthropology (0.4)
3. Peace (1.1)
4. Military (1.2)
5. Physics (1.2)
6. Disability (1.2)
7. Philanthropy (1.2)
8. Terrorism (1.3)
9. Privacy (1.5)
10. Society (1.5)

Maybe unfairly, it's easy to form a stereotype of a male US author talking on communications or technology. Big, complex topics (war and peace being ready examples) don't attract large audiences whereas gadgets and inventions appear to do just that. Generally uplifting topics—art, happiness, creativity, motivation—all see lots of views.

Benjamin Bratton is a professor of visual arts at UC San Diego. His TEDx talk was about TED, and he critiqued three aspects (this did not happen on the big stage, for obvious reasons). First, Bratton highlighted the oversimplification of complex ideas to fit into a time window and to appeal to an audience that doesn't engage with nuance. Summing up this point, he delivers a perfect TED soundbite: "I submit that astrophysics run on the model of American Idol is a recipe for civilizational disaster." The problem is that Chris Anderson never proposed such a venture. The straw man argument Bratton utilizes is exactly what he criticizes.

Second, and on much firmer ground, Bratton gets to the core of TED: its neospirituality. "I Think TED actually stands for: *middlebrow megachurch infotainment*," he says. "The key rhetorical device for TED talks is a combination of epiphany and personal testimony (an 'epiphimony' if you like) through which the speaker shares a personal journey of insight and realization, its triumphs and tribulations."[30] What Bratton calls "placebo politics" oversimplifies complex problems and offers a personal testimony of hope. Ultimately, these politics leave listeners thinking something has been conquered when in fact the intervention likely made things worse. The quasi-religious backdrop of hopeful optimism informs much of the TED narrative, leading to the third critique.

Technology, the *T* in TED, in Bratton's view tends to accentuate and amplify the flaws in underlying social relationships rather than exposing and correcting them. The techno-utopian thread in TED talks ebbs and flows, but it is always present, if only in the speaker's knowing relation to the video camera. A better *E*, he continues, would be "Economics," rather than "Entertainment," because all economic systems promise one thing and deliver something very different. Finally, *D*—Design—is where those technologies are realized in actual human contexts: "The potential for [phones, drones, and genomes (what we do here in San Diego and La Jolla)] are both wonderful and horrifying *at the same time*, and to make good futures, design as 'innovation' just isn't a strong enough idea by itself."[31]

Bratton ends by breaking the unspoken TED talk closing. He's not personal, not hopeful, and not exhortatory. Rather than wrapping up the idea with a bow, he expands it into multiple dimensions.

> I don't have one simple take away, one magic idea. That's kind of the point.... [I]t's not as though there is a shortage of topics for serious discussion.... Problems are not "puzzles" to be solved. That metaphor assumes that all the necessary pieces are already on the table, they just need to be rearranged and reprogrammed. It's not true.
>
> "Innovation" defined as moving the pieces around and adding more processing power is not some Big Idea that will disrupt a broken status quo: that precisely is the broken status quo. One TED speaker said recently, "If you remove this boundary . . . the only boundary left is our imagination." Wrong.
>
> If we really want transformation, we have to slog through the hard stuff (history, economics, philosophy, art, ambiguities, contradictions). Bracketing it off to the side to focus just on technology, or just on innovation, actually *prevents* transformation.
>
> Instead of dumbing-down the future, we need to raise the level of general understanding to the level of complexity of the systems in which we are embedded and which are embedded in us. This is

not about "personal stories of inspiration," it's about the difficult and uncertain work of demystification and reconceptualization: the hard stuff that really changes how we think. More Copernicus, less Tony Robbins.[32]

In the time since that critique, TED's moment at the center of the zeitgeist has passed. Civilized discourse at elevated levels of conceptual complexity is out of fashion, even (especially?) at the middlebrow tier. The world's population of superstar TED-type speakers is finite, and perhaps it's been mined out. Be that as it may, the dawn of online video brought the world its own equivalent of the Chautauqua movement,[33] a healthy portion of uplift and cognitive exercise unable to sustain itself over time, albeit without the picturesque scenery.

Online Video as Education for Commerce

Online video (including heavy but not exclusive use of YouTube) has been used for a wide variety of business purposes. In many ways, these videos are educational, whether they inform a prospect of a product's features and benefits, explain how to use it to maximum advantage, or aid in troubleshooting. While this happens to some extent in consumer markets, many decisions in this realm—which bread, sunglasses, or sweater to buy—are driven by brand awareness and price considerations. In business-to-business commerce, in contrast, brand plays a secondary role in many purchase decisions. Product attributes are often carefully researched before the purchase, whether the offering is legal services, industrial lubricant, or capital equipment such as an excavator or waterjet cutter. In both domains, online video's capacity to capture emotions and explain complexities has made it a powerful tool.

Consumer-facing companies have done both brand and product advertising. The former creates positive responses to the overall entity (such as Nike and "Just Do It"). Product advertising sells features and benefits of a particular model (Nike's ZoomX Vaporfly shoe). Business-to-business (B2B) selling has been less common on YouTube, though there are outstanding examples of B2B use, including Haas Machine Tools (expensive computer-driven metal-shaping equipment) and Bobcat skid-steer loaders (small track-driven machines used by landscapers, farmers, and construction crews). After the sale, online video can eliminate calls to the help desk. For example, Ikea posts videos on solving common problems. Configuration, assembly, installation, and troubleshooting are all much easier to demonstrate and explain in video than to draw and describe in print. Warranty repairs can also be expedited (or avoided) with simple explainers of how to find the serial number, how to winterize the unit, and so on. Should a return be necessary, explaining things like transit screws or draining liquids from the unit can prevent common issues.

In the early days of the web, when video was rare, a common characterization held that watching television involved a "leaning back" posture while reading the World Wide Web on a PC was a "leaning forward" mode of physical engagement. Tablets have certainly blurred that distinction, but online video generally appears to command a higher level of engagement than traditional television viewing. Advertisers have responded accordingly, breaking the bounds of the thirty- or sixty-second spot. The first YouTube video to hit one million views (in 2006) featured what looks like camcorder footage of the Brazilian footballer Ronaldinho juggling the ball in a warm-up drill, punctuated by medium-range blasts off the crossbar directly back onto his foot. It ran two minutes and forty-five seconds, a precursor of new video communications unconstrained by airtime schedules.

Nike has a tradition of expensive, original World Cup advertisements and the pinnacle may have been the 2010 edition. It lasted three full minutes and ran on both network television and YouTube. The theme of "Write the Future" allowed a full array of national heroes to each have a turn in the spotlight, each nearly making the putative historic play of the tournament, only to be denied by another global superstar. Directed (in a further nod to the global audience) by the Mexican filmmaker Alejandro González Iñárritu, it ends with a Christiano Ronaldo penalty kick cutting to black. Who will be the ultimate hero? In the end, Spain—an Adidas club—won the tournament, negating some of Nike's momentum.

2010 also saw a brilliant use of YouTube within a branding campaign. Old Spice had been purchased by Procter & Gamble in 1990 and launched a body wash in 2003. By 2006, intense competition in the category was making Old Spice an also-ran, so the advertising firm Wieden+Kennedy created "the man your man could smell like" campaign, which proved successful at the elusive task of appealing to both men (who use the product) and women (who in many households buy it). The campaign crossed traditional and social media boundaries, setting records and winning awards in both. More important for the client, Old Spice surged to become the top-selling body wash in the category.

The follow-on was the true landmark. The "Response" campaign was a pure social media play. Comments from the public and some celebrities were answered by Old Spice media star Isaiah Mustafa, a former NFL player, in video form. In a truly groundbreaking team effort, 186 responses were read, scripts were written, and videos were shot and edited in two and a half days. Mustafa became a phenomenon as it was revealed that the complex shots for the main commercial were shot in a single take, computerized effects and all. He was parodied on *Sesame Street* and elsewhere for his commanding presence and cultural ubiquity. "I'm on a boat" became a meme, showing the power of free global video distribution when coupled with insight and creativity.

Global brands also found creative ways to use the new capabilities. In 2009, Evian water released a YouTube version of a French TV commercial featuring roller-skating babies that fit into a long-term campaign dating to the 1990s. It drew 100 million views, an incredible return on the investment. Lego's use of YouTube is a perfect match of product and medium. The colorful bricks make for good visuals, and even the most experienced builder wants to learn new techniques. L'Oreal is capitalizing on YouTube's capacity to instruct, using videos to demonstrate cosmetics techniques and in so doing, show the features and benefits rather than announce them.

BMW experimented with short-form films in a series called *The Hire* from noted directors in 2001–2, long before YouTube. As of 2020, BMW continues to produce content that engages its enthusiast-driver target market. Car videos in general can rack up massive view totals. Rally driver Ken Block's trick videos have hit the 100 million viewer mark, indirectly promoting Monster energy drinks and his DC shoe brand more than the actual cars. Pepsi's "hidden camera" video featuring a disguised US stock-car racer Jeff Gordon going on a high-speed, high-skill test drive with the salesman along for the (allegedly) unauthorized ride also drew massive interest.

Vine, the short-video service, was shut down shortly after Twitter bought the company. One factor was an inability to fit advertising into the service's six-second clips. A few years later, TikTok solved the problem by extending its short videos to fifteen seconds. More crucially, TikTok's app architecture presents only one video to the mobile user at a time, and clever ads look enough like native content that viewers will watch rather than making the effort to skip ahead. TikTok's heavily young users are also amenable to being sponsored as "influencers," lending credibility to brands that go that route.

Does influencer marketing work? Ask any teen, and they will likely answer in the affirmative. Academic literature is less emphatic, if voluminous: a literature review published in 2020 found 154 articles in the previous three years alone.[34] Some, for example, point to the difficulty of being "seen" and promoted by the relevant algorithms; many aspiring influencers never break through.[35] There's also the delicate line between personal brand and promoted product: for the influencer to be credible, the product endorsement needs to be congruent with the overall identity of the individual. According to one article, influencers "need to appear authentic, yet also approach their followers in a strategic way to remain appealing to advertisers."[36] Finally, there is a tension between being authentic and "real" and, on the other hand, having fans engage in parasocial behavior (see chapter 5), an interaction with mental health implications on both sides of the screen.[37]

At the peak of the pyramid, there is serious money: TikTok stars can make more than $10 million a year (sometimes at $250,000 per post that mentions a brand). And in their league, the numbers back up the power of endorsement: Charli D'Amelio and her sister launched a sub-brand within the Hollister chain, and sales were up 10 percent in the year the deal kicked in.[38] It's also noteworthy that the Hollister deal was D'Amelio's tenth-biggest endorsement of 2021.[39] But for every million-dollar deal there are scores of people trying to get free hotel nights in exotic locales in return for a small number of views, and some hotels are banning all such visitors.[40] As with so much else, the power-law distribution will eliminate the long tail of people seeking free stuff and ever more heavily reward those few creators with looks, charm, and luck enough to command a massive audience.

Building a brand identity; engaging consumers with content that is entertaining, informative, or, ideally, both; and promoting a product are all familiar actions from television, amped up by more precise targeting and broader reach via online video. But other business processes are also well supported. Consider recruiting. When established firms recruit on college campuses, some of them fail to attract many applicants, so the recruiting manager complains to a campus administrator in charge of corporate relations. "Why don't your students want to work for our company?" they ask. A quick check of the corporate website usually tells the story: no or limited social media activity, paper-based business processes ("Call your representative for a quote!"), and potentially important but not-very-interesting widgets for sale all turn off young people accustomed to interactive and creative communications in the channels where they live.

Leaders in recruitment thus turn to online video for "day in the life" videos, profiles of actual successful hires, and technical explanations of the cool things their employees get to work on. If an office environment is genuinely playful, video office tours can show employee engagement far better than a stock photo of a ping pong table. YouTube videos have become a staple of campus recruitment, but the realty firm of Keller Williams uses them to interact with current and potential real estate salespeople. A combination of explanation, inspiration, and background data keeps people coming back—to the tune of more than 50,000 subscribers. The tone is well suited to independent contractors who can typically have their choice of local firms once they demonstrate sales and listing production. The Keller Williams channel is full of concrete advice, and a companion coaching channel takes a more personal approach that complements the main page.

Wegmans is a grocery chain of more than a hundred stores in the Northeast United States that is historically ranked as a top employer by employees. Its recruiting videos are brief and represent the company culture. They show how associates are given adequate training, put in place to succeed, and stay with the company far longer than the industry average. The chain is family-owned and professes to encourage a family-like feeling in the workplace. With views in the tens of thousands, the videos are far from viral but reinforce the same messaging prospective employees get from *Fortune*'s "Best Companies to Work For" rankings, the in-store experience, and positive word of mouth from both customers and employees.

Online video's usefulness in education has been discussed elsewhere in regard to TED talks and Khan Academy. In the business context, educating customers can be essential both before and after the sale. In B2B selling in particular, features and specifications matter more than most consumer scenarios, where brand or price can often prove decisive. In industrial adhesives, food additives, or capital goods like heavy trucks, showing and explaining both what the product can do and how to get the most out of the purchase has multiple benefits. They can improve customer satisfaction, reduce the load on the call center, and appeal to millennial engineers and other specialists. These employees must specify a purchase but may not want to engage with a traditional sales rep via golf or other business entertaining.

Three examples of sophisticated use of online video for B2B follow.

Haas Automation, Inc.

Haas is the leading US producer of machine tools, a market dominated by German firms over the years. Based in California, the firm sells highly complex and expensive computerized tools for shaping metal. Beginning in 2016, Haas began offering a "video tip of the day," delivered by a highly skilled and appealing presenter. Even for a nonmachinist, the videos are notably clear and useful, solving real-world problems. Over the years, Haas has built a library of hundreds of videos, creating a virtual postgraduate school of machine-tool expertise. The videos are well produced, stylistically consistent, and meticulously archived. Haas hosts the videos natively and on their YouTube channel, probably because the firm sponsors a Formula 1 racing team and has a consumer-facing digital presence in addition to its industrial customer base.

Bobcat

Skid-steer loaders are a particularly American success story, insofar as Bobcat created a market for small, maneuverable, capable tread-driven machines used in construction, agriculture, landscaping, and other applications. Beginning in 2016, the firm began producing product comparison videos against the competition: Which loader is the fastest? Which can drill the deepest fencepost hole? Which has the smallest turning radius? The video format is so ideally suited to showing product superiority that the company does not need to resort to smoke and mirrors for its machines to look good.

Such a move is not surprising. Bobcat joined YouTube in 2009, fairly early for a B2B marketer, and has amassed more than 18 million views over that time. In an industry dominated by trade shows and niche media, such exposure—with zero distribution cost—has to represent a decisive win. The cancellation of thousands of industry trade shows in the wake of the COVID-19 pandemic makes the B2B video channel that much more important.

Corning

Corning is known for being a glass company but is in fact a highly diversified material science enterprise that makes many varieties of glass into everything from fiber-optic cables to iPhone screens. In 2011, it created a slickly produced five-and-a-half-minute video of future scenarios for architectural, electronic, and appliance applications that a family might encounter in their waking hours. Teachers, for one, used it extensively in STEM (science, technology, engineering, and mathematics) classes, and the video was viewed between 20 and 40 million times (estimates vary). Corning then turned "a day made of glass" into a franchise, with several sequels. The firm's "Gorilla glass" was invented in 1960 but not used in electronics until Steve Jobs recruited the firm to help improve iPhone displays. Corning's branding success led to more video production, including the hiring of *Mythbusters* stars Adam Savage and Jamie Hyneman to make another online video with more than 10 million views.

Contested Knowledge

There's no way of knowing the ultimate ratio between online video's education and instruction compared to its misinformation (in broad strokes, falsehoods spread out of ignorance) and disinformation (actively disseminated lies and deceptions). Just as the lack of traditional gatekeepers enables new voices to be heard, it also opens the medium to both passive and active efforts to delegitimate scientific authority, defraud or disenfranchise different groups, and amplify one's prejudices. As great as the potential for things like Khan Academy and Lynda (a repository of video tutorials now owned by Microsoft as part of LinkedIn) might be, the need for human institutions to coevolve with applications of machine learning to address fact-checking and associated problems cannot be overstated.

Close to where I live, a white teenager drove to Buffalo, New York, to commit a mass shooting at a busy grocery store in a predominantly Black neighborhood in May 2022. As we will see in chapter 8, the pathways among online platforms for radicalization and recruitment of communities of hate are complex and poorly understood. In this instance, Discord, 4chan, YouTube, Google Docs, and Twitch were interwoven. The Buffalo shooter kept a diary in which he chronicled his path to white supremacist ideology and a detailed logistical plan. YouTube played a prominent role: one analysis of the "manifesto" document (itself heavily cut-and-pasted from the Christchurch shooter) showed that he studied tactics (39 videos), firearms (37 videos), and equipment (24 videos). A key discovery was how to modify his rifle to accept high-capacity magazines, which are illegal in New York, and to defeat a locking mechanism that would slow down reloading. He also consulted YouTube to learn how to shoot through different types of glass and how to use body armor.[41] All of these learnings contributed to the high death toll and sophistication of the attack. Whether in mass shootings, from vaccine misinformation, or in the wake of violent extremist content of many flavors, people are dying because of these tools.

Fraudsters can use the emerging capabilities of online video to deceive via deep fakes and related technologies. Note that some countries now require advertisers to announce if photomanipulation technologies have been used on human models. The next decade of online video will be strenuously tested by the intensifying battle between truth and falsehood, and by conventional consensus versus all manner of deniers (YouTube has at least one flat-earth channel, for example[42]). Thus, we are in the peculiar situation of being able to learn surgery[43] in the same venue where people insist the moon landing was faked.

Traditional suppliers of education, meanwhile, have mostly nibbled around the edges of making lectures available. MIT has substantial portions of a computer science curriculum online, absent homework and assessments, of course. This raises a question far too broad and deep to consider here: What does $5,000, $25,000 or $70,000 a year in tuition actually pay for? Is it the classroom lectures, or the professional networking, or the certification of completion? As we will suggest in the analysis of print's long-term impacts on knowledge generation and dissemination in chapter 8, educational institutions the world over will be challenged. Many will be forced to define, distinguish, and redefine what they do, including their business model, as online video grows in capacity and capability. Khan Academy is only a foretaste of what will be possible.

Conclusion

The teaching possibilities of online video were explored early and often in the rise of the new medium, and no doubt future innovations will expand this function further. Note how seldom existing educational entities were at the forefront. As we will see in regard to the printing press, innovation in business models often lags technological innovation. Let us turn now to a brief examination of how online video is transforming entertainment.

Entertainment

Between 2005 and 2020, video entertainment underwent several fundamental transitions. Both YouTube and Netflix shifted media consumption off programmed broadcast times. Online video in all its forms made the thirty-minute-multiple schedule that characterized those broadcasts an anachronism. People became famous both on and off network television for putting mundane aspects of their life on a screen. The popularity of watching people play video games led to an entire genre of videos in which viewers watched someone else watch and possibly analyze or critique an original performance. Most recently, TikTok trained hundreds of millions of people to create and consume fifteen-second clips that moved inside jokes, fads, and memes across the globe with staggering speed, absent official gatekeepers or tastemakers. Perhaps the only takeaway from the first years of online video is that stars, themes, and entire genres will evolve extremely rapidly and unpredictably.

Returning to Professor Mathias Bärtl's statistical analysis of YouTube content from 2006 to 2016 shows how tastes evolved. For one thing, the proliferation of uploads dropped median views per video by two orders of magnitude (see chart 12). The share of those views began to shift in 2016 toward the current landscape. Gaming steadily grew as a category, as did "People and blogs." Given that many of the top earners on YouTube either launched in game commentary or branched out of it to become brands, Bärtl's findings feel directionally correct even though he could only analyze a small sample of the service's content (see chart 13).

Different people find different things entertaining, so the term "entertainment" is vague. But whatever one seeks out to fill leisure time, online video is likely to have altered its shape, reach, and participants. From video

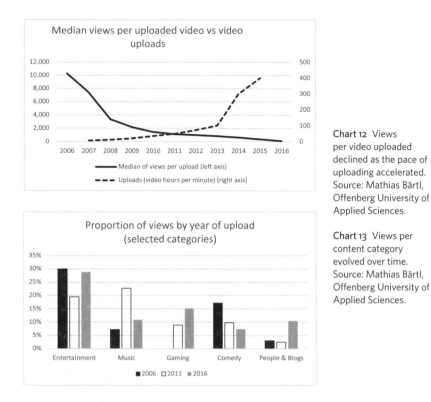

Chart 12 Views per video uploaded declined as the pace of uploading accelerated. Source: Mathias Bärtl, Offenberg University of Applied Sciences.

Chart 13 Views per content category evolved over time. Source: Mathias Bärtl, Offenberg University of Applied Sciences.

games to global football, from Hollywood to Bollywood, and from Prince to Psy to Pinkfong, online video continues to transform the entertainment landscape. As part of this systemic change, the nature of fame has also evolved, in both healthy and destructive ways. We will begin by analyzing music, where YouTube outpaces both Apple and Spotify in global downloads and TikTok has shaken up the industry. Then we will move to sport, skim some other entertainment issues, and conclude with an extended discussion of the consequences of Internet fame.

Music

The roles online video can perform in the music industry are many and complex. Some labels have uploaded extensive collections of artist videos while others aggressively block any whiff of content on YouTube and elsewhere. Cover bands and teaching videos can be taken down, for example. Even though neither is a threat to sales of the covered song and may actually stimulate demand for the original, the copyright owner has the final say. The concept of "fair use" is in retreat. The vast, low-cost distribution of online video music led to the Chicago band OK Go to sever ties with their record label in 2010 in the wake of their viral "treadmill" video.[1] More than a decade later, for example, the band continues to innovate ways to garner attention (in Super Bowl commercials and video game soundtracks, among others). As the band's website puts it: "Continuing a career that includes viral videos, *New York Times* op-eds, a major label split and the establishment of a DIY trans-media mini-empire, collaborations with pioneering dance companies and tech giants, animators and Muppets, OK Go continue to fearlessly dream and build new worlds in a time when creative boundaries have all but dissolved."[2]

Not all that long ago, the task of physical distribution of plastic discs to retailers with finite shelf space serving consumers with fickle taste made forecasting a key activity. It also forced the industry to address the issue of retailer returns of unsold inventory. The end of that era opens up many new avenues. Niche acts can find their audiences, established artists can mine their back catalog, and encyclopedic coverage of live sets can be practical.

The benefits are tangible. Online video has spawned many crowdfunding efforts to support musicians. Patreon is a crowdfunding platform launched by the husband-and-wife team that performs as Pomplamoose (see chapter 6). At Patreon, crowdfunders get tutorials, behind-the-scenes interviews, early access to new releases, and other benefits.[3] Current-day performers can get worldwide exposure, bond with geographically distributed fans, and release experimental material. Many sites feature merchandise ("merch") sales that help compensate for low streaming revenues. An example is the jazz collective Snarky Puppy, whose live version of their song "Lingus" has amassed 32 million views as of 2023—an astounding number for a ten-minute complex instrumental with little radio play.[4]

For all the video performed by living, touring artists, a vast segment of YouTube is devoted to old performances. Although jazz greats, pop music of many eras, and every niche audience imaginable can be found, the baby boomer generation's "classic rock" is heavily represented. Sounds connected to nostalgia may derive from video game soundtracks, modem handshakes, or even K-Mart in-store marketing audio. The role of YouTube as a resource for tens of millions of listener-rememberers bears mention.

One important function of these communities in response to music videos is to find solidarity in nostalgia (see chapter 8). Unlike the physical experience of a Coasters, Rolling Stones, or Celine Dion concert, one can connect with fellow fans in response to the richness of aural and video cues asynchronously and without any limitation on physical location. A common theme within these comments sections is to denigrate "today's" music (defined loosely) by praising the taste, talent, or popularity of a bygone performer. It is also common for a younger viewer to counter the criticism either by naming names of current artists thought to possess taste or talent, or by critiquing the performance being rhapsodized.

Another branch of YouTube is devoted to sounds that trigger a different, physical response. 2018 was the year ASMR broke out, almost entirely due to YouTube. Autonomous sensory meridian response is a mouthful of a title to describe the pleasant tingling sensations that typically migrate from the scalp down the neck and upper spine. It was named by an online forum participant in 2010. ASMR is in many ways a quintessentially Internet-centric phenomenon. Online forums supported virtual communities and YouTube became the home for videos designed to stimulate the response. One study estimated there were 13 million of them by 2018.[5] Practice far outruns theory. According to ASMR University, an online clearinghouse for materials on the phenomenon, only ten peer-reviewed articles address it. According to the *New York Times*, participants in the community tend to be female, and there is intense and ongoing discussion over whether ASMR should be considered as a sexual response.[6] Here we have a cultural phenomenon named, supplied, and consumed almost exclusively online, utilizing the many-to-many multimedia network in wholly new ways that defy conventional categorization.

It is not often expressed in these terms, but YouTube utilizes cloud computing to become a cultural repository, a shared attic of memory. Independent of every other function it performs—and there are many— online video's ability to hold and distribute billions of cultural memories is important but underrecognized. As the cultural critic John David Ebert notes, for centuries, those cultural memories were bound up in print. From stone carvings on tombstones to the works of Charles Darwin or Marie Curie, to be literate was to have access to the words, and perhaps drawings, of the past.[7] In a moment of historical time (less than five years), that changed.

YouTube's repository of video and audio recordings marks a milestone in the history of music (among other art forms that I will acknowledge but not discuss further here). Going back to the late nineteenth century, music was a key motivation for the development of the telephone. Books verging on science fiction envisioned a service whereby listeners could enjoy concerts without being in the hall. The performances were synchronous; the idea and invention of sound recording succeeded the hope for simultaneous remote transmission. It is impossible to recall, but not that long ago, that a person of means and cultural access might hear a given Beethoven symphony once in their lifetime. A short time later, the LP record made it possible to hear a Toscanini or von Karajan performance ad infinitum. It also spawned entirely new genres of music that marginalized the former canon. Roll over Beethoven, indeed.

Making music permanently available in copy form rather than only being ephemeral and synchronous changed the process of cultural inheritance. It also changed music from a communal experience to sometimes a small-group or individual one. Numerous illustrations from the 1950s feature a couple lounging in front of a hi-fi system. Magazines from *Gramophone* to *Audio* to *Playboy* advised readers on matters of equipment and listening choices. *National Lampoon*, for a time the most-read magazine in the US college demographic, served up a large helping of stereo ads in the mid-1970s to support such writers as P. J. O'Rourke (author of nineteen books, including *Parliament of Whores*), John Hughes (the hugely successful movie director), and Doug Kenney (*Animal House, Caddyshack*).[8] Later, after the iPod became popular in the early twenty-first century, listening became solitary. What had been a ritual for decades for young soldiers and students—buying and enjoying an audio system—faded from fashion as headphones and earbuds took center stage. Receivers and speakers, once ubiquitous in a certain demographic, became niche markets.

As of 2023, YouTube is by far the largest streamer of music on the Internet.[9] (This is not new. A 2011 "Critical Viewers Guide" to the service asserted that "music dominates YouTube."[10]) It is used daily by hundreds of millions of adults. It is primarily watched on mobile devices. Taken together, these facts begin to suggest how the service has helped reshape listening. Music is streamed rather than owned and often suggested rather than requested; in contrast to radio, both YouTube and TikTok facilitate interaction with the song, the artist, and possibly other listeners.

For several reasons, the algorithms have a much easier time with getting music to play automatically and coherently than they do with other types of content. While the selection is broad and deep (including bootlegs and B-sides in some cases), it is not inclusive. A number of artists have estates or offices that take down any material associated with the act. These exceptions have not diminished the site's popularity, and the volume of available material can satisfy most any listener, anywhere: global mass and local niche markets alike are well served. Part of this popularity relates to price; Spotify boasts more subscribers than YouTube, but without the cross-subsidies at work in Google, Spotify's long-term lack of profitability raises concerns. In terms of overall users and not only subscribers, YouTube is five times the size of Spotify.[11]

In 2021 an unintended side effect of automated copyright screening emerged. Beverly Hills police officers who did not want citizen video of their behavior posted online played the Beatles song "Yesterday" into the camera-phone microphone. Given their proximity to the entertainment business, the officers knew that videos containing the familiar melody would automatically be removed by Instagram and YouTube. (Both employ automated takedown algorithms on behalf of music rights holders.) At least three episodes were reported, another tactic in a long-running battle between police officers and those who seek to hold them accountable for their actions.[12]

Where YouTube differs from radio or iTunes, however, is in the comment function. Listeners can post technical information (time and track listings), trivia (who was the uncredited saxophonist?), affirmations or denigrations, and memories. This annotation function means that communities can form around a song that carries special emotional weight. These communities have no intention, no formal organization, and no premeditation. As NYU professor Clay Shirky presciently noted in *Here Comes Everybody* (2008), coordination goes from being an organization's function to being a feature of the infrastructure.[13] People can contribute as much or as little as they like, when they feel so moved, with no awareness or forethought of when other people might be listening, available, or interested.

Online video thus replaces stereo playback systems (at the individual or small-group level), radio (in some respects), and record stores (either physical ones or those online, like Apple and Amazon) as a new kind of distribution network, expert recommender, and fan club. Seeing the service only in its role as streamer (distributor) is understandable but misses what Shirky calls the "collaborative infrastructure" that provides inchoate social groups the ability to coalesce and communicate, perhaps only ephemerally. For all the attention rightly paid to the prodigious upload and download numbers attached to YouTube's videos, the huge crowdsourcing effort also present on the site can get lost if one isn't looking for it.

Consider just a few examples. A Dutch uploader found a Scopitone (a 1960s video jukebox popular in Europe) clip of Procol Harum's "Whiter Shade of Pale." After some cleanup, the video has been viewed more than 100 million times. The comments appear to come from many parts of the world, connecting tens of thousands of people (30,000 comments) who will never cross physical paths and few of whom were alive when the song was on the radio. About the same year, Atlantic Records released the dance tune

"Tighten Up" by Archie Bell—an Army vet—and the Drells (of Houston, Texas). The song, viewed nearly 9 million times, remains infectious and original. Here, the comments tell a different story. Pop Dada wrote:

> archie , I was in nam in 68 ... one night we was dancing to tighten up .. some of the guys..next day we lost 4 of my squad ..ambush .. we fought all day and night.. but I always remember that night and day .. one minute we were back in the world „ hours later some of us had left it behind and died at 20..i didn't know I had ptsd till maybe 15 yrs later .. I was driving with my wife and "tighten up" came on the radio ... all of a sudden I thought of that night . the guys dancing then losing them the next day and my eyes swelled up with tears because the memory of them was so strong .. we were with Charlie co. 2/506th 101st Airborne Div. we were the 1st Platoon. thanks man your song carries a lot of weight with me brother.. ... you got hit too.. yea man me too.

More than a hundred people wrote back with affirmations, sympathy, and thanks for Pop Dada's military service.

Aretha Franklin, a force of nature in any medium, is a powerful figure on YouTube, with multiple videos getting 10 million or more views. One stands out as a kind of landmark. In 2015 she performed "(You Make Me Feel) Like a Natural Woman" at the Kennedy Center Honors performance, paying tribute to the song's cowriter Carole King, one of the night's honorees. The TV special was viewed by 7.5 million viewers[14] who saw Franklin deliver a stunning performance; King herself was clearly moved by the seventy-three-year-old's rendition. In only five years, YouTube viewers had seen the performance roughly 25 million times, highlighting the importance of the service for broadcast-like reach as well as effectively infinite selection.

Sakamichi no Apollon (Kids on the Slope) is a Japanese anime that aired in 2012. Jazz specifically and music generally are a central force in the storyline, based on a prize-winning manga of the same name. In one episode, one of the aforementioned kids is playing Art Blakey's jazz standard "Moanin'" on an organ in an empty church. The young priest silently enters and joins him on drums in a skilled, emotionally rich improvisation. The clip is of course available on YouTube, as is the Blakey original, and the respective comment threads tell the story of bidirectional trans-Pacific cultural transmission. Each video has more than a million views, and there are clearly people being introduced to entirely new art forms in a way no other medium could have facilitated.

Another change also set the stage for YouTube's music presence. With the decline of physical music media, downloaded files from both legal and illegal sources assumed primacy for a short while—maybe less than a decade. With the rise of streaming services (e.g., Netflix, Amazon, Spotify) many music listeners never "owned" or "had" a given song. Playlists became like radio, in a preferred vein but not typically programmed tune by tune.

This participation in the preservation and repetition of past musical performances and styles is also important in the context of the history of popular music. Between the late 1990s and possibly until the present day, public performance of music in the United States (live and via electronic distribution) has been dominated by aging rockers, established country acts, and a handful of hip-hop superstars who have become the dominant face of their genre. Nothing in genre terms has broken through the way rock and roll did in the 1950s, hard bop jazz did in the late 1950s, acid rock did in the 1960s, punk did in the 1970s, or hip-hop did in the 1980s. That's upward of thirty-five years in Western culture without a major shift in musical direction, maybe slightly less if electronica/techno/rave is counted as major.

Rather than innovations in musical *style*, the twenty-plus years of music on the Internet have been characterized by *technological* innovation. The late 1990s initially saw MP3 file sharing through Napster, which then evolved into BitTorrent (and its gray-area variants), plus legal services that include Apple's iTunes and Amazon Music. More recently, the notion of a music "file" has been eclipsed by streaming media, including YouTube. The innovations have come far more in the technologies of distribution and consumption (headphones and earbuds) than in any artistic realm.

Online video's technological facilitation of nostalgia serves many social functions beyond the individual frissons of memory. People can bond over shared tastes or memories, they can feel and assert a sense of meaning (many combat veterans recall where they were and who they were with when certain songs were playing), and people situate themselves (and identify with others) with temporal anchors: I was X years old in Y school when that song came out, possibly driving a Z car.

YouTube also facilitates new kinds of content that previously lacked a name or a vehicle. One example is music commentary. Rick Beato is a fifty-something former music professor and record producer. His YouTube channel, which is nearing a thousand titles, has more than 3 million subscribers. After beginning with history and theory topics aimed at music industry insiders and professionals, Beato has expanded into other types of content that have increased the reach of his channel.

His top-twenty countdowns (best rock drummers, best guitar sounds, best vocalists) combine the authoritativeness of a music professor discussing mixolydian modes, the insider memories of an industry figure who worked with major artists (and cowrote a Billboard number one hit), and the enthusiasm of a true fan. More recently, his more than one hundred videos of "what makes this song great" break down well-known tracks from a variety of genres, showing how a clever sound effect, unexpected chord change, brilliant instrumental technique, or other factor contributes to the song's long-lived popularity.

On the way to his fame, Beato has learned much about how YouTube works. The service employs algorithms that search out possible instances of copyrighted material, and content owners can and do block even instructional copies of a teacher playing a single riff. Song names are seldom included in his metadata, even on the "what makes this song great?" videos, and certain note sequences must be varied considerably from the original to avoid takedown. Production value is rewarded. If a thumbnail photo is off by even a pixel or two from the 1280 x 720 template, it can be ignored, whereas early adoption of 4K video uploads was rewarded by the surfacing algorithm. Finally, Beato has his own gold mine. As recorded multitrack tape was transcribed onto compact disc masters in the 1990s, workers at studios took the time to load the isolated tracks (typically up to twenty-four of them) into the digital Pro Tools editing suite. Hard drives were then swapped and circulated, and often forgotten. Beato's collection of isolated tracks makes for fascinating insight into how a song was constructed ("that's a tuba playing way down in the mix—here it is solo"), to the point where he has received calls from artists clamoring to know where he got the original multitrack files of their records.

Beato uploads new material frequently. After quitting record producing to make YouTube his full-time job, he creates material in several subcategories on his main channel. (A secondary channel allows him to test takedown-prone material without getting a copyright infringement "strike" against his main channel as well as to experiment with different styles of both music and presentation.) How-to videos might highlight microphone placement techniques. "What makes this song great?" has expanded to include "deep cuts" that while not iconic are musically compelling. History videos dig into the evolution of instruments and genres over time. Interviews with historically important figures are a byproduct of Beato's influence in the music business. Just in 2021, Pat Metheny, Ron Carter, and Joni Mitchell spoke with him. Podcasts might be released on both audio and YouTube platforms. Personal content—"This day changed my life," "My twenty-year

101

Entertainment

overnight success," "I don't want to hear your excuses"—shows up regularly as well. Given the appetite for music of the 1960s through early 2000s, there is no shortage of material going forward, and the audience continues to grow. Reaching his first 100,000 subscribers took thirteen months while going from 900,000 to 1 million took only twenty-nine days.

The fame part of Beato's YouTube presence is visible. As for fortune, that's more complicated. Several factors are in play. First, per-view royalties don't add up to a livelihood. Published estimates vary but a million views earns in the vicinity of $5,000, and this might be split with a rights holder— in this case, a band's record label or management. Second, ad placement cuts several ways and Beato has thus far eschewed commercial sponsorship. Finally, physical merchandise can comprise an attractive revenue stream, but involves the channel owner getting into supply chain issues of procurement, warehousing, and fulfillment. In Beato's case, the main differentiator is his PDF Beato Book, a copy of the self-published textbook he used in his college teaching. Digital distribution involves only virtual inventory and selling direct removes all intermediaries from profit dilution. Beato keeps every penny of the book's selling price, along with lesson software and other virtual goods. He also has a club for viewers, one benefit of which is having Beato react to your uploaded composition or musical technique via digital coaching.[15]

For its part, TikTok's rise to cultural prominence has centered on music: lip-syncing, dance clips, and similar content wrapped around some musical content. Unlike YouTube, TikTok performs extremely well with kids as young as ten or eleven (too young to legitimately sign up for the service) but so far not well with viewers over thirty. It's a great tool for artists to get noticed, especially if the song goes viral with many viewer remakes or remixes. Artists are flocking to the platform—Lil Nas X (who we will encounter again in chapter 7) and Lizzo were early examples, and the Korean pop stars BTS debuted a song on TikTok in February 2020—just as record company lawyers were negotiating with TikTok's parent company ByteDance to get royalties paid to songwriters, music publishers, and performers.[16] The rapid rise of the app, the problematic youth of its demographic, and the uncertainty of both China's and the US government's demands on ByteDance all combine to make the legal status of TikTok going forward extremely complex and unpredictable.

Spectacle

Whether they are billed as tricks, stunts, pranks, or "science," online video has long been home to extreme events that gather large viewerships. Some events are shocking, and as elsewhere, I will note these without comment. Others are part of franchises: Dude Perfect is the name for five college buddies from Texas A&M who started making make trick-shot videos. They now earn a reported $20 million a year across multiple platforms, including a $100 million theme park. Mr. Beast, who we met earlier, counts to 100,000 on camera and was buried alive in a casket for fifty hours.

What counts as spectacle evolves rapidly. "Challenges" in the vein of 2014's ice bucket fundraiser[17] are now a staple of TikTok. Flash mobs were a thing for a while, especially in the Netherlands, until they weren't (the COVID-19 pandemic did not accelerate the trend). As we will see, trying to one-up yesterday's spectacle has proven to be the undoing of several people who could not exceed extreme events with even more extreme events.

Popularized science can also generate large viewership. Diet Coke and Mentos account for hundreds of millions of views via multiple channels. NASA has 11 million followers and satellite coverage of a volcanic eruption generated 93 million views. Blippi, a kids' YouTube channel, includes a "which things sink and float" video with nearly 350 million views. Visual effects videos often see tens of millions of views. Using "science" as an excuse for pyrotechnics has a long history: Purdue's George Goble lit a barbeque with liquid oxygen in one of the first Internet videos, spread in the days of dial-up modems, about a decade before YouTube.[18]

Sport

It's become a truism that television helped make American football the dominant sport it has become in the United States over the past sixty years. The pace of the game, the scale of the field, and the color of the jerseys all contribute to a compelling viewing experience. After 1960, it soon became clear that football provided better audiences to advertisers than baseball, the alleged national pastime that lost considerable cultural traction during the NFL's ascendancy. What will new online video media mean for sport in the twenty-first century?

Athletes Go Direct to Fans

Along with other social media platforms, online video has become a way for sports stars (defined very broadly) to communicate. No editorial layers of interpretation, media neglect, or rationing of access interpose themselves between players and watchers. Whether related to professional "wrestlers," Olympians, or pro athletes in media-friendly sports, fans will seek out and consume hours of programming. The sports figures might discuss a social cause, a charity, their training or dietary regimen, or the state of their career directly with their public. Conde Nast's GQ property (magazine? website?) launched a YouTube channel in 2019 focused on off-field personas, whether it be an athlete's tattoos, watch collection, pets, or, predictably, clothing collections. Vice Media hosts a channel devoted exclusively to sneaker culture, often featuring celebrities and athletes alongside designers and collectors.

In the United States, college athletes are using social media channels to capitalize on their fame. Prior to 2021, campus stores would sell a uniform replica with a well-known player's number on it, but the player saw no royalties. With the advent of NIL (name, image, likeness) legislation and other rule changes, athletes can monetize their fame through product endorsements, appearances in video games, and social media revenue streams. While TikTok and YouTube are core to the new status quo, social media more widely defined was a major driver of the sea change. It's difficult to conceive of NIL reform absent direct-to-fans media options that bypass traditional television network and related gatekeepers.[19]

Online Video Is a Memory Bank

We will discuss the larger issues related to nostalgia in chapter 8, but past sporting moments are hugely popular. Google found in 2017 that seventy of the top one hundred sports videos on YouTube included the words "great," "greatest," or "best" in the titles. Ipsos research shows that 84 percent of soccer fans surveyed watch historical matches from World Cups and other tournaments, and 68 percent of Olympic viewers on YouTube say the same of their content. In 2018 Google asserted that viewing of historic sports video had increased dramatically over the five years prior. This searching for past sport performance includes searches for big-game ads as well, whether in the World Cup or Super Bowl. Google reports such searches tripled between 2016 and 2018.[20]

Online Video Is Changing What We Consider Sport

YouTube hosted millions of hours of video gameplay and commentary footage long before ESPN began covering online gaming. Twitch seized on the movement further, focusing on live versus recorded gameplay streams. Other sports and games have thrived in light of online exposure: Dambe, a traditional African combat sport, has been revived by YouTube exposure.[21] Extreme sports, whether they involve flying, going fast, or another big risk, have been catapulted into mass consciousness less by mainstream broadcasting and more by GoPro and other ruggedized high-resolution cameras (for capture) coupled with YouTube (for distribution).

Headquartered in Austria, the makers of the Red Bull energy drink may have played the YouTube card better than anyone. Their aggregate view count of more than 1 billion dwarfs all other beverage companies. Red Bull has built a broad portfolio of adrenaline sports sponsorships ranging from wingsuit flying to Formula 1. It even boasts a space program: the company sponsored a balloon launch to record altitude, from which daredevil Felix Baumgartner jumped for a ten-minute freefall covering 39 kilometers (more than 24 miles). The company has created an effectively unlimited storehouse of video content for free distribution. That content is well archived and organized so playlists flow well. Some people stream a Red Bull channel during parties as entertainment.

The brand's target market is hard-core but not well reached by traditional media. Having hours of extreme skiing is perfect for YouTube, but not so desirable for networks, even one such as ESPN, which must still abide by schedules for programming and audience metrics for ad revenue. The brand's logo is inescapable, as is the messaging. The energy drink powers everyone from ski jumpers to aerobatic pilots to race car drivers. The global reach of online video saves the brand from having to negotiate network deals in every country they want to reach. A reported 9.5 million people worldwide watched the Baumgartner Stratos jump live on YouTube.

Online Video Is a Virtual Coach

Fifteen years ago feels like another world in many ways, but the story of Kenya's Julius Yego remains incredible. His country boasts a rich tradition of distance running but has had little success in field events such as the high jump or shot put. In 2009, Yego was frustrated by his progress with the javelin, so he spent time in the cybercafe watching every javelin-related video he could find, with particular attention to training programs. In 2011, he became the first Kenyan to win a title in a field event at the All-Africa Games. By 2015, he was world champion. Yego then earned a silver medal at the 2016 Olympics despite suffering an ankle injury. There is no way an athlete from a developing economy could master a technique-intensive event looking at books. Yego's medals show we are living in the presence of not only a new medium but a new distribution system, a new curation method, and a new scale of knowledge exchange.

Whether couch-potato fitness or Olympic javelin-throwing, everyone can learn their sport online. From curveball throwing to "running faster," queries for sport technique videos are popular, doubling in the year to 2017.[22] Every fitness program one can conceive of (along with associated fad diets) is represented. Trick shots are an entire subgenre, whether in billiards, basketball, or bow and arrow—and audience feedback is an essential part of the channels' popularity. Experts can emerge from anywhere. In response to the query "how to throw a football spiral," NFL Films produced a video with 2.3 million views. At the same time, an assistant coach at the University of North Dakota has a 2011 video with 1.4 million views that YouTube surfaced on the first page of results.

Part of coaching is performance analysis. Whether it's a swimmer, a jump-shooter, a rower, or a thrower, numerous outlets break down the mechanics of athletic performance. This critiquing extends to video gameplay as well. Millions of views have been collected by both well-known and self-made observers who can break down a given performance for both performance enhancement and educational entertainment. Video analysis is yet another Internet genre that would have been impossible in 2004.

Online Video Contributes to the "Second Screen"
Smartphones and tablets have merged with broadcast television viewing. Twitter feeds, statistics lookups, and past highlight videos all get called up to complement what's happening on the big screen. Videos can range from "funny" clips to athlete interviews to feature material on the athlete's hometown, rehab from injury, or path to the big moment. As early as the 2014 FIFA World Cup, global video sites served up an estimated 37 billion views for football-related content. Big broadcast audiences drive proportionately big online traffic.[23]

Women's Sports Can Break Out Online
Whether related to soccer, tennis, Olympic sports, or adrenaline sports, online channels can bypass traditional media gatekeepers. YouTube itself streams some events in which traditional rights holders do not have interest or broadcast reach. Just because Austrians, hypothetically, watch women's skiing live doesn't mean a US or Japanese video outlet will carry a given race in those countries. Time zones and local broadcast restrictions are falling for many varieties of live events, with female athletes being one beneficiary of the increased audience.

Sports is a classic long-tail phenomenon. The hits at the top generate global superstars, but even a neighborhood croquet tournament might be available somewhere. Online video is a perfect match for subject matter that involves both participation and fandom, leisure and conditioning, trash-talking and technique. The passion people bring to sport generates both intense memories and the willingness to curate and create compelling content. Sports talk podcasts proliferate endlessly, and many of them find an audience. All of this adds up to a body of material ideally suited to the crowdsourced ethos and business model characteristic of online video.

Other Entertainment Vehicles

A full accounting of the migration of entertainment-related content to online video platforms is well beyond the scope of this project. (For the sake of context, prepandemic 2019 worldwide revenues in various entertainment channels are shown in table 1.[24])

In 1996, professors Adam Brandenburger and Barry Nalebuff published a book on game theory and business strategy entitled *Co-Opetition*; it remains in print twenty-five years later. Google and various entertainment companies appear to be engaging in simultaneous cooperation and competition as YouTube transforms the entertainment landscape. Back in 2007, as Viacom was suing Google over copyright, it also desperately wanted twenty-somethings to watch Comedy Central snippets that Viacom itself was uploading. Fast-forward fifteen years, and NBC (part of Comcast) has dedicated channels for shows such as *Today* and various *NBC Sports* talk shows even as that same content is hosted at NBC.com. *Saturday Night Live*, a battleground since YouTube's first year, is now available for purchase by episode on YouTube.

Most major entertainment providers realized they must coexist with YouTube; ESPN, the Oscars, Fox Sports, Comedy Central, the NBA, cable channels including TLC and Lifetime, and individual entities such as Selena Gomez and the Baltimore Ravens all are readily available. Note that a team (Baltimore), a league (NFL), and a broadcast network that covers sports

Table 1 Worldwide revenues for entertainment by type, 2019.

Medium	Global receipts (in billion USD)
Recorded music	21.5
Movie box office	42.5
Streaming video	83
Video games	120
Television	243

(ESPN) can all be represented, rather than only one exclusive entity. The same goes for recording artists and labels; self-made online video stars (Jenna Marbles or Bella Poarch); movies, actors, and studios; and gaming platforms (Nintendo's Pokémon). Whereas familiar gatekeepers organized a particular domain in the past, now the online video medium is a more level, albeit chaotic, field of competition.

Disaggregation was a common buzzword in the early years of electronic commerce.[25] Online video is a textbook example. Not only is a television show now parted out into subunits (interviews on talk shows, sketches on *SNL*, highlights of sporting events), but the familiar audience aggregators are joined by new co-opetition allies and adversaries. Google does not publish video games or host gameplay, but YouTube was hugely important in the rise of e-sports. Similarly, Amazon (not a console manufacturer or game creator) bought Twitch, an online game streaming service, for nearly a billion dollars in 2014. Despite Amazon not being a traditional player in the industry, the synergy between game streaming, consumer reach, and Amazon's cloud computing platform made for what appears to be a successful acquisition.

The notion of "watching somebody else play video games" has snuck up on mainstream culture (see chapter 6). As of 2018, young US gamers spent 3 hours and 26 minutes a week watching video gameplay. This is almost identical to television viewing of traditional sporting events by the general population, which averages 3 hours and 18 minutes. Importantly, the viewers identify with players: they are watching people play a game that has been launched as "e-sports." YouTube is a vital part of this trend, both in its support for livestreaming tournaments and in the rise of PewDiePie and other gamer-celebrities. These rising stars come from all over the world—Chile, Spain, El Salvador, Canada, Brazil—and often use the gaming content as a springboard into other genres, including comedy and personal vlogging. A key part of their attraction is in the way they are perceived to increase the enjoyment or perhaps skill of the watcher of the video game being played. Game trailers, released in the gap between a title's completion and its general availability in physical media, have become more popular than movie trailers, at least in YouTube view count.

Twitch is a major force in online video that may be less visible to people born before 1995 or so. It pulls dominant numbers among millennials: 70 percent of this demographic has played or watched a video game in the last sixty days. Fifteen million viewers log in on an average day, during which time more than 2 million hours are streamed across roughly 100,000 concurrent channels. The audience skews 80 percent male versus 20 percent female, and harassment of female and LGBTQ streamers and players remains an ongoing issue for the platform. Live streams are especially popular on Twitch despite being available elsewhere. As of 2017 Twitch accounted for more live streaming than ESPN or any other entity, and by 2022, it made up 76 percent of all live hours being watched online.[26] Viewers are loyal, log in for long periods, and constitute a rich hunting ground for advertisers in search of the 18–34 demographic. Twitch and Reddit stand alone in this regard, outpacing Facebook, YouTube, and ESPN.

Twitch has capitalized handsomely on the rise of online game streaming. Early on, the service provided gamers with tools for monetization, including gamification of the viewing experiences, cash "tip jars" for fans to support streamers, and virtual assets like badges and tokens for purchase. The intimacy of the chat function clearly accelerated the feelings of parasocial engagement—notably, the side-channel augments the ostensible broadcast content. Furthermore, these interactions could occur in the "flow" state so named by psychologist Mihaly Csikszentmihalyi, increasing their salience. The second screen, watched by the viewer, was only slightly removed from the primary locus of action, the video game being streamed.[27] As a result, participatory video streaming helped form extremely large online audiences bound by intense and shared experiences.

As a result, more than either YouTube or TikTok, Twitch has used video as an anchor of a community. Game players interact with fans, who follow players more than games. Game developers test, promote, and track performance of new titles. Gaming is a structure in which video occurs, so advertisers are sometimes more comfortable entering a better defined online community environment than the chaos of Reddit or the vast and sometimes problematic context of YouTube.[28] According to MIT professor T. L. Taylor, Twitch is part of a complex ecosystem where "new entertainment products . . . mix together gameplay, humor, commentary, and real-time interaction with fans and audiences."[29] To anticipate our examination of cross-platform issues in chapter 7, video gameplay migrates across devices. Live game streams exist in an ecosystem alongside televisions, game consoles, tablets, and smartphones.[30]

Why do people watch gamers play video games? Taylor identifies six motivations.

1. Aspirational: to improve game skill
2. Educational: to learn about game titles and genres
3. Inspirational: to express fandom

4. Entertainment: to enjoy humor and/or gaming skill
5. Community: a collective experience of something larger
6. Ambience: gameplay can be background presence.[31]

Twitch serves both the gamers and their fans by satisfying all of these motivations. Fans can donate to the gamers they enjoy, the gamers can create storefronts and announce upcoming streams (across multiple social media), and crowdfunding can support the creation of new game titles or hardware. This was an astute move by Twitch management given that game projects have long been among the best supported projects on the Kickstarter crowdfunding platform.

The net result is a nearly boundary-free entertainment market. In early 2019, Netflix made headlines when it noted the threat from video gaming to its business. The company's annual letter to shareholders asserted that "We compete with (and lose to) Fortnite more than HBO." How much of this represents competitive posturing (especially relative to WarnerMedia, HBO's corporate parent) remains to be seen, but the point is a valid one. The online environment has erased traditional distinctions between television and movies, between network and streaming television, and between upload platforms and providers of studio content. Both Twitch and YouTube are courting gamers. TikTok spreads new music the way MTV and MySpace Music used to. After winning three Oscars in 2017, Amazon won seven Emmys in 2019 (compared to NBC's two). The NFL signed a promotional deal with TikTok in 2019. Physical DVDs constituted 64 percent of the US home video market in 2005, compared to less than 10 percent in 2020. Streaming and online video can accommodate all previous electronic media.

Similarly, Google does not make movies but is an essential part of the promotional ecosystem and yet an uneasy presence in the Hollywood world of content creation. Takedown notices routinely target users interacting with studios' copyrighted movie clips. The place of theatergoing in daily life is changing in the United States and elsewhere; accordingly, the role of YouTube in promoting a movie is also evolving. Theater attendance is in a long-term decline that the 2020 pandemic only accelerated; streaming is eliminating the role of DVD sales and rentals; and the war for talent has bid up the cost of writers, directors, and name actors. Movie-watching in 2030 is likely going to look very different from 2015—particularly after the COVID-19 experience—and online video's role in that industry will likely be crucial.

Overall, online video can be seen as an entertainment channel in its own right as watch times continue to rise, competing with everything from

gameplay to binge-watching. It's also a complement to other media properties that make and distribute original content. (As it was building its US
audience, TikTok was the leading purchaser of Snapchat ads in 2019.) Google
continues to experiment with its own original content, though not nearly at
the scale of Netflix (with a 2019 content creation budget of $15 billion), Apple
($6 billion), or Amazon ($7 billion). Disney remains the industry heavy-
weight champion at $24 billion. Facebook, meanwhile, launched Watch in
2017, a service that overlaps both Netflix (with original content, budgeted at
a reported $1 billion for 2019) and YouTube (snippets from various external
partners). Quibi, a Hollywood-backed short-video channel, flamed out in late
2020 after only six months live.

User-generated content, long a YouTube mainstay, is expanding to new
mediums, most notably TikTok. Vine, which was live between 2013 and 2017,
featured six-second video clips from users, some of whom became incredibly popular despite the constrained format. A rumored successor has yet
to appear. Facebook's video features serve a different function compared to
YouTube's (given the primacy of the former's social networking mission),
and the counts are hard to parse given the short length of the videos and large
number of truncated views. In addition, Facebook's TikTok copycat, Reels,
has not stemmed user defection in the under-25 demographic. Monetization
for video creators is also less robust on Facebook, so overall, Meta's video
content appears to be of minor concern to Google's global behemoth.

Parasocial Parasitism?

Given the tendency of online phenomena to assume power-law dynamics,
and the vast scale of both uploaded content and viewership, it's predictable that there will be a small number of really popular celebrities. Some
of these people translated Hollywood fame into the YouTube variety. Will
Smith and Kylie Jenner are both highly visible, as is Dwayne Johnson. But
especially among teens, TikTok and YouTube "stars" are more popular than
Hollywood personalities. This relates to something called parasocial relationships, which are one-sided personal attachments directed at another
person who is unaware of the feelings. Because YouTube is a different kind
of medium, the relationships it fosters are also different. (The anthropologist
Michael Wesch noticed this dynamic very early in the service's existence.[32])
Fame and fandom are important examples.

Parasocial relationships have long been a subject of media studies,
originating with television (the seminal paper appeared in 1956[33]) although

movies undoubtedly fostered similar responses before they were named as such. These relationships can affect everything from body image in adolescent boys and girls to the ability to learn from external examples. Via cable television and social media, Kim and the other Kardashians showed the commercial power of allowing viewers to feel they know you. (We will see how online video beauty influencers are among the next generation of parasocial celebrities in chapter 7.)

Via Internet video, the effect appears to even stronger than with TV. Even though they technically cannot sign up for YouTube, children consume vast amounts of content and bond readily with friendly faces doing fun and interesting things. They also lack critical apparatus to understand that friendly faces are not real people in the viewer's life. Scholars at the University of Amsterdam have highlighted the role of parasocial relationships in children's consumption of advertising.[34] Teens report feeling closer to YouTube personalities, who score higher on indexes of both approachability and authenticity. (These Q scores are proprietary and not systematically reported either by sector or chronologically. See qscores.com.) As of 2014, the only actor to crack the top six most influential celebrities among thirteen-to-eighteen-year-olds was Paul Walker, the actor in the *Fast and Furious* franchise who had died the year before.[35]

Consider the differences. Hollywood stresses illusion, whether through makeup, sound effects, or editing. Online video stars are generally not professionally lit or filmed. Hollywood stresses glamour and, in some senses, remoteness; YouTube and TikTok stars are average to pleasant looking but not exotic (some fashion models notwithstanding), and they are rewarded for talking about mundane activities like shopping for everyday goods. Some of the most popular YouTubers are gamers whose fame derives from commentary over video gameplay. Felix Kjellberg, known on YouTube as PewDiePie, eschewed editors until well after his career was launched. His popularity—at one point the most successful YouTube celebrity anywhere, with 100 million subscribers—derives precisely from his distance from Hollywood norms. He comes across as genuine, unscripted, and authentic, which can translate to naïve, careless, and boorish. His audience loves him precisely because, as *Variety* called him, he can be "aggressively stupid."[36] Logan Paul, another white male YouTuber famous for being dopily accessible, inspires similar affection. At a press conference promoting a pay-per-view boxing match with another YouTuber known as KSI, one young female in the crowd told an ESPN reporter, "He's inspiring, I like the way he respects his fans."[37]

As we will see in beauty vlogging, parasocial relationships are not only formed with traditional celebrities (Will Smith, Kylie Jenner) or with video gamers. Virtually every genre features people who come across as approachable, unscripted, and relatable. What happens as a result of this global level of exposure, outside traditional "star-maker machinery" (to quote Joni Mitchell's apt phrase), can prove to be unsustainable.

Kjellberg was accustomed to interacting only with rudimentary video capture and on screen. In 2013, he naively walked into a crowd at a gaming event, against the advice of his security detail. "I remember there were five security guards yelling at a crowd to back up—it was out of control," he recalled. "It was shocking to find myself in that situation, where I was that celebrity person."[38] Online, his fans (many of them barely teenagers) felt considerable proximity and loyalty that was to be tested.

When Kjellberg was called out for antisemitic and racist "jokes" in 2017, his fan base attacked the bearers of the news, including the *Wall Street Journal*, whose website was hacked. The fame clearly had done what fame so often does—turned a human being into a larger-than-life phenomenon, to which human reactions are often insufficient. Some of his fans, however, had second thoughts. One sixteen-year-old had been watching his videos for years so was familiar with the modus operandi. After a series of incidents, she retreated from fandom. "It's like if you had a pretty good friend of many years and you found out they were a racist: what would you do?" she was quoted as saying. The reporters of the story summed up the parasocial dynamic perfectly: "The thing about being a fan of a YouTuber is that it makes you feel like you belong. When the media reports on PewDiePie, for his fans, it can feel like an attack on a friend."[39]

The Price of Fame

Logan Paul (who sometimes appears with his brother, Jake, another video persona) is a US-based YouTuber who is neither the biggest nor the best talent in his genre, but his history nicely illustrates the dilemmas of YouTube fame. His story began in some ways in 2006, when Google acquired YouTube. Given the vast quantity of pirated material on the site and the legal implications—ranging from a steady stream of litigation up to threats to the site's very existence via court or legislative action, Google soon began to emphasize original content. Early in 2012, at the Consumer Electronics Show (CES), YouTube announced a $100 million investment in original content from such established figures as *CSI: Crime Scene Investigation* creator Anthony Zuiker and self-help guru Deepak Chopra. The latter remains a presence on the site, but his view counts are modest. Google, it appears, could not pick winners. The premium channels were shut down two years after launch.

The next iteration was YouTube Red, a $9.99-per-month subscription service that stripped out ads and married professional production with homegrown YouTube personalities such as Felix Kjellberg and Lilly Singh, a Canadian entertainer. Red stretched the videos longer and longer, distancing YouTube from its origins as a repository of short videos of cute cats or everyday pratfalls. As of 2015, the plan seemed to be working for all concerned. Creators could earn a lot of money, Google had less to worry about with copyright infringement, and both viewership (in numbers of people and time spent on the site) and upload numbers continued to grow. New genres emerged. Comedians adapted to the medium. Countless prank videos attempted to follow the fate of Dude Perfect, a long-running top-five channel. Toy unboxing and reviews could earn a preteen millions of dollars a year. Traditional strengths continued to draw well. On *Forbes*'s list of top YouTube earners for 2017, four of the top six positions were male gamers.

In 2016, YouTube changed the recommendation algorithms and some of these newly popular video stars saw a sudden and inexplicable drop in revenue. People who were burning out or having trouble coping with extreme and sudden fame questioned the site and their role in it. Anthony Padilla was half of Smosh, a YouTube comedy duo that earned double-digit millions of dollars out of nowhere. "I associated that more views meant that my effort paid off," he said. Then came the changes to the algorithms; effort and outcomes no longer tracked. "I could put hundreds of hours of work into something," he continued, "and the views could be much lower than I was expecting." Not surprisingly, it took a toll on Padilla's mental outlook when he equated view counts with his "sense of self-worth."[40]

The mysterious changes to the algorithms drove some content producers to get ever more outrageous, to create videos no algorithm could ignore. Kjellberg's anti-Semitic videos were exposed in 2017 and some advertisers left the platform. Jake and Logan Paul moved from Vine, the short-video service that closed in 2017, to focus more heavily on YouTube where they took Jackass-style pranks to another level, including having Logan pretending to be shot in front of a crowd of his fans. When critics such as Kjellberg called them out, the Pauls produced diss (disrespect-driven) videos that fueled the charges of irresponsibility still further.

Kjellberg, both a force and a pariah by this point, reiterated the critique in 2018 after Logan Paul controversially published a video featuring a suicide outcome in a Japanese forest. Paul mildly apologized but by this point, everything was about view counts, a state PewDiePie knew well.

> The problem with being a YouTuber or an online entertainer is that you constantly have to outdo yourself. I think a lot of people get swept up in that . . . that they have to keep outdoing themselves, and I think it's a good reflection of what happened with Logan Paul. I don't think Logan is necessarily a bad person; I just think he really got caught up in that idea that he has to keep pushing himself to get those numbers. If you make videos every single day, it's really tough to keep people interested, and keep them coming back.[41]

Paul's premium channel had its ad revenue shut off two months after the suicide episode: the "creator" (his term) was so remorseful and changed by the incident that he posted video of himself tasering dead rats. It was for that breach, not for disrespectfully videoing a human corpse, that he was demonetized.

Ethan Klein, a New York YouTuber devoted to vaping videos, spoke for many in his own video: "This is the state of YouTube, guys. These people aren't like, 'How do I make good content?' It's more like, 'How do I make dangerous, risky shit that's so over the top that people have to click it?'"[42]

Paul, meanwhile, lives on the ratchet of trying to be ever more provocative and outrageous; someone branding himself as "Maverick" (the name of his clothing line) seems unlikely to play by Google's rules and prone to doing things like mugging with a dead body on camera. At one point, Paul estimated 80 percent of his life was being captured on video. "I'm a maverick. I'm unlike any other creator on the internet. I'm an athlete, I'm funny, I'm creative, I can tell a story, I'm likable. I can sing, I can act, my physical comedy is on point. I can do the splits. I don't know if there's a person on the internet who can fulfill the things I just said."[43] Given the incessant demand for content, Paul confessed, sometimes "you come up with the most random, outrageous s—— you can, break some plates, call it a day." The fame was addictive; the pressure unsustainable. "I was becoming such a skewed person due to the internet and the type of content I was making, and it being encouraged every day over and over again by 7 million people watching my daily vlogs," he says. As Google changed the recommender algorithm, Paul careened between (and eventually over) any guardrails that might have preserved his completely unreal life of self-exposure. After the Tokyo suicide incident, he stopped vlogging, but had grown so addicted to the lifestyle that he lacked any sense of what to do except turn a camera on himself.[44]

But Logan Paul is not an anomaly, he's an apotheosis. In an era in which smartphones improve in battery life, camera performance, and wireless connectivity every year, the temptation to document one's existence runs up against the desire to *live* that life. "Pics or it didn't happen" used to apply to extreme events, but now the undocumented life often looks pale in comparison to what one's social media followers see. Scott Welch was a passenger on a JetBlue flight in 2014 that experienced an engine malfunction. After he pulled on his oxygen mask, he pulled out his smartphone and began shooting video, soon turning the camera on himself. According to the *New York Times*, "I was considering the fact that my family might not see me again," he said. "After I started filming, that's why I turned it on myself." He added, "I wanted my family to see me smile."[45] It also made him just another fifteen-minute celebrity.

History continues to repeat itself. Looking back to the PBS television series *An American Family* (1971), we can see fifty years of US video programming premised on watching the "reality" of one of our number. In this early case, the broadcast was edited from three hundred hours of footage captured over seven months. The Loud family gave the audience plenty of drama. The wife asked the husband for a separation on camera, and one of the children came out as gay—shocking stuff in the early 1970s. The show was a sensation, one for which the family was unprepared. The psychological toll was tangible, not just in the couple's divorce. Living a life on the screen changes many facets of human life and interaction, rarely for the better.

Jump ahead to 2022, and, like Logan Paul, another YouTube celebrity has made a lot of money but finds himself at a crossroads. David Dobrik was twenty-three and living in a $9.5 million house in Los Angeles, capitalizing on multiple aspects of the zeitgeist, including photo-editing software, a pizza franchise, a network TV series, and several major corporate endorsement deals. In early 2021, allegations of sexual misconduct were made against a friend in Dobrik's circle, and stories circulated portraying Dobrik as bullying and culturally insensitive. The latter is public in a 2015 Vine video that features Dobrik pretending to be an amputee in a wheelchair. In April 2021, Dobrik's Vlog Squad mate Jeff Wittek asserted that he had been badly injured at a video shoot in which Dobrik swung Wittek, hanging on a rope, from an excavator.

Once again, the pressure mounts to create something compelling for a vast audience. Dobrik told a *Rolling Stone* reporter that "you want to be able

116

to put on a bigger show, and it can get really dangerous because you get lost in it. It was just like, 'How can I make this bigger and better than the last thing?'"[46] The reporter summarizes the situation well:

> The central problem [is] Dobrik and others like him making money off a platform that rewards those who are motivated by the central question of how to make something bigger and better than the last thing. [These efforts are] bombastic gestures intended to capture the attention of an increasingly distractible online audience. And not even the cancellation of David Dobrik can change the fact that his brand of content—the pranks, the stunts, the thrill of knowing someone is going to be genuinely surprised, or the schadenfreude that comes with knowing someone is genuinely uncomfortable—is one of the motors that keeps YouTube up and running.[47]

In the end, the disconnect between human scale and fast-moving, lightly regulated, global video distribution has implications for audiences and creators alike. We squirm when we see someone pranked, yet we tune in for more. The creator must top today's click-attractor with tomorrow's, competing not only with countless imitators and similarly empowered "influencers" but with one's former output. The psychological costs are considerable, but only rarely tallied.

Conclusion

The broad availability of entertainment on YouTube and TikTok addresses almost every conceivable interest group. It also redefines our cultural inheritance. If the Internet serves as our collective memory (implied by the European Union's right to be forgotten, a legal protection of an individual's request for personal data to be removed from a platform), how does any mere mortal cope with millions of hours of available programming? With the algorithmic fragmentation of mass audiences into micro-niches, what will constitute shared experience?

Once we see and experience something via online video, how do we remember it? If "data never dies," as my former boss told me, how do I remember or otherwise internalize so many thousands of clips, mashups, TikToks, or streams? Will digital memory look different from what previous generations held in their minds from movies, from radio, from broadcast TV? Will we remember anything digital if we are not told we remember it? Or do we learn to adapt to what Wendy Chun called "the enduring ephemeral" in the preface? Maybe all we will be left with is the last clip we saw.

Online video has dramatically changed the way people watch content on screens, the way they listen to music, and the way they follow sports. Even more than that, essentially every form of leisure—board games, travel, cooking, and many more—has also been affected by the global reach and instructional power of crowdsourced content. Video's advantages over print make it a natural choice for many forms of communication, and the innovations do not appear to be slowing any time soon. What happened to video gaming, or teaching, or music promotion will spread to new domains, and seeing which ones are transformed next will make for still more compelling viewing. For our purposes here, we will next turn to exploring a sample of the ways technology changes artistic content.

How Does Technology Shape Content?

Art, culture, and technology have been intertwined since the first cave paintings, and possibly before. The state of the tools dictates what the artist is capable of recording, whether in clay, watercolor, stone, or print. Painters in the Italian Renaissance had ready access to canvas given that it was made in large quantities for boat sails. Mass-circulation newspapers gave rise to the serial novels of Tolstoy and Dostoyevsky, Dumas and Flaubert, Dickens and Conan Doyle, Melville and Stowe. Louis Sullivan couldn't build skyscrapers without Elisha Otis's elevator.

More recently, the video technologies of the twentieth century gave rise to new forms of storytelling and historical documentation, typically after a period of adjustment: the first television programs were radio plays with the readers visible. It took innovators like Lazlo Kovacs, Nam Jun Paik, Spike Milligan, Ed Sabol, and others to begin to stretch broadcast television into what it became at the height of its influence before streaming altered the conventions and possibilities of the medium.

Because of the vastness and cultural velocity of online video, no attempt will be made to be encyclopedic; there are undoubtedly innovative expressions emerging in many languages beyond English to which I simply do not have access. Even limited to English-speaking video, tracking the latest TikTok motifs is impossible. Even so, it's important to acknowledge how an emerging technology creates possibilities for artistic expression that simply did not exist prior to the technology's availability. Three examples are presented here; there are, and will be, many more.

One: A Forerunner

In 1996, two college friends created a parody of a children's book. It's recalled that "five or ten" copies were printed, possibly at Kinko's, but the authors had no higher aspirations. The main character, based on Atlanta Braves second baseman Mark Lemke, was named when one of the authors, not a sports fan, called the player a "home star runner for the Braves." After college, coauthor Mike Chapman enrolled in a masters program in photography but did not finish; younger brother Matt had studied film, and they began to experiment with Macromedia Flash, a new animation tool. After registering the "home-starrunner.com" domain in December 1999, the "Brothers Chaps," as they have come to be known, launched the website in January 2000.[1]

What began at the turn of the millennium still persists nearly twenty-five years later. The four characters introduced in the 1996 children's book parody are all present, joined by others that were built in a 1996 Mario Paint video about a wrestling match, set in Japan. That clip could be watched as a linear video, but the main thrust of the site was based not on animation but on the hybrid of capabilities introduced by Macromedia Flash. From day one until the deprecation of Flash by Adobe (its owner since 2005) in December 2020, Homestar Runner blurred old boundaries. Yes, there was linear video that later translated easily to YouTube. But there were also video games, minigames, Easter eggs, clickable links—sometimes obvious, sometimes hidden—and other, multiple layers of interactive content that stands as a "what might have been" when considering online video writ large.

Between 2000 and 2005, content was added to the website at a rapid pace. April Fools and Halloween often got special uploads, and the fan base was taking shape. Bearing in mind the site's hybridization of gaming, pop-culture parody and commentary, and character-driven humor, as well as the stage of the Internet's development, it's notable how the fans embraced the site. For a certain type of nerdy teen and college student in the early 2000s, weekly content drops were must-see material. To this day, any article about the site gets massive fan commentary, much of it in the form of inside jokes and recollections that "this site got me through adolescence," or a crappy job, or a hard patch of life.

The Brothers Chaps returned the affection: after fans started dressing up for trick or treat as sometimes obscure subcharacters and uploading photos of the costumes, "fan 'stume" videos were posted, often by early December. Even when the brothers were busy with life (spouses and children) and careers (several projects for Disney and other major outlets) and the site seemed to be dormant, fans kept dressing up and the brothers posted reactions even in years when very little else was happening with the site.

What were the brothers posting? Thanks to the Homestar Runner wiki, we have a week-by-week chronology. Early videos were typically in the two-minute range, given that (as we saw in chapter 2) most people not on college campuses were accessing the site via dial-up. Easter eggs were already common: an alternative ending, an added scene, or some inside joke might be revealed by a well-aimed mouse click. Existing characters were given back stories and additional nuance while new characters were added.

By the mid-2000s, the cast had grown from the original four to about a dozen recurring characters, but there were also additional franchises such as Cheat Commandos (a G.I. Joe parody) and Teen Girl Squad (black-and-white line-drawn reflections on high school social life). Not one but two rock bands entered the universe, one an '80s hair-metal quartet called Limozeen and one a play on the moody indie-rock scene called Sloshy. After music videos came karaoke videos; after video games came video game commentaries and even physical products. The character of Trodgor is a fire-breathing dragon that incinerates "thatched-roof cottages" (sung in a heavy-metal screech). He gets not only a song but a full-scale King's Quest parody video game called Peasant's Quest, which itself is a spin-off of a live-action movie trailer. Trogdor also starred in a Kickstarter-powered board game: the funding goal of $75,000 was exceeded when more than $1 million was raised, and it's now available at the website, Amazon, and elsewhere.

On August 22, 2001, what became the site's most popular feature debuted. An original character dating to the 1996 Mario Paint animation, Strong Bad is Homestar Runner's nemesis. He wears a Mexican wrestling mask and boxing gloves and was recruited into a long-running bit in which he answered fan emails on screen. Strong Bad emails, shortened to sbemails, dropped once a week when the brothers were at their peak productivity, and quickly became extremely popular: even the computers on which he typed became their own characters. Later, even without the benefits of the Easter eggs that Flash made possible on the original website versions, sbemails proved popular on YouTube. But the experience is undeniably and meaningfully different.

The site's most ambitious upload was a live-action movie trailer for a movie that was never made. On February 6, 2005—Super Bowl Sunday—the site made public a massive 13.4 MB video file. Simply entitled "Peasant's Quest," it was the ultimate low-budget affair chronicling the adventures of Rather Dashing, a peasant seeking to slay Trogdor. Cast and crew consisted of the Brothers Chaps (plus Matt's wife, Jackie Chapman) and assorted friends, including future *Archer* producer Lucky Yates and future Emmy nominee Craig Zobel. The video, filmed near the Chapmans' home base of Atlanta, contains the usual barrage of pop-culture references: *Monty Python and the Holy Grail*, the Doom and Half-Life 2 video games, *Kill Bill*, the *Lord of the Rings* trilogy, and director Spike Lee are all paid homage.

The fans' fervor plus the poor broadband infrastructure of the day shut down the website. On Monday morning, the big file was taken down and a few hours later visitors were presented with a screen listing three download options: 10.3, 5.4, and 2.6 MB respectively. Other experiments in video downloads had already occurred, including BMW's eight *The Hire* minimovies in 2001–2, but the Peasant's Quest upload was noteworthy for its timing: one week later, the YouTube domain was purchased. One can now view the full-size Peasant's Quest trailer on YouTube, bringing the story full circle.

By 2005, many of the updates had to do with merchandise: after initially selling a few T-shirts to people who mailed checks to their father, the brothers expanded to a wider range of available products and were able to earn enough to quit their day jobs and work on the site full time. The site has never hosted any advertising: developing sufficiently compelling characters and iconography appealing to a merch-buying demographic was a sufficient monetization mechanism. In addition to e-commerce, booths were set up at comic book shows, reaching one segment of the site's fan base. In 2005, the brothers archived the first hundred sbemails to DVD, then also released three DVDs of "Everything Else." Since that time, there have been lapses but the bit doesn't die: "sbemail 209" dropped on April 1, 2022.

The merchandise continues to sell, as befits a cult favorite. Sarah Silverman wore a Homestar Runner star T-shirt on television, Rush's Geddy Lee was photographed wearing a Trodgor The Burninator T-shirt on stage, and celebrity pastry chef Duff Goldman has Homestar Runner elements appear in his shows. The series finale of *Buffy the Vampire Slayer* features Trogdor as a character within a game of Dungeons and Dragons. Cult favorite band They Might Be Giants (we can detect a trend here) has collaborated on songs with the Brothers Chaps, and artists ranging from Beastie Boys to My Chemical Romance have somehow saluted the Homestar Runner universe. Two Homestar Runner musical pieces were included in Guitar Hero video games.

The site's appeal is absolutely niche, by design. Many of the jokes are inside references to previous content, or to pop culture. (Strong Bad's dissection of the independent movie world remains devastating almost fifteen

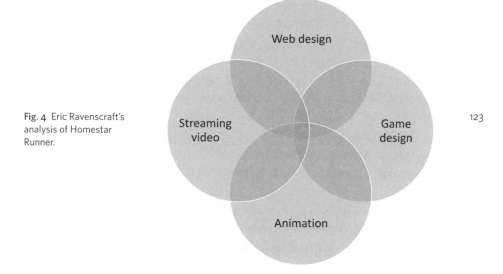

Fig. 4 Eric Ravenscraft's analysis of Homestar Runner.

years after it dropped.[2]) In one demonstration of the site's multilayered geekiness, Sloshy releases a song for Record Store Day. It's called "The B-est of B-sides," poking fun at bands' releasing offbeat material for Record Store Day.[3] Three years later, in a nod to all the offbeat formats bands were releasing tracks on (cassettes are once again a thing, for example), the Brothers Chaps 3D printed "The B-est of B-sides" on a plastic disc playable on a children's Fisher-Price record player.[4]

In 2021 a YouTuber named Eric Ravenscraft uploaded a video entitled "Homestar Runner: How to Master a Dying Art Form." Among his insights was a Venn diagram depicting the intersection between animation, web design, game design, and streaming video similar to the Venn diagram in figure 4.

Homestarrunner.com delivered live video, and games, and webpages, and animations. But Flash enabled these elements to interact with each other and users to interact with the Brothers Chaps' universe of gaming, music, inside jokes, fan uploads, and other elements. It really was a chimeric vision, for a brief moment before YouTube and Facebook defined the platform landscape, of a different architecture: of interactivity, participation, possibility, and blurred boundaries. As one comment put it, "Homestar Runner felt like, at the time, a peak [*sic*] into what type of entertainment would be common on the internet in the near future. Instead we got social media and everything controlled by algorithms to keep us addicted to scrolling."[5]

Krister Johnson has won an Emmy and is working on multiple Netflix and other projects. In an interview on *Vulture*, he articulates the enveloping and seemingly infinite nature of the Homestar Runner franchise:

[Interviewer]: *You did get the sense, especially when they were uploading more regularly, that you would never, ever reach the bottom of the content.*

[Johnson]: Ever! And you just keep clicking and discover more things. Even the interface, which you can still see on their website. If you go to the main page, and you roll your cursor over the main buttons, these voices come out: "Toons!" And the animated graphics pop out. But if you go away from that page and come back a second later, it's a completely different interface. Suddenly it's old-timey, or whatever. It's not just the funny videos they created—they created the entire apparatus to be entertaining and unusual and surprising. If you clicked a button on an image of a VCR, suddenly a tape pops out and you've found a video. It was this incredible treasure chest you could dig around in.

Going back to something we were talking about earlier, I loved the sort of pixel-hunt aspect of the site, where you could click on a word in the email and get taken to this whole other thing.

It blew me away. It was the first time I was able to interact with a website like that. I'm still in awe of how much effort they put into those details, because they were so easily missed. They were putting work into creating these experiences that a lot of people would never even see. It's not like they made a video explaining, "Be sure to check for this, that, and the other." They just hid all this gold in various places. And if people found it, that was great. And if they didn't, that was fine too.[6]

It's tantalizing to imagine an alternative universe in which online video is more interactive, less algorithmically programmed, more original, less linear. But Flash, while a great authoring tool for a small and technically light creative team, also harbored serious security holes that made it impractical. Putting all those controls into a cross-platform environment came at a cost: more than 1,000 vulnerabilities had been reported between 2005 and 2017— almost 600 of them after 2015.[7] The rise of the smartphone at the expense of the desktop market certainly has something to do with that situation; at its core, Homestar Runner remains, for better and for worse, a website, one of very few that hasn't philosophically or technically become an app. It remains a monument to the act of going to the designated desk or table, sitting down at a keyboard, and using a computer in the circa 2000 sense of the phrase.

Two: The Evolution of the Mashup

Beginning in the 1980s, DJs began to move beyond linear segues from song to song, instead overlaying one onto another. An early example mashing up Michael Jackson's "Billie Jean" with Steely Dan's "Do It Again" started in Italy with Club House and was later copied by Detroit-based Slingshot. The trend gathered momentum through the 1990s and 2000s. In the early years, the effect traveled with the DJ, who could replicate it in performance. Later, records were pressed in the 1990s and 2000s, often using the "vs" nomenclature to indicate the two source tracks. A key example was British record producer Freelancer Hellraiser's bootleg of Christina Aguilera's "Genie in a Bottle" and the Strokes' "Hard to Explain." "A Stroke of Genie-us" helped launch the mashup genre in 2001. The word "mashup" itself dates to the 1850s—Charles Dickens had characters named Mr. and Mrs. Mashup—but the more contemporary sense seems to have originated in Jamaican dancehall culture: "Mash it up" functioned similarly to "Put your hands in the air!"[8]

The record labels spotted an opportunity and launched a wave of "remix" albums, often consisting of extended dance mixes, once an album had achieved initial popularity. Madonna's *You Can Dance* (1987) and Michael Jackson's *Blood on the Dance Floor* (1997) sold well, as did the Beatles' *Love* (2006). Jennifer Lopez's *J to the L-O! The Remixes* (2002) debuted at number one on the Billboard 200 chart.

A 2004 landmark in the genre was the creation of Brian Burton (aka Danger Mouse): he mixed Jay Z's raps on *The Black Album* with Beatles instrumentation on *The White Album* to create *The Grey Album*, which became the target of lawsuits from Beatles copyright holders. Burton gave the small run of CDs away, but copies could subsequently be found on eBay, making the project commercial in legal terms. In protest, about two hundred websites offered free downloads of the album on February 24, 2004. Even though the sites were also targeted with legal threats, more than a million copies of the album were downloaded. Burton thus did not see much revenue from the project, but his name was made; he later produced music for U2, the Black Keys, Norah Jones, and Beck. With CeeLo Green, Burton formed the act Gnarls Barkley.[9]

The mashups, meanwhile, violated copyright in many countries, though sometimes the original combination was argued to be "transformative" and thus immune from prosecution. In addition, the different artists whose songs were combined probably were under contract to different record labels, complicating accounting. There were minor successes: The Source featuring Candi Staton's "You Got the Love" was based on a DJ mashup and peaked at number four on the UK charts. Different Gear vs The Police's version of "When the World Is Running Down" cracked the UK top forty and is still available on Spotify. The English producer Richard X had a hand in three singles that reached the US top ten after 2001—the artists included Chaka Khan, The Human League, Tubeway Army, and Adina Howard.

In addition to Internet distribution, another technical factor in the popularity of the form was widespread availability of mixing software that could, for example, speed up the beats per minute without changing the pitch of a singer's voice.[10] With the launch of YouTube, however, the mashup entered a new phase. Anybody had access: that software for beat matching, cross-fading, and other effects decreased the skill necessary to create a convincing blend. The sheer number of tracks available opened access to those without extensive music collections. And, crucially, the music video became the source of a new kind of multimedia mashup.

The creativity expressed by a global army of remixers is stunning. Michael Jackson remains popular; "Billie Jean" segues seamlessly into Eric Clapton's "Cocaine" cover. Someone else combined "Beat It" with Iron Maiden's "The Trooper." Bob Marley proves that reggae can mix with almost anything, including Billy Idol: "With a Rebel Yell, She Cried 'Don't Give Up the Fight'" is infectious. Daft Punk vs The Doobie Brothers has about 9.5 million views nine years after its release. Bill McClintock, who has released dozens of clever mashups, may have hit his creative peak in the pairing of Marilyn Manson with Mariah Carey. Wax Audio's most-viewed contribution pairs AC/DC and Bee Gees in "Stayin' in Black."[11]

The cultural juxtapositions are telling all by themselves. Brazil-based Milk'n Blues did a live recording mashing up the Stones' "Miss You" with Pink Floyd's "Another Brick in the Wall" in 2017. What comes out is infectious and skillfully played, especially the blues harp, sounding at once British and not at all British. It's amassed 37 million views. Another of the band's mashups is all-American: George Gershwin and B. B. King.[12] Seven million viewers found that it works. It's worth taking note of how this is happening: no record labels, no radio stations, somewhat random and yet very comfortable in its own world-shrinking way.

In the hands of talented DJs using sophisticated software, the video mashup became a new kind of art, transcending music, video, television, and performance with something that combines all of these. UK-based Ithaca Audio has produced several great videos, some of them based on live events.[13] Significantly, the firm has expanded dramatically and away from its DJ roots to include immersive physical environments with sound and light as well as innovative campaigns for such global brands as BMW, Bang and Olufsen, and Mercedes Benz.[14]

Jack Stratton and his band Vulfpeck also merit mention here. The band has consistently innovated in the video era, eschewing a record label and building a bottom-up fan base that showed out in a sold-out Madison Square Garden performance; there was no headliner, no booking agent, and no radio play to hype the tour—YouTube was the distribution engine. (One commentator called the concert "the 'Stop Making Sense' for this generation"; the insight is apt. In each, an innovative, unstoppably funky band of nerds pioneered a whole new visual concert experience.) Part of the innovation has been Stratton's use of the video mashup: his "Sound of Two" series juxtaposes artists from across time and often genre to create an original musical moment that can be uncanny. Many highlight the legendary drummer Bernard Purdie providing a rhythm track for a completely unrelated performer: keyboardists Cory Henry and Herbie Hancock lock into Purdie's beat completely seamlessly, for example. Stratton also mashed up his own band's "Disco Ulysses" with Katy Perry's "Teenage Dream," to the astonishment of the band's hip fanbase.[15] (Though they aren't mashups, Stratton's visualizations of Motown bassist James Jamerson also show how online video facilitates entirely new representations of existing art.[16])

Speaking of innovative music acts who used YouTube to change the music industry business model: Pomplamoose is a duo who helped found Patreon. As opposed to Kickstarter's support of a specified project, Patreon gives fans a channel to support artists' being artists by funding their art without defined outcomes. The band creates innovative videos of many sorts and Patreon members get behind-the-scenes lessons, software plug-ins and stems, and other benefits. Pomplamoose works in clever covers, and some are mashups: Jamiroquai's "Virtual Insanity" was performed as a mashup with the Bee Gees' "Stayin' Alive" and 18 million viewers tuned in. Pomplamoose also make Eurhythmics' "Sweet Dreams" a perfect complement to the White Stripes anthem "Seven Nation Army."[17]

Many of the most-viewed mashups on YouTube are one-off hits: an uploader may have one video with millions of views and many others in the tens of thousands. There seems to be very little brand loyalty to the mashup makers. Faroff seems to be an exception. Their biggest hit mashed up the biggest YouTube video in history (at the time) with a thirty-year-old movie theme, and "Gangnam Busters" was born. Other popular combinations merged Britney Spears and Metallica; the most ambitious added MC Hammer, Eurhythmics, New Order, Talking Heads, and Donna Summer. DJs From Mars crossed the 6 million view threshold with something original: Beethoven's Fifth Symphony and Chemical Brothers' "Galvanize."[18]

DJ Cummerbund also struck a nerve with a series of inspired pairings: Earth Wind and Fire's "September" clicks with Ozzy Osbourne's "Crazy Train" to the tune of 4.7 million views. The '70s funk band Wild Cherry has no business accompanying Germany's uber-metal Rammstein, but that mashup qualifies as "transformative" use of prior art.[19] There's even a "choose your own adventure" mashup game on the site.

As much as there's a story in the hits, the accessibility that allows anyone to remix audio-visual culture is also noteworthy. Not long ago, both the means of video production (the studio) and distribution (networks of movie theaters, radio and television stations, or record stores) were out of reach for the proverbial garage band or self-produced singer-songwriter-rapper. In a moment, all of that changed, and the empowerment, disinformation, rethinking of copyright, and a dozen other issues that come out of that democratization are only beginning to be explored.

Three: Watching People Watch Things

From the early days of both YouTube and TikTok, videos of people talking about things they're watching have been a staple of the genre. In fact, the *New York Times* noted the phenomenon as early as 2011.[20] By the late 2010s, the phenomenon had become extremely widespread. No statistics are available, but one could find reaction videos to almost anything: music videos, Hollywood movies, Bollywood movies, high school yearbooks, cooking shows, schools, almost any sport that is unfamiliar to the watcher (and broadcaster), travel videos, standup comedy, Internet memes, old television clips, and more that I haven't discovered yet. (A subgenre of reaction videos concerns shocking material and I will only note it here without analysis or comment.)

There are competing theories as to the origin of the genre.[21] Some say that there is a long-standing tradition in Japanese variety shows. Early in YouTube's history, "kids react" (itself a remix of an old US meme of "kids say the darnedest things") became popular and lives on in the channel now simply called "React."[22] My theory is that people imported practices from the video game world: many of the biggest YouTubers of the first fifteen years of the site overlaid snarky, instructive, or condescending commentaries onto other peoples' gameplay. The format carried over: a small video window shows the original screen while the reactor is more visible. That inset window can now contain any of dozens of things that aren't game play.

Reaction to the reaction genre is divided. I might enjoy seeing someone ostensibly new to something that I treasure come to love it themselves; lots of people steeped in hip-hop have launched channels showing their reactions to classic rock tunes. Other people can maintain in-group status by seeing newbies fail to get the joke or appreciate some nuance of the original performance: reinforcing stereotypes can be deeply satisfying for some. Then there are those who detest the genre altogether.[23]

Much of the reaction genre plays on cultural distinctiveness: Nigerian sisters comment on K-pop, European visitors react to US peculiarities (essentially reversing the trope of Michael Moore's *Where to Invade Next*), tourists react to the scenery/cuisine/mores of a country other than their own. In this regard, the reaction video is as old as travel.

But there's also vicarious discovery in the best of the genre (which is a minority): even people in the practice of making reactions often say that most such videos are, politely, "not very good" or, more directly, "terrible."[24] That said, people who are engaged, insightful, and skilled presenters and entertainers interacting with interesting material can be itself an engaging experience. The surge in popularity of the form during the pandemic suggests that human interaction, of whatever kind, had value, especially during periods of lockdown or high uncertainty.

There's a widespread perception that reaction videos are staged—"There's no way that person has never seen XYZ music video/film clip before. This is all fake." Some presenters are transparent about how much research they did before filming the segment and about whether they've seen or heard the artifact before. Similarly, there are times when fresh eyes are a novelty and times when domain knowledge would be more than welcome.

How much of the genre's appeal is voyeurism? Several academic articles raise the question but no consensus emerges.[25] As we will see with regard to parasocial relationships, the intimacy of a video camera in someone else's study or dining room is a new kind of connection of viewer to star (or wannabe star). There's also an element of nostalgia, as we will see in a more general discussion in chapter 8. Seeing someone get the experience of seeing or hearing a personal touchstone for the (ostensibly) first time takes us back to that moment of discovery and our world view never being the same afterward.

How, in the world of online video, does technology change content? Briefly, in at least eight ways:

1. YouTube, Twitch, Vimeo, and other services are a massive repository of old video to remix. In 2000, one would have had to own a VHS tape of the desired footage or gone to a repository such as the Museum of Television or possibly a network.
2. Whether through unboxings, challenges, reactions, vlogs, or other formats, online video presents creators with community-defined genres within which to work, most of which were not practical options in 2000.
3. As gatekeepers evolve from owners of content distribution channels such as radio stations or newspapers to algorithms, there is new leeway in what is said, and there is much more diversity in who is saying it: marginalized populations have access to a global audience. These new constituencies bring new history and context, new cultural knowledge, and new agendas. Two examples—diss videos by gang members and the revival of sports such as Dambe—are noted elsewhere in the book.
4. Having content to remix would matter little absent a distribution and monetization channel—online video provides content creators with both. Having access to a livelihood, and potentially more, provides strong incentive to make videos as opposed to, let's say, sculpt.
5. In ancient libraries, books were chained to the building, whereas after World War II, paperback books made many titles available to massive markets. In a similar fashion, online video allows new people to interact with humanity's video record in new ways, whether by remixing or watching as many times as one wants for free, at times of one's own choosing. There was also, from 2000 to 2020, the era of Flash that allowed the genres of watching, gaming, and audience participation to commingle in new ways that now appear to be lost.
6. The platforms dictate the format of the videos they will display: duration, orientation, size, and (to a degree) content are a function not of one's camera or computer, but of TikTok or YouTube. Vine's six-second limit may have been just a little too short, and TikTok has repeatedly stretched the time limit of its videos. When papyrus was scarce and

expensive, writers didn't compose multipart epics like *Lord of the Rings*. Creators always adapt to available media.

7. Online video facilitates audience participation. Not only is it hard to sing along with music on paper unless you're pretty well trained, but there's no way to capture my singalong for you to see, like, or critique. Singalongs (in this example) thus become a whole new genre.

8. Our algorithms tell people what will become popular before it's popular; view numbers are a lagging indicator to measure algorithmic effectiveness. In response, content creators engage in a dance with the computer as they name, script, capture, and edit a video; the inanimate audience matters in some ways more than flesh-and-blood humans. Most modern appreciations of the Brothers Chaps marvel at the fact that Homestar Runner tracked no audience or other performance metrics.

In each of the three examples, online video has allowed a new population of content creators to make and distribute new kinds of cultural artifacts that would have been impossible without innovations like high-speed Internet, cheap video production, and billions of hours of existing footage from which to learn or sample. While there are technological capabilities under discussion, the personal, social, and cultural implications of Flash, mashups, and reaction videos are real and vastly understudied. This is not the forum to do proper analysis but rather, as elsewhere in the book, the forum to raise them as topics for further study.

7

Cross-Platform Ecosystems

In addition to questions relating to platforms and content moderation, a third challenge to framing this stage of the Internet's development relates to cross-platform behaviors. In particular, they are difficult to study or to measure. Each platform is to some degree a "walled garden," with limited public information about user behaviors. When people move between platforms (sharing a TikTok link on Facebook, for example), the two companies involved can see the interaction, but the aforementioned proprietary architectures combined with the overwhelming scale of the issue means that third parties have a difficult time assessing what is going on, and why.

Many people use many platforms, but how the platforms' functions interrelate and interact is largely unknown in public. To use US teens as a case study, according to Pew Research Center, 97 percent of US teens use the Internet daily as of 2022. YouTube is by far the most popular platform, with 95 percent of teens using it; 19 percent characterize their use as "almost constantly." TikTok is second at 67 percent, with Instagram (62 percent) and Snapchat (59 percent) close behand. Facebook fell from 71 percent in 2014–15 to 32 percent in 2022, and Twitter, Twitch, WhatsApp, and Reddit all fall between 14 and 23 percent.[1] Simple math proves this is not a zero-sum game: most teens use two or more platforms, probably owned by different companies, likely for different purposes, but few researchers can see the cross-platform patterns.

Within their respective categories, the major Internet platforms are in winner-take-most scenarios. So far, video is an exception. Outside China, the world's number two photo-sharing site usually doesn't matter much, nor does the number two search engine. (Inside China, the market dynamics are different for many reasons.) As a result of so many near-monopolies in various silos, Internet cross-platform dynamics usually don't play out as competitive market share statistics the way consumer products (Crest versus Colgate) or automobiles (Hyundai versus Toyota versus Ford) have traditionally worked. Instead, it's a difficult task to understand how users maintain identities on multiple services: one might view Snapchat and Instagram as competitors, but there are likely many teens who use both, in different ways.

The story of "Old Town Road," a country-hip-hop track by the Atlanta-based Montero Hill (stage name Lil Nas X), points to the possibilities for creators. Just as importantly, the song's success highlights the difficulties that the decline of gatekeepers and the proliferation of platforms pose for analysts and scholars trying to comprehend this cultural moment. In late 2018, Hill bought a banjo clip that he heard on YouTube for thirty dollars from a music producer in the Netherlands via the Soundcloud transaction platform. After writing some clever lyrics melding the worlds of country and hip-hop, he spent twenty dollars at a local recording studio to capture a performance. Hill then took to Twitter, where cowboy memes were plentiful at the time. Those memes were popular in part because of the high profile of Red Dead Redemption 2, a popular video game title from earlier in the year.[2]

On February 16, 2019, a high-profile TikTok influencer named Michael Pelchat used the track for his own clip. A wave of imitative TikTok clips followed, combining the genre-defying music with cowboy attire. At this point, radio stations wanted to promote the song, but Hill had no record deal. Getting creative, some stations had to download YouTube copies of the song to get it onto the airwaves. Those airwaves drove sales, but then Billboard (the music-industry source of popularity measures) didn't know how to characterize the song. For a few weeks, "Old Town Road" was on top of the country, Hot 100, and hip-hop charts, but then Billboard pulled it off the country charts, most likely because of the singer's race. At the same time, many hip-hop stations didn't play the record either. No matter what the label applied to it, "Old Town Road" set a record for the longest tenure at the top of the Billboard Hot 100: nineteen weeks.[3]

In this one episode, we have a confusing convergence of gaming, the two big online video platforms, a massive clip repository and market, radio, and Twitter. Hill was extremely skillful in assessing his audiences' cultural context and crosscutting multiple platforms to drive interest, respond to fans, and force the radio gatekeepers to play his game rather than he theirs. In the end, Hill signed a record deal with Columbia and continues to enjoy prominence in the entertainment industry, traditional categories notwithstanding:

he has corecorded songs with both country singer Billy Ray Cyrus and rapper Cardi B.

In light of this new world, we can consider several cross-platform patterns that would be useful to understand in more depth were the data available.

1. *Platform Migration.* Do people leave YouTube for TikTok the way people abandoned MySpace for Facebook in the mid-2000s? Or do the two services coexist as complements, much the way that Staples and Target do? The two stores share a large number of items for sale but the business models and use cases are sufficiently different that both companies could conceivably thrive—often in the same physical plaza.

2. *Platform Competition.* In credit cards, this idea is called single-homing (everything I charge goes on my Visa) versus multihoming (gas goes on Discover, groceries on Mastercard, travel on American Express). This dynamic can apply to different sides of the platform. In some cities, most Lyft drivers also drive for Uber, arbitraging opportunities and pricing. Some riders use one service (because it's a corporate account perhaps) while others compare the apps to see which one performs better for a given ride. For our purposes here, how do online video creators think about their role in the larger social media ecosystem? How do they decide when and where to post videos when they have multiple options?

3. *Platform Infrastructure.* Here, language is imprecise.[4] Square and Stripe are payment platforms, but they can be used in support of content platforms like Twitch. Similarly, Reddit is a social media platform, but YouTube creators use it both for content ideas and to cross-promote online video uploads. The lines get blurry: "Sign in with Facebook" takes an aspect of a platform and converts it into infrastructure. The larger question asks what services for payment, authentication, geolocation, and related support functions occur where? Much like physical infrastructure, we can think of Internet service providers, content delivery networks, payment processors, and content moderators as the preconditions for commerce and communications.

4. *Multiplatform Tactics.* From the video creator's perspective, there are two main ways to get—and stay—visible. One is to work to understand and accommodate the "preferences" of the matching systems, essentially optimizing behavior *within* a given platform for algorithmic visibility. The other is, like Lil Nas X, to use one's presence *across* multiple online platforms as a collective, mutually reinforcing system. How this works largely remains understood only by random examples. Data collection at scale is expensive and difficult, not to mention a privacy conundrum. If a given user is

visible on, let's say, Pinterest, Instagram, Facebook, and YouTube, is one presence—the Instagram maybe—the central identity, with the others serving to reinforce a primary "brand"? Or do some users create an identity that is relatively equally (measured how?) distributed among those four online platforms? Another possibility is that the same person emphasizes different facets of their identity on different platforms, basically compartmentalizing the whole person into subunits. From the standpoint of the discovery and visibility challenge, using multiple online identities definitely confers some advantages for the video creator even as it makes the research problem practically impossible.

Before they can become *users* of a platform, people are *choosers* among platforms. Why YouTube and not Vimeo? Why TikTok and not Vine? It can be argued that platforms have an obligation to these users-with-choices that is often neglected. Recent scholarship by the University of Colorado's Casey Fiesler and Bianna Dym tracks the platform migration of community members who create fan-generated cultural artifacts (mashups, fan fiction, etc.). Given the nature of their discourse—these people develop loyalty both to other community members and to the platform itself—they travel as something of a collective across Internet platforms. Why do people defect, either individually or as part of a larger movement? According to the authors' summary of survey results, "common reasons given in interviews for leaving a platform were design changes, policy changes, technical problems, or just that there was a new platform that was better."[5]

The platform owner, meanwhile, obviously makes countless decisions to attract, to retain, to exclude certain categories of users and behaviors. In the fandom universe, for example, how is copyright administered? How much say is given to authors who threaten to sue fan-generated adaptations or alternatives to the published work? How is anonymity treated? What censorship, if any, is applied against sexual, violent, or abusive material? None of these choices is simple, and every platform balances competing objectives. Fiesler and Dym do an excellent job of highlighting the primacy of such design and policy decisions for this particular community, and by extension, YouTube and TikTok platforms and creators as well.

The complexity of the multiplatform problem is illustrated by the methods by which harassment and abuse are delivered. In 2021, Amazon's Twitch game streaming service announced it was cracking down on "hate raids," which are bot-powered deluges of hate speech typically directed at LGBTQ+ and Black streamers, by suing offenders.[6] By 2022, the harassers had upped the stakes, placing false emergency calls to police departments in the

135

target's physical location. So-called swatting is not new: in 2017 prank callers sent the tactical response team to the wrong address and an unintended target was killed by officers.[7] The 2022 wave was directed at trans gamers, one of whom reported multiple attempts *per week*.[8] Note the many layers of complexity: so-called doxing (publishing an online persona's real-world address and other data), online then physical-world harassment, local police departments and the platform not being coordinated in their responses. Anti-swatting law was proposed in the US Congress in 2018 but has not been passed as of press time.[9] In short, minority online populations can be targeted with multiple forms of abuse, and both detection and punishment are apparently unlikely enough to fail as deterrents.

A final aspect of multiplatform behavior relates to wayfinding. As we saw in chapter 2, YouTube solved the then-difficult technical problems related to the uploading, hosting, and distribution of online video. The issue that remains—navigation—is formidable, requiring and to date resisting the application of machine learning techniques to address the problem of wayfinding amid the millions of hours of video that have been made available. Just as the vast holdings of the Library of Congress would be worthless without the institution's cataloging system, so too does Google face the challenge of matching users to content with algorithms and bot crawls very different from the technologies that worked for text on the World Wide Web—that is, text-string matching augmented by hyperlink analysis.

TikTok, as we have seen, solves the curation problem by presenting viewers with no choices, only a single full-screen video at a time. The user's behavior relative to that video is minutely dissected, cataloged, and used to feed the next video fifteen to sixty seconds later. The challenge from the research perspective is to try to understand how viewers get served their full cafeteria tray of content from multiple platforms. How much does TikTok know and weigh my Twitter identity? When do changes to my physical location trigger content delivery changes, and how do those algorithms differ across platforms? How soon will my action on platform X influence the algorithms on platform Y?

Because the global scale of online video is too vast for anyone outside the big platforms (which have deep analytics they do not share) to map or analyze, the best anyone can do is to sample some subcultures. Even in English, one of about seventy-five languages available, there is so much volume, and it changes so fast, that nothing remotely accurate can be asserted about "online video" as a coherent entity. Google itself changes how it represents its store of YouTube content: historic cumulative view counts are no longer reported as a guide to videos ("most viewed") as of 2019 and possibly earlier, likely because of the potential for click fraud. Subscriber counts were also truncated in 2019; 1,234,567 actual subscribers will appear as 1.23 million.[10] Bearing in mind that "the singular of 'data' is not 'anecdote,'" here are four subsegments, each of which illustrates a larger point about the place of modern large-scale digital platforms within larger digital and physical ecosystems.

Beauty Influencers

Before discussing the impact of online video on the global cosmetics industry, it is useful to understand some demographics. As we noted in the introduction, the Pew Research Center analyzed the behavior of 43,000 "high-subscriber" YouTube channels in 2019. The Pew researchers found that YouTube viewership followed the power-law distribution familiar to Internet analysis of Wikipedia contributions, Twitter audiences, and historical YouTube viewership. That is, a tiny percentage of creators accounted for a disproportionate share of audience attention, while a vast number of creators attracted audience views in single digits.

A final piece of context helps set the stage for a discussion of beauty vloggers. Much as was true in the early days of Facebook, it is clear that preteens and teens are heavy users of both TikTok and YouTube. (The stunning statistics relating to Lego's popular videos suggest as much, given that no other brand has half as many views.[11]) In the realm of the ostensible target market, 96 percent of 18-to-24-year-olds use YouTube. As for TikTok, 69 percent of US teens are on the service, and beauty is the number four most popular hashtag there (following pranks, fitness/sports, and home reno/DIY).[12] Across all demographics, average daily viewing time was more than 8.5 minutes on YouTube, with millennials particularly voracious consumers of how-to content; Google asserts that YouTube viewers are three times as likely to look for a video as they are to read the product's manual.[13] For comparison, among all US TikTok users, the average monthly viewing time was 858 minutes—almost a half-hour every day. Among 4-to-14-year-olds, according to TechCrunch, US viewing time almost triples—to 82 minutes per day as of February 2020, just before the pandemic drove TikTok usage still higher.[14]

This brings us to the confluence of factors at work in the cosmetics and beauty sector of YouTube and TikTok.[15] Young people watch online video a lot, they look for instruction, they come from all over the globe, and a small number of vloggers in a given subject area typically amass very large subscriber bases. The Korean beauty vlogger Hye-Min Park—known globally as Pony—had generated 350 million views as of fall 2021. Even though Park speaks in Korean in the videos, the clear teaching technique and subtitles mean that her audience comes from many countries. Tati Westbrook, a former image consultant and makeup artist, began making beauty videos in 2010. After reaching a million YouTube subscribers in 2016, she was approaching ten times that number three years later. James Charles, a longtime YouTuber, expanded his content to TikTok where he had 36 million subscribers—a big number until one realizes his aggregate YouTube views totaled 3.8 billion as of winter 2023.

These beauty experts produce videos illustrating different techniques, comparing different products, and suggesting looks for special occasions such as a job interview, Halloween, or an outdoor party. They gain their following by being believable and relatable, then audience engagement drives algorithmic visibility as well as subscriber return visits. In many instances, the content verges into self-help and positive thinking. Many vloggers share personal stories of goals attained, barriers overcome, and self-doubts vanquished.

The beauty genre has dramatically expanded in popularity since 2013. According to an analysis of YouTube statistics by the BBC, average daily views of beauty-related videos surged from fewer than 100,000 to more than a million in the five years ending in 2018,[16] then TikTok ratcheted up that count further: 33 billion TikToks have beauty hashtags as of early 2023.[17] Not surprisingly, the most successful beauty influencers have additional revenue streams beyond per-view cash flows from Google and ByteDance. Pony Syndrome cosmetics are sold direct at Memebox, a collection of Asian brands targeting the US market. Westbrook launched a line of vitamin supplements in 2018, while YouTube beauty pioneer Michelle Phan moved from the video channel she launched in 2007 to roles at Lancôme and L'Oreal before starting her own cosmetics subscription service IPSY, valued at roughly $800 million in 2015. Phan then went through personal and financial transitions, leaving IPSY to focus on EM Cosmetics, which she had earlier launched with and eventually bought from L'Oreal. As of early 2023 Phan had returned to YouTube after a hiatus, attracted 8.8 million subscribers, and also had 2 million followers on Instagram.

In a few years, YouTube and TikTok have inverted the global cosmetics business model. Products ranging from acne treatment to mascara report double- and triple-digit sales spikes in the aftermath of viral TikTok videos. In 2022, a $600 Dyson hair dryer went viral on TikTok, racking up 4 billion views in a matter of weeks.[18] CeraVe cleansing products were previously recommended by dermatologists and available at many drugstores, but a positive TikTok review by the highly influential Hyram Yarbro helped empty store shelves nationwide. In addition, TikTok beauty videos can also emphasize the do-it-yourself ethos so viewers can mix their own formulations of many products, sometimes using common household ingredients.

Beauty vloggers can now not only partner with established brands, but in a few cases, they can become a brand themselves. Phan's IPSY model sells direct (five products arrive every month for $13, sold to 3.5 million customers). This means lower prices for customers, higher profit margins, no guessing as to demand forecasting, and no fighting for space on retail shelves at department stores or pharmacy chains. Rather than celebrities and models being named as the "face" of an established brand, the influencers bring credibility and relatability to the market. The worldwide, free content distribution network of online video bypassed traditional gatekeepers at ad agencies, magazine publishers, fashion weeks, and the like. Furthermore, print media cannot convey the amount of information that a simple demonstration video can.

Both technical expertise and personal relatability shine through the best online video content in ways they cannot on a flat, static page. This impact is then amplified by word of mouth that travels farther and faster than phone calls, personal contact at work, or other physical modes of transmission. The net result is a more responsive (in time), inclusive (in populations), and dynamic beauty industry at the global level. The rise of beauty influencers is a wonderful case study in the rise of a new class of entrepreneurs made possible by direct interaction with the end market, and the marginalization of old gatekeepers.

Brands are, of course, responding. Google's research team identified three types of YouTube beauty videos that gained traction with viewers: (1) inspiration (mood-setting rather than technique-imparting), (2) education, and (3) access. The last category is a potentially big win for the brands. Few "influencers" can go behind the scenes at Dior's reception at Paris Fashion Week, for example, or show how the products are not tested on animals. The advice to brands was blunt: "Do what the creators do." That is, upload content regularly, create content catering to an audience's needs, and encourage viewers to share (across multiple social media platforms) and subscribe. None of this is difficult, and it will bear watching over the next few years to see how well "fresh and independent" voices fare in the face of "heavily resourced and highly motivated" global giants.[19]

In the end, the final word should go to the beauty vloggers. Sophie Bishop studies digital humanities at Kings College London. In response to scholarship that bifurcated algorithm studies into investigations of expert coders versus outside-the-firewall users, she embedded herself with a group of beauty vloggers. These women and men were dependent on YouTube, Instagram, and other sites for their livelihood, so understanding the algorithms' quirks and "tells" was of utmost importance. What Bishop called algorithmic gossip used the capabilities of social media, email, and other digital infrastructure to create investigations into and narratives representing the evolving algorithmic landscape. A vlogger will ask on Instagram or Facebook what their followers see on the YouTube screen, for example, seeking cause and effect, then compare results with other vloggers. In this way, we can see that the cross-platform behaviors of online micro-celebrities are at once entrepreneurial, collaborative, investigative, and evolving.[20]

Such studies are only a beginning.[21] Getting macroscale measures of traffic among and between platforms is important for child safety (relative to predators who have gravitated to these platforms), advertisers, and antitrust enforcement, among many other goals. Once again, understanding any one platform will require great strides in being able to measure and analyze that platform in a dynamic digital and physical context.

Men's Rights Activists

Research by my colleague Sarah Bolden has taught me much about the particular behaviors of the men's rights movement in online environments. Defining the movement itself is complicated given that there are many factions, including some involving women, that occupy a continuum of positions. These include the search for better male role models for boys ("better" of course being a matter of opinion), pursuing equality of child visitation or custody after a divorce, efforts to define gender roles in a way that favors men, statistical gymnastics trying to prove false rape accusations are more common than reported, arguments over the flaws in paternity testing and accompanying lawsuits, and the need for a male oral contraceptive. People even argue about whose suicide problem is worse: men's (who succeed more often) or women's (who attempt more unsuccessful suicides than men). Rhetorical violence of an appalling variety and quantity can readily be found, and depending on one's critical position, the movement itself may be considered to be misogynous, whether a given individual is or is not.[22]

The point here is not to characterize the entire men's rights movement to the satisfaction of anyone. Such a diffuse body of thought and discussion is impossible to pin down to a summary. Rather, the use of online platforms by men's rights activists raises important questions about the nature of those platforms: (1) Who builds them? (2) Who moderates them, and how? (3) How much transparency is required or provided by platform owners moderating the users' content? and (4) How do users navigate on and among multiple platforms? The short answers are: (1) the users and potentially somebody's bots; (2) a combination of bots and people struggle to solve the content moderation problem, which appears to end in either an abdication and shutdown of comments or an unsustainable cat-and-mouse game; (3) more is required than is typically provided, but platforms treat moderation as a trade secret; and (4) in ways we don't understand very well.

Bolden's research convinced me that the video format does not materially change the discourse of this community the way that video enhances instructions for performing surgery or assembling a bicycle. In fact, some videos very closely resemble printed postings from other platforms, most likely Reddit. As in many (but far from all) instances, the most important contribution of YouTube to men's rights activism is less likely the videos and more likely in the use of the comments section. These comments, in turn, form one node in a larger ecosystem of multiple platforms, among which users migrate, cross-pollinate, and support and defect. There is much more to learn about cross-platform ecosystems, but for the moment it remains a daunting methodological challenge.

One major strand of discussion that Bolden identifies concerns the use of the platform itself. Specifically, how was Google observed by commenters to be facilitating or impeding activist discourse? If YouTube (or Facebook, or Reddit, or . . .) was thought to be failing to promote men's rights activist voices, what should be the consequences?

Here's one example. User RedPillPhilosophy had a 2018 YouTube post referring to a BitChute video that "proved" YouTube was cutting his traffic.[23] The discussion had hundreds of replies. As with so much other men's rights discourse, there was intense difference of opinion. Some denigrated the poster for their poor-quality videos, saying they didn't deserve an audience. Some posters took the accusation (or "proof") of censorship to be further evidence of a greater conspiracy. This knowledge in turn often drove a survivalist strategy of off-the-grid bunkers or related structures, replete with bottled water, rations, and (of course) arms and ammunition.

Other responses to the perceived nonpromotion or suppression of men's rights ideas took the form of migration to other platforms. In the video realm, the most commonly mentioned platform was BitChute, an allegedly peer-to-peer video-sharing architecture launched in 2017 and headquartered in England. BitChute is friendly to far-right video channels that have been demonetized on YouTube; the Southern Poverty Law Center asserts that the site hosts "hate-fueled" material. Men's rights content would be in keeping with the site's overall tenor, but the site's claims to peer-to-peer decentralization appear to be false. Because of its apparently centralized serving architecture, it is vulnerable to attack in ways a true peer-to-peer architecture would not be.[24] The site's purported resistance to suppression ought to be an important marketing tool when the audience includes a substantial population of people who believe unnamed forces are out to prevent them from being heard.

It is important to view this platform migration in a broader context. Not only are extremist speakers banned from YouTube, but these people are also deprived of financial contributions as PayPal, Patreon, Stripe, and Indiegogo also shut them down. The apparently friendly hosting environment of BitChute fails to provide a revenue stream independent of these payment utilities. Men's rights activists wrote about monetization frequently, both approvingly and with concern or condescension. "They" are a frequent bad guy: "they" are coming for your guns, "they" aren't telling us the truth, "they" won't promote X or Y kinds of voices. In this way, Google, as YouTube's parent company, is both hiding certain kinds of content but also denying those channels the revenue that would come from an unlevel playing field in which YouTube promoted some material over others. In the end, it's worth following the money to understand the motivation for some of the critiques.

Besides BitChute, other alternative platforms came up in comments. These included DTube, Mindz, Bittube, Gab, Freenet, and Snaptube. At the macro level, we can see the brilliance of Mark Zuckerberg's acquisition of Instagram in 2012 for the at the time incredible price of $1 billion. In retrospect, spotting and buying an adjacent platform not only prevented the rise of a Facebook alternative but also appealed to a new generation of social media users. Unlike most Facebook or YouTube users, however, men's rights activists are part of an out-group, one with many repugnant beliefs and sometimes threatening behavior. For them, the choice of and trust in a platform relate directly to the conspiracy narrative central to the group's formation and ongoing identity.

This nuance was for me the most important insight of Bolden's research. Often, the discussions of men's rights (or, in parallel subgroups, Thai cooking, Israeli politics, or English Premier League football) stop being primarily about the nominal function of the group. Instead, when the postings become complicated by considerations about the stability, durability, and trustworthiness of the platform on which the discussions occur, the nature of discourse changes. Some of the accusations were likely true—Google does of course take down extremist content—while other videos lost promotion and viewership in the same algorithmic evolution that affected beauty vloggers or butterfly collectors. Even so, concerns about the precariousness of the platform serve both to undermine the original discussion (fake paternity, the myth of a male-female wage gap, or whatever) as well as to reinforce the out-group's identity: if "they" are trying to slow us down, we must have something powerful to say.

The men's rights activists' suspicions line up with what's happening in Google's search business. After public embarrassments and complaints from major advertisers, Google is reportedly hand-tuning results more than ever before. "There's this idea that the search algorithm is all neutral and goes out and combs the web and comes back and shows what it found, and that's total BS," a former executive was quoted as saying in a *Wall Street Journal* article. "Google deals with special cases all the time." The article also claims Google maintains a manually implemented list of bans on auto-complete text queries; it also won't search on the word "download" in the context of a movie or other digital entertainment asset to prevent searchers from finding pirated copies.[25]

This kind of attention to the platform, a metadebate driven primarily by speculation, falls into a long line of both concerns about media gatekeepers and responses to new media technologies. Gutenberg was partially responsible both for increased Bible-reading and for pamphlets that broadened distrust of the Catholic Church. The newspaper did not immediately provide serialized novels. Television did not create live sports, talk shows, or sketch comedy as its first offering. In our day, we have no idea how social media platforms will drive new forms of information transmission, and new art forms that exploit those technologies. (We will have much more to say about the printing press in chapter 8.)

Where does this leave us? Digital platforms are a form of public commons, owned by private entities intent on profiting from the users' behaviors, primarily on the consumption side. Legal guarantees of free speech do not apply, and privately implemented bans and uplifts of certain forms of speech are anything but transparent. The activists' concerns of selective promotion and demonetization are impossible to assess without transparency from Google (and Reddit, and Facebook, and Twitter). Distinguishing between an algorithmic policy change, a software glitch, a trigger word or action that crosses some invisible line, and randomness is currently impossible. In the vacuum, conspiracy theories will continue to find fertile and troubling soil in which to grow.

144

Kony 2012

Any study of online video must come to terms with what is now a nearly forgotten episode that proved decisive. *Kony 2012* was a documentary film about an African warlord that involved a variety of online and offline platforms, redefined virality, altered US foreign policy, and paved the way for later charity-driven social media phenomena. It also provided another episode in which YouTube's extraordinary reach and capacity for emotional resonance moved a human being (in this case, the film's creator Jason Russell) into extreme public visibility with mental health consequences. YouTube can feel like person-to-person conversation but is in fact on par with traditional media reach, without the psychological and other protections such infrastructure can sometimes provide.

Kony 2012's overnight success began many years earlier. Russell was involved in evangelical church activities from a young age, meeting his future wife when they were children in a drama program. (He later cowrote a script for a musical that was bought by Steven Spielberg.) Russell's church, like many such groups, was focused on evangelizing Africa, so he was exposed to this region early and traveled there as a missionary to Kenya during college. His first documentary exercise after graduation from USC's film school was focused on Sudan's civil war. Russell's film crew sought Sudanese interview subjects in neighboring Uganda and began hearing about warlord Joseph Kony there.[26]

By then (2004), the power of the story to be told overwhelmed the Christian evangelical mission. Ugandans, Russell told a reporter, "know Christ far more than I or anyone in the Western world and in the Christian church knows Christ." Invisible Children was founded to tell that story, and Russell toured across the United States in 2006 to schools and colleges building what would be a grass-roots network of 80,000 mostly millennial social media natives (across a hundred US cities) primed to spread the Kony story after they viewed a rough cut of Russell's "Invisible Children" film. In 2007,

The Rise of the Algorithms

the campaign retained its US focus, claiming mobilization of 68,000 people in fifteen cities, while in 2008 Invisible Children went global with a rally called "The Rescue" in ten cities that drew 85,000 people. The 2011 campaign, "Break the Silence," toured eighteen US sites and claimed 90,000 attendees.[27]

As of 2006, Invisible Children was a nominally secular enterprise. According to its website's FAQ as captured on the Internet Archive:

> *Is your organization a Christian organization?*
> No. The three filmmakers believe in Christ, but do not want to seg-regate themselves in any way. They believe that this story is not theirs to own/brand. They strongly believe that every person needs to hear this story regardless of race, religion, gender, or culture. Invisible Children is about invisible children, and is not exclusive to people who believe what the filmmakers believe. It's about the "orphans, the widows, the hungry, and the oppressed." It's about children that are born into a horrific situation, with no voice.[28]

Despite this formal disclaimer, the leadership of Invisible Children remained strongly Christian. It included leaders of what they call "emerging churches" that diverge from traditional denominations, most of which are witnessing an exodus of aging members (to the hereafter) and millennials (to new forms of religiosity). Invisible Children, meanwhile, eschewed doctrine and ritual for direct engagement and political action, busing more than 3,000 young people to Washington, DC, to meet with legislators and help advance legisla-tion targeting Kony's Lord's Resistance Army (itself a Christianity-influenced movement seeking to rule Uganda according to the Ten Commandments). President Barack Obama signed the anti-Kony legislation into law in 2010.

By 2012, Invisible Children had a story, a network of advocates adept at social media, and a filmmaker inspired by a sense of mission. Once the video launched, it rewrote both the record book and the playbook for future efforts. First, the record book. Invisible Children aspired to amass a million views in a year; it got 120 million in five days, resetting the bar for the fastest video to reach 100 million views.[29] The demographics, which showed the power of online media among teens who watch little to no television news, were also noteworthy: 58 percent of eighteen-to-twenty-nine-year-olds surveyed by Pew Research Center had heard of the video within a week of its release and 23 percent had viewed it. Compared to 36 percent of those people who found out about the video from social media, only 9 percent of the sample found out about it by talking to someone. Pew Research Center also found that the video was mentioned in nearly 5 million tweets in that same week, with 66 percent of the Twitter sentiment supporting the video's message.[30]

As for the playbook, Gilad Lotan of the media analysis group Social Flow analyzed the data and identified several important and nonobvious factors. Lotan, as it happened, was speaking at SXSW, the big interactive conference in Austin, Texas, just as *Kony 2012* was surging across the web. One audience member reported that Lotan found that "a core of highly connected users seem to have been key in launching the social media campaign. Gilad sees evidence that these users were clustered in a couple of communities, notably in Birmingham, Alabama, and sees evidence that many of these users identify strongly with their Christian faith. This aligns with explanations of the viral spread of the video, which point out that Invisible Children has done great work organizing a core of supporters who they were able to mobilize to support this campaign."[31] Some of the social media support came before the film was launched, indicating that the supporters were close enough to the Invisible Children organization to know of the distribution schedule.[32] According to Lotan's SocialFlow analysis, the campaign's supporters were frequently overtly Christian youth with biblical psalms in their social media profiles. He concluded, "I've never seen this tactic being used on such a large scale. You see it with bots, but organizing actual humans? I hadn't seen that yet." In addition to this small core of committed, focused (on-message) promoters, the *Kony 2012* campaign astutely targeted celebrities including Oprah Winfrey, Ryan Seacrest, Justin Bieber, Alec Baldwin, and Taylor Swift who tweeted or sent Facebook messages to their large fan bases.[33]

What really happened? Why was a publicity campaign to "make Kony a celebrity" such a massive phenomenon? What were those 100 million viewers doing with their time, attention, and support? Invisible Children's goal was to use US military and logistical support to arrest Kony and deliver him into the International Criminal Court's prosecution process. The publicity campaign sought to elevate Kony's profile in order to mobilize public sentiment to motivate action at the nation-state level. Despite the campaign's apparent success, nothing changed. As of 2023 Kony, if he is alive after having been reported to be in ill health, remains at large. The US government did offer a $5 million reward for information leading to Kony's capture and allocated troops and aircraft to the cause; the level of commitment clearly increased after the movie's publicity.

McKensie Wark, a professor at the New School (in New York City), aptly summarized the *Kony 2012* phenomenon as a "weird global media event."[34] The weirdness has many facets, not least of which was the filmmaker's public psychotic break, captured on video that of course went viral. Jason Russell was arrested in San Diego, naked and pounding the streets in rush hour, and charged with indecent exposure. Weird or not, *Kony 2012* also served as a coming-out party for online video in the realm of public affairs. Yes, YouTube had streamed presidential debates, but television remained the principal channel. Much like the Kennedy assassination and television, *War of the Worlds* and radio, or the instigation of the Spanish-American war by tabloid newspapers, *Kony 2012* crystallized the transformative power of a new medium to affect public debate in wholly new ways.

Part of the weirdness relates to the episode's global character. As numerous experts noted upon the film's release, pushing the United States to aid Uganda to capture Kony made little sense given that Kony was likely operating elsewhere. In the heat of post-9/11 politics, Kony had been designated as "specially designated global terrorist" in 2008, notwithstanding that his crimes did not affect US interests. Presidents George W. Bush and Barack Obama both signed directives targeting him, a tribute to the influence of Invisible Children and related lobbying groups. Ugandan political realities were of little consequence as the film drew support from much of the English-speaking world, including Australia, where the film aired on a national TV network. In African countries, meanwhile, there was much outrage at both the premise and the portrayals. At a screening in Uganda, viewers threw rocks at the screen.

In its essence, *Kony 2012* was a media event rather than a religious, political, or moral one. It occurred almost entirely within social media. Physical-world events in the film's aftermath drew sparse crowds even though the thirty-dollar "action kit" (which sold out but was available on eBay afterward) included such essentials for social change as a T-shirt, button, poster, and sticker. People were given a vastly oversimplified and emotionally charged telling of the story complete with the filmmaker's son used as a narrative device. Newly motivated, they were then told they could do something about this horrible evil by clicking, tweeting, or otherwise demonstrating moral outrage from their keyboard. For its part, Invisible Children was completely organizationally unprepared for the massive response: the public relations staff at the video's launch consisted of one intern.[35]

The aftermath of *Kony 2012* is far less visible but still noteworthy. The film was a launching pad for a new kind of Christianity, at least briefly. The CEO stated that "Invisible Children wants to be attractive to anyone from any background, period. We want to build loyalty around a lifestyle brand." Doing so with little money and a founder with an image problem proved difficult. Donations on the scale of Oprah Winfrey's prior $2 million were not forthcoming and the sequel to *Kony 2012* has received only 2.9 million views in the eleven-plus years since its release—and comments are disabled for both videos.

Drill Music

Many of the themes we have already discussed converge in fascinating ways in the world of "drill music," a genre of rap originating in Chicago. YouTube plays a, and probably *the*, central role in the coalescence of gang warfare, social media popularity (including algorithmic manipulation), parasocial relationships, and manufactured personae. Numerous tensions are in play: successful rappers can gain global attention but are severely limited in their local travels; the representation of social menace via video often contradicts the lack of violence in an artist's real life; for all the notoriety and fame online celebrity can bring, the rappers can see surprisingly little economic benefit; and while social media platforms may date to the 2000s, cultural projections of and fascination with ghetto exoticism date back at least a century before that.

I draw heavily on an extraordinary work of scholarship for this discussion. Beginning in 2014, Forrest Stuart, at the time a young sociology professor at the University of Chicago, began interviewing participants in his after-school violence-prevention program. These initial discussions led him to embed with a South Side gang, from whom he learned the rituals, intricacies, and surprising consequences of modest success in drill music popularity. His insights into this subgenre illuminate the larger discussion of online platforms from multiple perspectives.

Drill music traces its origins to Chief Keef (Keith Cozart), born in 1995, whose 2012 track "I Don't Like" became a hit in Chicago. It attracted both major names (fellow Chicagoan Kanye West remixed the track) and highly visible record labels—Interscope signed him to a $6 million deal before he turned eighteen. Chief Keef's YouTube-driven rise to popularity paralleled Justin Bieber's, absent a famous name who promoted him. There was much talk at the time about the death of cultural gatekeepers, and Cozart's ability to bypass record company production and retailer distribution allowed him to find a fan base with little intermediation. Many of the genre's features were evident early on: repeated encounters with the legal system for firearms and violent-crime accusations; disrespect for fellow rappers voiced via social media; disrespect for victims of violence, expressed via both rapping and social media; and a curated social media persona enhanced by the aforementioned criminal justice history.

While Cozart is still alive in 2023 (unlike several of his label-mates), his career never climbed to the peaks his early success might have predicted. Nevertheless, he inspired a generation of Chicago teens to emulate his formula of raw, often ferocious lyrics, a distinctive snare and bass sound conveying martial and insistent overtones, and video production emphasizing the hard life of someone surviving on the streets. Contributing to the emulation was the ready presence of a brand. The violence in Chicago is often referred to as "Chiraq," so the drill rappers channel the dire circumstances connoted by the label. This is a war zone, the implicit narrative goes, and we are the lords of our turf, more powerful than those who seek to take it from us (37).[36]

Surprisingly, that turf is not defined by the drug-selling that characterized gang life thirty years ago. Today's street drugs are different in many ways—effect, pricing, supply chain, legal sentencing—from the crack cocaine of the 1980s. Law enforcement has made established drug-sellers hesitant to recruit and establish young sellers. For teens, finding drugs to sell, buyers to purchase, and firearms is made much more difficult by this hesitance. Stuart reports some teens tried selling only to their friends, who demanded discounts, so that the business soon shut down after repeated financial losses (26). For their part, the older sellers fear the social media personalities encouraged by Facebook, Twitter, and Instagram (11). Black teens create more social media content than any other demographic,[37] and law enforcement is now tracking these accounts carefully to spot firearms, gang identity, and other pieces of the prosecution puzzle.

As a result, gang lordship can now be heavily conveyed by videos and social media, but the disses and threats broadcast therein often lead to physical violence. As Stuart notes, as of 2016, of forty-five gang factions in a six-square-mile area, thirty-one had an online presence that both claimed territory and accused rivals of posing and of other failures of urban dominance (viii). In some cases, the posturing—posing with a large group of young men and often firearms—may actually *reduce* the odds of physical violence, while at other times, similar behavior can invite retaliation or testing (216).[38]

For the rappers as individuals, the path to fame has been marked out by Cozart and others like Montana of 300 (38). The teens Stuart interviewed spent hours deconstructing lyrics, beats, video techniques, and social media rules of engagement that have proven to work. View counts were a commonly cited yardstick. Much like blues musicians in the twentieth century who were exploited by record labels, the rappers themselves seldom control a YouTube channel at the start of their career. Instead, more technically experienced and better capitalized videographers and other members of the ecosystem see the checks from Google. To make money, rappers might be featured on an out-of-town artist's effort to cash in on Chicago's drill credibility, or they might do live shows. The latter is problematic close to home, however, given the geography of gang identity. Chief Keef was banned from performing in Chicago, for example. Even walking to school can be dangerous once one's face has been linked to one of those forty-five distinct gang identities. At the same time, getting arrested on gun charges raises one's street credibility.

The teens were resourceful and astute in using the recommender algorithms to their advantage. Starting out, with no name and no back catalog of work for Google to cue up in a playlist, one can hope to land a "feature" or guest appearance from a performer with more algorithmic weight. This typically costs money. Instead, a more common tactic is to include the names of better-known entities in the title. The only way to do this while maintaining the gangster persona is to insult them: diss tracks are a clever way to associate one's new, unknown name with someone more famous (53). The other way to "scaffold" one's brand is to claim connection to someone who dies in urban violence. Citizen Z who just died was a member of my network, the logic runs, and so I represent that I live under similarly dangerous conditions (whether I do or not) and that I will uphold their honor, implicitly by violence.

The rappers may have made their fame as individuals, but behind every successful individual is a fascinating web of supporting characters (45). Given the poverty of their surroundings, aspiring rappers lack both social and financial capital. Even as YouTube provides an ostensibly free distribution platform, music recording and video production both require some access to equipment and expertise. The technical experts in these fields may come from the gang, or they may be hired. The neighborhood guy who's "good with computers" might earn sixty dollars an hour on an intermittent basis, whereas the city's top videographers earn two to five times as much and have steady demand for their services (52).

Beyond technical services, the network of affiliated people grows wider. Neighborhood residents and informal associates often serve as extras on camera. Known as "the guys," fellow gang members can also support the driller by providing Wi-Fi passwords, drugs, or access to guns. Tasks might include tracking the police radio scanner, standing guard on a key street corner, or getting access to a car. Proof of loyalty at the earliest stages (often dating to elementary school lunchrooms) will be remembered once the rapper achieves stardom. None of these roles, it should be stressed, involves physical violence.

Firearm possession is problematic for anyone on parole or hoping to avoid prison time, so every performer needs at least one or two "shooters" who will follow through on the promises of violence stated or implied in the videos. Because of the legal issues and personal danger involved with the role, shooters were not a stable population in a given neighborhood. People changed living arrangements for a variety of reasons, necessitating the recruitment of new people to fill this niche in the ecosystem (93). Shooters did not always appear in the videos, but rappers often shouted them out in the lyrics. As Stuart writes, shooters performed an essential function, and "drillers typically considered taking matters into their own hands, carrying out violence themselves, only when they were completely unable to muster their triggermen" (94). The reality of gang life is that a small percentage of people are connected to the bulk of violence, online media portrayals to the contrary.

This fact raises a matter of central importance: many drill rappers did not live the life of which they spoke in their videos. One of the surest ways to lose face is to be discovered as living at odds with what one portrays, being outed as a "computer gangster" (129). This can happen in a variety of ways. During the filming of one video, an associate had to educate a driller about the proper handling of the gun that was being waved around as a prop. This was not a matter of naïve firearm safety—something that nearly got Stuart shot in a different setting—but rather of street authenticity. Viewers of the video would have been able to see the incorrect grips, reloadings, and other giveaways of a disjuncture between lyrics and experience (78).

The ecosystem of drill music extends far beyond the city blocks where it is produced. Aspiring rappers from many places across the world—London, Los Angeles, Atlanta—network to the "authentic" Chicago voices, trying to share their fame. Bloggers, journalists, and other nonperformers aggregate and repackage drillers' material, including social media posts, to feed a wider audience following the various beefs among the drillers. DJ Akademiks, a Rutgers graduate in mathematics, has more than 2 million followers on both Instagram and YouTube. On his channel, he primarily summarizes industry news, music sales figures, and personal details of hip-hop artists' lives and careers. Googling the phrase "Twitter beef" provides a steady flow of perceived and documented slights that could escalate, spread by parties often far removed from the protagonists (143).

The nonfinancial rewards of drill music microcelebrity, of even appearing in a video much less starring in it, were at once predictable and surprising. Getting noticed, particularly in an environment with few viable economic pathways, provided a boost to self-esteem. In addition to the elusive and unlikely music fame that accrued to only a handful of the aspiring drillers, Stuart was surprised to find that a potent behavioral payoff was being noticed by females. Armed with minor fame and ample charm, drillers "finessed" female admirers into lodging, sex, money, and other favors. For their parts, the females benefited by borrowing the drillers' "clout" as they posted photos of themselves with the young man to their social media streams (109–13).

While drill microcelebrity has similarities to that experienced by social media "influencers" and beauty bloggers, for example, Stuart is careful to point out important differences. The rappers he observes lack any semblance of a financial safety net. There is no sense whatsoever of resuming one's "day job" if social media fame doesn't work out. The drillers are committed, lending more credibility to their raps about the hard life on the streets. Yes, some might be found to be "computer gangsters," but compared to the more visible YouTubers and Instagrammers who have been studied by previous academics, most drillers are "all in" by economic necessity (103).

Stuart concludes by emphasizing three macro-level points. They are subtle and worth summarizing. First, the digital production practices of different groups can vary significantly. Just because white North American males were among the first to colonize the Internet in the mid-1990s does not mean their habits and practices will serve as a universal norm. Similarly, the paternalism embodied in the "one laptop per child" movement failed to recognize the many different ways a social group can use technology. Projections of upward social mobility derived from access to computers proved terrifically naïve. Furthermore, what was once called the Internet's "death of distance" has played out in reverse in these communities.[39] In the case of the drillers, amplifying the social stigma attached to their neighborhood had the effect of attracting attention to their music among a wider public and at the same time, making it so the drillers' faces were quickly recognized as they tried to traverse the turf of competing gangs. Drillers could fly to Atlanta or LA to capitalize on their fame but had to be extremely careful walking more than a block or two, or taking mass transit, away from their homes. Social media makes tracking peoples' habits and locations easier than ever (203).

Second, commercializing urban Black identity—portraying what sociologist Elijah Anderson calls the "iconic black ghetto"—allows the drillers at once to capitalize on stereotypes just as doing so hardens extreme perceptions (204). This dynamic operates at multiple levels. At a social level, creating and distributing videos based on hyperviolent personas, potentially highly fictionalized ones, reinforces negative stereotypes created by media coverage, movies, television, and urban legends. Much like Italians and the Mafia as depicted by media stereotypes in previous generations, many Black Americans now live under the umbrella of implied or imputed violence and lawlessness. As individuals, meanwhile, the drillers found it difficult to move on in life, growing into adulthood constrained by the self-generated media portrayals. Several men in the study had to quit jobs that involved long commutes across competing gang's boundaries. The danger of "being found lacking"—being identified and forced to humiliate oneself and one's [former] gang, most likely on camera—was too great once the men got signaled they had been spotted on the subway or wherever (129, 143).

153

Third, the drillers' flight to the extreme edges of their reality not only attracts audiences, it also contributes to the broader "poverty knowledge" (understandings of ghetto life taken to be fact that may or may not be based on firsthand observation) and stereotyping that informs policing, public policy, and social discourse. In courts of both law and public opinion, the videos' content and ethos reinforce the "facts" of urban life and, in turn, the supposedly adequate and appropriate responses to that "reality." Poverty knowledge impedes real progress in numerous ways, from distracting policymakers to fueling stereotypes for white fraternities' theme parties (205).

For our purposes, the use of online video by a distinctive and highly visible online population—as I write, the various versions of Chief Keef's "I Don't Like" have attracted more than 100 million views—helps illuminate the wider online video environment in several ways. Like many of the other YouTube stars we have encountered, drill rappers found fame came with decidedly mixed outcomes. First, people who knew the drillers only via their online persona could assume interpersonal closeness that carried both benefits (including sexual ones) and bizarre interactions. One driller was flown to Los Angeles by a wealthy white fan who had assumed the persona of a Beverly Hills driller, dressing in expensive hip-hop style, flashing gang signs (including those of the visiting drillers' mortal enemies), and speaking casually of activities and issues that were much more consequential on the Chicago streets. The parasocial relationships we discussed in chapter 5 operate in very similar ways among the drillers (80).

Also like other suddenly famous YouTubers, the drillers lacked the protective infrastructure provided by a character, a stage name, or a movie or television studio. The pressure to live up to one's online persona, even as the capriciousness of algorithmic promotion could vaporize that fame in a very short time, took a toll. People struggled to create a persona that both found wide viewership and remained sufficiently stable that they didn't have to keep changing emphasis and style (82).

That fame was in turn built on a delicate dynamic. Authenticity was commercially viable only when it was both accessible to outsiders and convincing of its interior grit. As Stuart wrote, "for those with limited resources, this means finding new and innovative ways to demonstrate they *truly* embody the negative stereotypes of the stigmatized social group" (6). Successful drillers managed this tightrope by their use of artifice. Whether by images, lyrics, soundscapes, or persona, they convinced their audience of both their commonality with the poorest of the poor *and* their superiority and uniqueness.

Finally, the drill rappers illustrate how online video is but one corner of the larger digital landscape. The fame of the rap subgenre is not only appealing and comparatively accessible—the odds of these young men attracting a million views are not much longer than their chances of completing an Ivy League college education—but it is the rare economic ladder out of the poverty dominating these neighborhoods. Unlike most white students, these high-school-aged kids have little safety net and little room for error. The community possesses less housing and financial capital, sees more people incarcerated, and lives under more overtly racist policing policies than white districts.

As tough as the context is, the fame is no guarantee of a ticket out. As we saw, that fame is both fraught with pitfalls—among them, getting shot—and precarious given the economics of online video popularity. Even when fame comes, a double standard applies. As Stuart notes, when Black male teens flash firearms, they attract heavy attention from police and prosecutors, whereas when white teens pose with firearms, they often become celebrities and attract "atta-boys" from police. What he calls the "digital disadvantage" (9) is a much more satisfying and empirical reading of the ground truth than to simply bemoan a "digital divide" that both assumes a technocratic benefit and ignores the realities of Black and Hispanic Internet adoption, which for years has tended much more toward mobile devices than stationary cable modems.[40]

Conclusion

These four narratives—all global in impact and three of which are far from decisively concluded as of 2023—can only hint at the complexity of perspectives, trajectories, and audiences that online video can empower and mobilize. So-called real life continually interacts with online video, further complicating the challenge of understanding and attempting to manage cross-platform flows and behaviors. To take only one example, when can and should a platform use GIS (geographic information systems) or credit score data to influence a viewer's online experience?

This diversity of platforms and patterns of their use is multiplied by the increasing number of adjoining online platforms that video creators use for infrastructure, inspiration, promotion, and feedback. Gray areas that would be troubling but manageable on some local scale can become violent fissures given the velocity and emotional power of global video in ad hoc virtual neighborhoods. For their part, the global platforms have learned from these experiences and developed plans, processes, and protocols for dealing with things that go very wrong very fast at this scale. As this game of move and countermove evolves, it is time to try to take partial and preliminary stock of the place of online video in contemporary life.

8

Situating Online Video

In many ways, we end where we began. Recall that media studies, critical theory, computer science, and other fields use the term "platform" in slightly different ways. To understand online video, or more realistically, to begin to think about how to think about YouTube, TikTok, and the other megaplatforms, we need to use an array of conceptual frameworks. All of the above, plus sociology, history, and sociotechnical studies, are useful; each is also incomplete. One final useful nuance is added by incorporating the notion of infrastructure. Historically, this referred to technological commons—wires, roads, canals, bridges—there were either publicly owned or regulated by the state as was the case with power companies and AT&T in the mid-twentieth century. More recently, "infrastructure" has been expanded by some scholars to include human aspects such as work practices or organizational culture.[1] Platforms ride on today's technological commons and can attain the status of infrastructure ("log in with Facebook") but are privately owned and generally much more lightly regulated than public utilities.

Questions

Two of the most provocative questions emerging from various strands of research relate to these online platforms. First, outside the platform owners, who are reluctant to share data for both competitive and regulatory reasons, nobody really understands how people relate to these platforms and to the other people on them. The fact that many people are communicating unknowingly with bots, for example, is poorly understood. Furthermore, agency remains difficult to discern. If person A posts a video on YouTube and person B views it then harms themself or others, what is the relation of A to B, B to A, B to A's advertisers, and both A and B to YouTube and Google? Put more simply, what do platforms do relative to the behaviors of their uploading and downloading members? Who sees, knows, understands, or regulates these activities? Foremost among these platform-centric activities are the processes of curation, both in removing prohibited material and surfacing or promoting what the algorithms and human curators determine should be the winners.

Second, and more problematic from a research perspective, is the question of measuring and analyzing people's behaviors *across* platforms. We saw in chapter 7 how men's rights activists migrated from YouTube to BitChute for video content but announced their intentions on Reddit or elsewhere. Facebook understandably wants to keep its users on the platform with video functionality at both Instagram and Facebook proper, but it would be naïve to think there wasn't substantial cross-pollination from video properties elsewhere.

Because of its vastness and because Google is hesitant to release indexes and other summary statistics related to its subsidiary, efforts to limn this cultural resource are futile. More recently, given the rapid rise in the popularity of TikTok, we know even less about its operations, controlled as they are by a Chinese company. That said, certain truths have emerged.

First, online video services take advantage of video's conveyance of human facial expression, tone and timbre of voice, body language, and "how-to" demonstrations of particular operations to supplement print's five-hundred-year primacy as the world's most accessible asynchronous mass medium.

Second, YouTube is participatory, and TikTok even more so given its reward structure for making videos in response to other videos. Google produces very little video content and TikTok even less. The uploaders make the service what they are.

Third, at the same time that uploaders *create* content, the platforms largely determine a video's viewership. Google contributes considerably to the shape and direction of YouTube via search and auto-play algorithms, while TikTok's "For You" playlist is even more addictive and effective. YouTube is not currently indexed in the way Google crawled the print/hyperlink web. The videos are suggested to viewers partially on the basis of limited metadata (relating to the video's actual content) and primarily on the basis of previous viewers' behaviors. How many people clicked on a thumbnail, how long did they watch, did they leave a "like," a rating, a comment? It's important to understand the major online video services as part of the planet-scale behavioral experiment being conducted, without consent or oversight, by Amazon, Facebook, and governments,[2] among others.

Fourth, online video is too big to grasp. Even English-language or US-native content is too big to analyze, or even measure. Longitudinal analysis of such volumes, outside the platforms themselves (who have hired many talented academic researchers), is expensive and difficult.

Fifth, participation within YouTube is complex. The simple act of watching a video all the way through is significant for the uploader's ranking and possibly revenue stream. Another option is to make a video in response to a video. Before 2005, this was a practical impossibility, to interact with broadcast video via video. Now it is core to TikTok's popularity, supported as it is with filters, tips, and directions from the platform. Further, extensive comments sections facilitate a different mode of interaction of the viewer with the uploader and other viewers.

Sixth, the networks formed within YouTube and Twitch are of a new sort. People's primary (strong) ties are well-known and extensively studied: intimates, family, the closest of friends. Loose ties, the friends of friends and people we knew long ago, were named in research in the 1970s by the sociologist Mark Granovetter drawing on work by Stanley Milgram among others. More recently, Paul Adams at Google identified a class of "temporary ties," people who connect to each other briefly, possibly anonymously, for the purpose of completing a task.[3] The traffic-awareness app Waze is a textbook example of a network of temporary ties. TikTok, meanwhile, has overtly little reliance on social graphs but can further create in-group identity through cultural artifacts (songs, clothing, turns of phrase) across time and space as videos become a form of storytelling.[4]

Inside YouTube, the comments section constitutes a social network unlike any other. While able to scale globally, these networks are microtargeted. One need not identify with a larger community (tool-users, techno music listeners) to interact meaningfully with other viewers of a Makita cordless drill teardown or fellow Chemical Brothers fans. They can be either immediate or long-lived. People will often reply to a years-old post. Posters can express any or all of their identities—cat fancier, Halal cook, Manchester United football fan, cancer survivor—in response to a given video. At TikTok, users do not need to create an account or log in, partially because the service tracks devices and other proxies for a user ID. It is not necessary for users to consider themselves as part of a network of connectivity, although this identity can emerge.

Google does not report many numbers related to YouTube even as it collects billions of data points, which it uses to rank and deliver the service's videos. TikTok is in even murkier water, particularly given the evolving ultimatums directed at it by a former US president, the management instability that coincided with those ultimatums, and the shifting winds of Chinese governmental involvement.[5] Herewith is an assortment of statistics collected from a wide variety of sources, each of which points to a larger story, insight, or question.

How Profitable Is Online Video?

Because YouTube is not broken out as a separate business in Alphabet accounting, precise financials are unavailable beyond the $15 billion in 2019 revenues announced in early 2020. Further, because Google services share a login, it's fair to question whether a user's activity (both cost- and revenue-generating) is closely allocated to the various subproperties. If I use Gmail to send a friend a YouTube video related to a national park I found on Google search, to which I send her directions using Google Maps, all on my Android phone, there are many ways that session could be apportioned. Expenses for storage, bandwidth, and computing are greatly reduced by Google's overall expertise and scale. The company owns many thousands of miles of fiber-optic cable that were laid but never lit in the late 1990s Internet boom by companies that no longer exist, for example. Google also uses (and owns) the VP9 video codec, another source of both cost and technical overhead savings. In short, a startup trying to duplicate YouTube would need to cross a very broad, deep moat. The company can justify financial losses (if there are any) by the traffic the video service drives to other Google properties.

Because TikTok is privately held and belongs to a Chinese parent company, financial reports are only estimates. ByteDance had a very successful calendar 2020, according to the BBC which quoted an internal memo that the firm confirmed. Total revenues rose 111 percent to $34.3 billion. Gross profits were announced at an internal company meeting to be $19 billion, which would be an extraordinary 56 percent margin. Like Google, ByteDance operates a wide range of platforms, many of which share reliance on the company's machine-learning expertise.[6] TikTok numbers were not broken out. Even if they were, the internal cross-subsidies would be difficult to control for.

How Popular Is Online Video, Really?

According to the Pew Research Center, here are some numbers that explain YouTube's popularity among advertisers:

- 83 percent of US adults earning more than $75,000 annually use YouTube
- 93 percent of US adults aged twenty-five to twenty-nine use YouTube
- In the United States a larger percentage of men use YouTube compared to women (78 percent to 63 percent), while women out-participate men on Facebook by a narrower margin (75 percent to 68 percent)
- YouTube outperforms Facebook in total users and in most demographics (all levels of education, for example), though Facebook users log into that service more frequently[7]
- According to *Forbes*, 80 percent of YouTube traffic comes from outside the United States[8]

Here are similar numbers that testify to TikTok's popularity:

- The app has 689 million worldwide monthly users, 100 million in the United States [9]
- 90 percent of users check the app more than once a day. As of 2018, teens checked it about forty times a day, or almost three times per waking hour[10]
- The app is available in 155 markets, in seventy-five languages[11]
- TikTok was the most downloaded app, worldwide, in 2020[12]

What do all these figures really tell us? Do people stay on these services over many years, or does a steady stream of new users churn through? What does that 80 percent non-US traffic mean for curation, for monetization, for advertising revenue? (Do one million US views generate more or less revenue than one million Japanese or Brazilian views?) The popularity helps explain the willingness to absorb potential financial losses at a business unit level, if that is in fact the case at either parent company. Growth rates—in time spent on the site, in viewers, in ad dollars spent—all appear to trend in a positive direction, and the services present potential challengers with daunting barriers to entry. The infrastructure, the brand, the massive and loyal user base, and Google's ability to build synergies across (and thus cross-subsidize) its properties all make YouTube a formidable franchise. One of TikTok's many challenges will be to avoid problems with its too-young viewer base, and to increase the appeal of the service among adults with potentially warier views on data privacy.

Why Does It Matter That YouTube Does Not Behave like Google's Search Engine?
According to YouTube's chief product officer, speaking in 2018, 70 percent of user time spent on the site consists of watching recommended videos.[13]

The search model made popular by Google begins with a query. At YouTube, recommendations begin with a behavior. As with any long-tail phenomenon, shelf-browsing does not scale to navigating a massive selection. Furthermore, Google does not consistently index videos the way it indexes text. Searching for a video based on words included in its *Google-generated* captioning will not necessarily return that video. Rather than resembling a reference librarian, the site recommends (or automatically begins playing) videos that it predicts will generate more time spent on the site, and therefore more ad revenue. Accuracy with regard to the initial query, or similarity to the initial video which we might have found via a link shared on social media, does not appear to be a success criterion.

Definitions

Perhaps it is appropriate to attempt to consider YouTube and TikTok by what they *do* rather than what they might *be*. Both services, because they are video, entertain in a manner different from text. As we work to understand the big video platforms, the fundamental differences between video and still images or text are important for analyzing TikTok and YouTube's impact. For all the criticisms it has attracted over the years, Marshall McLuhan's work remains valuable. He saw, quite early, the numbing potential of the medium, and his characterization of television as "cool" (versus print's being "hot") highlights the different ways audiences participate in the reception of information. The discontinuity of televised images he characterized as a "mosaic," requiring audience participation to construct meaning out of discontinuous streams. Also unlike print, this stream could be never-ending, and online video amplifies this reality of endlessness.[14]

The mosaic imagery is appropriate as we try to grasp online video. One important aspect of online video, from the outset, has been music. Music and television form emotional touchstones, again in ways text cannot, so YouTube is an enormous reservoir of nostalgia. (So is Vine among a narrow demographic. TikTok is young and moves its memes fast, but we can expect it to spawn a retro variation of some sort as its audience ages.) Online video educates and, in part because of demonstrations and animations, it explains. Finally, all the video platforms support a large number of independent content producers. TikTok and YouTube do this less by paying royalties and more by providing exposure to everyone from beauty vloggers to political pundits.

At its founding, YouTube was envisioned as "Flickr for video." (Flickr was a photo storage and sharing site launched in 2004 and acquired by Yahoo in 2005. It peaked at slightly over 100 million users in the early 2010s.) In part because of video's emotional power and its explanatory capabilities, the site soon became much more than that, in positive ways by helping reshape US election coverage and in negative ones by contributing to homophobia, racism, bullying, and misogyny. The early tagline—"Broadcast Yourself"—was soon outgrown as anyone who saw the traffic would understand the limitations of the broadcast metaphor. Even when a video receives (reportedly) billions of views, it's hard to call YouTube a broadcast medium. Media studies scholars Daniel Herbert, Amanda Lotz, and Lee Marshall, in an article on comparative approaches to streaming media industries, say as much (though I disagree with their characterization of gatekeeping): "YouTube is excluded from our analysis, which may be somewhat surprising given that it has been the largest streaming website for both video and music by some metrics, but YouTube does not actively curate (gatekeep what content is included) so much as function as an open access distributor. While YouTube is undoubtedly affecting practices within the industries we discuss, it remains external to them and subject to its own logics that require a distinct analysis."[15]

Writing about another platform in the *Atlantic*, Robinson Meyer says something that could help us understand YouTube and TikTok: "Twitter has been a mess of speech-like tweets interpreted as print, and print-like tweets interpreted as speech, for as long as most users can remember. This whiplash between orality and literacy is even part of what makes it fun."[16] If we substitute "instruction" and "entertainment" for "print" and "speech," there's a similar polyvalence to online video. It is rant and record, escape and engagement, timely and time machine. Much as Twitter blurs old distinctions between conversation and broadcast, YouTube presents us with an apparently universal archive of cultural moments. (Indeed, a telling exercise at YouTube's fifteenth birthday would be an inventory of what is *not* available, and why.) That archive, however, is unlike anything we've ever seen.

The archive is effectively infinitely large. The Museum of Television and Radio in New York hosts 150,000 artifacts. YouTube has, by one report, 1.3 billion videos—and counting. It's both top-down—NBC posts "official" old *SNL* videos and takes down most everything else related to the show—and bottom-up. New "genres" have emerged, such as unboxing. Who would have ever predicted that a nine-year-old kid could post reviews of toys—and earn $29 million in one year doing so?[17] Meanwhile, to navigate this unfathomable mass of content, finding what one is looking for is not an extension of text- and web-searching patterns to which Google has acclimated us. In many facets, online video is at once foreign and familiar.

Accordingly, online video must be seen as both continuity and discontinuity. It does resemble "Flickr for video" in some respects, except that it's way bigger and involves way more money than its forebear. It does resemble network television—in its moving images, many of which originated in its broadcast cousin. But online video platforms are owned by companies (Amazon, ByteDance, and Google) that don't produce much content and that serve everything algorithmically or by request, almost never by schedule and rarely to aggregated audiences. A "channel" on Comcast and a "channel" on YouTube really don't have much in common at all.

"Participatory"

Like Facebook, online video is literally nothing if not participatory. (The early scholarship related to YouTube was fixated on the notion.[18]) Absent uploads, there is no service. All three companies court and support key content producers while encouraging a broad base of upload participation. But what exactly does that mean, and what does it imply? Several existing analytical frameworks are useful, if only to see how online video platforms break them. These platforms combine multiple forms of participation into something we have never seen before. The scale of both contribution and viewership, the algorithmic gatekeeping, and the emergence of the mobile smartphone all combine in the many uses to which online video is put. To comprehend this new medium, let us examine three scholarly frames: the notions of communities of discourse, communities of practice, and the social construction of technology.

Communities of Discourse

In 1977, the historian David Hollinger attempted to defend his field of intellectual history from charges that it was immaterial, elitist, and irrelevant, particularly in contrast to the vividly gritty social history of previously marginalized groups. In contrast to an antiquated concept of a history of ideas, Hollinger sought to return his field's focus to people. These agents took action, left artifacts, and caused consequences. A large part of intellectual history, in this view, studied how historical actors engaged with the questions of their era, particularly in relation to other thinkers, writers, and speakers. As Hollinger said nearly forty years later, "I wanted to remind colleagues of the value of the kind of history that focused on the questions thinkers are trying to answer and on how various individual thinkers answered one another's questions and thereby participated in a community of sorts."[19]

Much of that discourse took place in letters and conversations, of course, but a good deal of textual evidence at the disposal of the intellectual historian consisted of printed matter: books, clippings, articles. These were published in an environment of scarcity. Books have traditionally been expensive, journals and magazines have page constraints and word counts, and access to print is tightly controlled by editors and publishers. Online video, in contrast, can be considered to consist of millions of communities of discourse as commenters reply both to the original video but also to other comments. In fact, given the purely virtual nature of the enterprise, the communities can consist of almost nothing *but* discourse, words on the ephemeral screen. What used to be elite, slow-moving, and available only to a few has been thrown wide open to any mass that wants to converge and discuss anything from Oprah to Indigenous peoples to eye shadow to Fortnite. "Discourse," Hollinger wrote in 1979, "is a social as well as an intellectual activity."[20] Digital platforms radically enlarge the playing field upon which discourse occurs. Paradoxically, online video can also change the use and reach of print, as the TikTok community BookTok demonstrates.[21]

Communities of Practice

Beginning in 1991 and continuing through the present, the Swiss educational theorist Étienne Wenger has studied how people learn and concluded that the group in which the learner is situated—their "community of practice"—significantly shapes the knowledge. The phenomenon is not new. Wenger and his coauthor Jean Lave were originally studying how young tailors learned more from other apprentices than from the master craftsperson, the ostensible teacher.[22] While the same dynamic has been observed in photocopier repair people,[23] for example, or among accountants in Wenger's later work, the study of the idea goes back to the American pragmatist philosophers, notably Charles S. Peirce (who wrote of a "community of inquiry" in 1877, referring primarily to scientists) and later John Dewey, who applied the idea to education.

In part because the 1990s spawned rapid growth in enterprise software systems, the consulting genre of "knowledge management" focused much of its attention on the communities of practice in a given organization, whether corporate or governmental. As a key article in the field put it, knowledge management is "primarily . . . a problem of capturing, organizing, and retrieving information, evoking notions of databases, documents, query languages, and data mining."[24] Not surprisingly, social network mapping software was applied to enterprises in the pursuit of communities of practice, whose members could then be identified as "subject matter experts" or as sources of the elusive "best practices" with which managers were so concerned in these years.

What is a community of practice relative to online video? Practitioners may not actually practice the skill until *after* seeing the video. Rather than the enterprise computer seeking to identify experts, novices can learn from more seasoned practitioners and perhaps surpass them. There are many worldwide virtual communities where this is happening, including street dancing and unicycling. In more traditional communities of practice—including surgical residents—YouTube is also proving to be a key contributor to improved performance, knowledge recall, and other traits.[25]

Sociotechnical Studies

Since shortly after World War II, a school of technology scholars has spoken of technology as an artifact embedded in and coevolutionary with human contexts. As summarized by my colleague Steve Sawyer and Mohammad Jarrahi, "The sociotechnical premise can be articulated as: (1) the mutual constitution of people and technologies . . . ; (2) the contextual embeddedness of this mutuality; and, (3) the importance of collective action."[26] Whether it is 1950s English coal miners who were the first object of study using this lens or organizations struggling with enterprise software implementation, technology in organizations is in this view best understood as a dynamic of complex mutual coevolution and coadaptation. Designers' intentions and builders' skill both matter but are not decisive. Families, tribes, work teams, labor unions, and other groups use a given technology in particular, evolving, and often unintended ways, changing both the nature and behavior of the artifact and some dynamics of the human group.

In contrast, as Microsoft's danah boyd points out, in "Web 2.0" systems such as YouTube, Facebook, and various Google services, software is treated as a perpetual beta. No digital platform can ever be understood to be "done." Software in the wild is therefore not a hardened artifact with which to coevolve. It is plastic and impermanent, very much unlike a rock drill or even an SAP system. The users not only *adapt* to the introduced technology, they help *make* it.[27]

The traditional software engineering approach of "design, develop, deploy" is completely subverted. Users not only make the site possible via uploads, but they continually redefine the environment. A classic example occurs intermittently in Amazon product reviews. A gallon of milk launches an elaborate set of literary parodies,[28] a pair of running shoes sparks a fierce defense of women's reproductive rights after Texas legislator Wendy Davis wore this particular model for a filibuster,[29] and a $1,500 audio cable is scathingly derided as the worst form of pseudoscience.[30] As at YouTube, a set of "temporary ties"[31]—contrasted to Granovetter's famous naming of "weak ties"—defines a community in relation to a particular artifact for a window of time. Commenters typically share no institutional membership, or even knowledge of each other's names. These communities are defined only by the cloud software deployed to host the uploaded videos and comments, not by membership, locality, computing platform, or other traditional attributes.

As these three departures suggest, online video fails to fit any extant theoretical model. It is bigger than, different from, governed unlike, and situated far from any media, communications, or computational environment we have ever built or encountered. Neither telephone nor television, social network nor World Wide Web, online video at once borrows from each of these technologies while replicating none. Part of the difficulty we face in governing or regulating online video is that nobody really can define precisely what it is today—or what it could evolve into tomorrow.

Gatekeeping and Curation

Online video also illustrates the power of a new form of agenda-setting. In light of the billions of hours of available content, the gatekeeping of editors, producers, and publishers has been replaced. Following Kevin Hamilton and his coauthors, I hesitate to call the algorithms a "black box," but the principles and processes by which videos find recommendation or even visibility are unclear, evolving, and consequential.[32] Content creators are frustrated about unpredictable visibility while subscribers to a creator are not guaranteed to see their newest material. In light of the lack of content indexing and reliance on readily gamed behavioral measures of viewer response, the contrast between the vast amount of available material and the non-content-centric principles of visibility and surfacing must be taken seriously.

Online video can form communities around artists, around issues, around household repair problems, and around a new kind of media celebrity. One of these types of communities consists of content creators trying to decipher the changing promotional algorithm. Just as in the cat and mouse game of search engine optimization (SEO), in which firms engaged self-declared experts in site rewording, relinking, and restructuring in the pursuit of better ranking within keyword search results, the content creators are trying to see behind algorithmic curtains. Ad hoc networks of creators, often utilizing side-channel communications with audiences, are emerging, sometimes in closed Facebook groups. The dialogue follows some variant of "If I did X with my video, Y used to happen but after the first of the month, now Z happens. What about you?"

This behavior has precedent. High-rent image and public relations consultants could land an op-ed slot in the *New York Times*, *Wall Street Journal*, or *Washington Post* for a CEO or potential political candidate. Now that process has moved substantially down-market. There are always gatekeepers, and as in any ecosystem, new species evolve to thrive in unfilled niches. Here, it is often the practitioners themselves decoding the algorithm from the outside in, in the absence of much guidance from the platforms directly. (Consultants much like the ones who did SEO back in the day are also available for hire.[33]) As of 2019, YouTube watch data appeared to be valued much more highly than creator-supplied descriptive verbiage. Because roughly half of views are terminated within twenty seconds, the algorithm appears to reward long watch times. Longitudinal patterns matter—channels with frequent uploads fare better than those with inconsistent schedules of new content.[34] As of 2025, or some other random date, the factors will change, most likely with little or no notice from Google or ByteDance.

This difference from text-based search must be emphasized. The grounds for surfacing a video are opaque and ever-changing. Theories and anecdotes abound. Because of the immense scale of online platforms, video creators are in some cases dependent on them for their livelihood. Seemingly capricious changes to the algorithm can strike directly at one's wallet. In addition, YouTube (and Google) hosts the video as well as indexing its properties, so the SEO analogy has limits. Going forward, the problem of finding videos will see evolving solutions. Given that print had been in place for more than five hundred years and hyperlinks were only about ten years old at Google's founding, the dynamics of searching video will take time to be more robustly understood. As we noted, TikTok is driven by a vision to eliminate the need for search entirely.

We have had centuries of experience with text- and video-based gatekeepers. Many different species have evolved. Save for their function as rationers of scarcity, many of these gatekeepers have little in common, be they peer reviewers in an academic humanities journal, a small-town newspaper editor, Hollywood producers and directors, television networks' choices for interview subjects on Sunday morning shows, agents and editors that stand between fiction writers and the printed page, a PhD dissertation committee, or schedulers for slots on everything from *Ellen* to the *Tonight*

Show. Information industries have traditionally been capital-intensive, and access to that capital was not remotely democratic.

Compare those gatekeepers and many others to the platforms' algorithms. The new scarcity is attention, not production or distribution capacity. In contrast to printing press supplies, broadcast studio time, cable channel slots, shelf space at newsstands or libraries, or radio frequency allocations, Google and ByteDance appear to be able to scale video storage indefinitely. The uploading public does not seem to tire of creating or repurposing content for handoff to the enormous private clouds. As a result, the solution to scarcity—no longer rationing production or distribution but rationing attention—reflects a profound underlying shift in the economics of media creation after 2000.

A crucial difference between the algorithmic gatekeeping and its historical forerunners is its opacity. Google published an eight-step guide to YouTube brand building—for established brands—in 2015. For the many independent content producers, the guidance was much less concrete, extensive, and directive. Deep in YouTube's help documentation lie four bullets:

- Create descriptive and accurate titles and thumbnails
- Keep viewers watching with video techniques
- Organize and program your content
- Use reports to see what's working[35]

Each of these subheads has only a few sentences of elaboration, and in no case is there any sense of how the promotional algorithm treats long versus short videos, titles in all caps versus mixed case, or any of the other aspects of video production under creators' control. After reading the vague recommendations, the creator has no sense of "what happens if I don't?"

At TikTok, the advice is much more directly contextualized in algorithmic behavior. Vertical format video works best. Captions, hashtags, and music choices can all drive viewership. Give the video enough time to circulate and possibly catch on before trying something different. Here's what the help page said about watch time in late 2021: "Watch time factors into how a video gets recommended, so capturing viewers' attention early and maintaining it throughout makes for watchable, shareable content. Our recommendation system takes watch time as a signal that users are enjoying your content—keeping this in mind as you create will help you make videos that are deeply engaging from beginning to end and, as a result, positioned for strong performance."[36]

Regardless of how it is presented by the platforms, algorithmic promotion or indifference is also disembodied. The aforementioned human
gatekeepers might not have been public figures, but their structural roles
were known and visible in their subnetworks. In contrast, the tendency
to refer to algorithms as "black boxes" takes us beyond *Wizard of Oz* con-
ceptualization—there is no longer a human behind the curtain—and into
anthropomorphization. The algorithm now "wants" certain things and
"penalizes" others.

Radicalization?

An example of this disembodiment can be seen in the characterization of
YouTube's recommendation algorithm in regard to political radicalization. On one hand is a conception of viewers as undecided, with content of
increasingly higher "engagement" being fed to radicalize them. According to
authors of a critique of this position (which is largely propagated by media
summaries of more nuanced scholarship; no credible study has shown cau-
sation): "YouTube audiences are at risk of far-right radicalization and this
is because the YouTube algorithm that was designed to maximize the company's profits via increased audience time on the platform has learned to
show people far-right videos."[37]

In contrast, two Penn State political scientists begin by setting YouTube's
far-right political content in the context of cable television. Since 2017, viewership of extremist videos on YouTube has surpassed television hours as
people seek out the viewpoints. In this formulation the YouTubers are filling
an unmet market need. People with white supremacist and related views are
not being "infected" by YouTube nearly as much as it is providing viewpoints
that cable television cannot or will not, at least in the desired proportions.
The recommendation algorithm might potentially radicalize some viewers,
certainly, but the larger population has already committed to the views: "We
argue instead that YouTube has affordances that make content creation easy
for fringe political actors who tap into an existing base of disaffected individuals alienated from the mainstream, encouraging parasocial relationships
that serve as a stand-ins for real sociality."[38] Note the return of the unhealthy
identification we saw in chapter 5. The extremists, it appears, seek emotional
rewards as much as political affiliation.

Turning from algorithmic game theory and concerns about falsehoods
and political polarization, let us try to situate online video in a longer arc.
We will do this first by examining the role of nostalgia in the appeal of online
video, then we will turn to an assertion that online video has the potential

to change the world much like print did. As it turns out, the effects of print were more complex and far reaching than one might assume, but there are clear lessons to be learned.

Nostalgia

Nostalgia—*nostos* (return home) plus *algia* (pain or longing) equals "home-sickness"—is making a strong run in scholarly circles in the past twenty years or so. What used to be a dismissive characterization of one unable or unwilling to embrace the present (and implicitly, modernity) is now the subject of cross-disciplinary consideration as a "sanctuary"[39] or "psychological resource."[40] Other scholars accurately connect nostalgia to commodification and consumption.[41] One core function of online video is to spur nostalgia, whether with old television commercials, online recordings, or movie and television clips. Asserting this is simple, but let's spend some time explaining how it works and why it matters.

Surprise

Every generation, for millennia it appears, has worried that its cultural touchstones will be lost to history—how else do we explain the persistence of time capsules in the cornerstones of major buildings?[42] When we look at the great political biographies of the past few decades—Caro's Johnson, Blake's Disraeli, Goodwin's Lincoln—and consider the state of email versus diary-keeping, telephones versus letter-writing, and the surge in popularity of the paper shredder in the 1980s, we wonder what future historians will have as evidence for their documentaries of our times. How will the future remember our evanescent, disposable present?

After 2005, however, it was as though the planet's attics were unlocked and digitized. Home movies, videocassettes of television programs, and even networks' videotape archives were uploaded and shared. Exquisite 1959 footage of Miles Davis playing live in black and white. Mary Lou Retton's 1984 Olympic gold medal performance in gymnastics. Euell Gibbons's much-parodied Grape Nuts commercial. *Sesame Street*'s spin on the Old Spice "the man your man could smell like" ad campaign. *SNL* bits from whenever you thought it was funniest.[43] Millions of tidbits and opuses, ephemera and mountaintop moments, all suddenly (in historical time scales) made available, often decades after we thought we'd never see them again, much less free, on demand, on a smartphone.

Ambiguity and Contradiction

The "who" of nostalgia is obviously complex. In part, it straightforwardly involves one's personal recollections. Everyone's history is unique, but no one travels life alone, so the power of YouTube's nostalgic triggers combines individual memory with a variety of collective memories and feelings (hence the power of those comments we noted in chapter 5). "I was in high school/ the military/working in a restaurant when this song/program/event was popular," the thread might begin. The implicit "Where were you?" prompts a response.

A second ambiguity is nostalgia's subject. As Svetlana Boym (an insightful professor, filmmaker, playwright, and artist) argued, it involves more the longing for a past *time*—to which one cannot return—compared merely to a sense of *place*. Because past time is past and we cannot live backward, nostalgia involves both a sense of loss and a mythologization of what happened. Golden ages are a key aspect of nostalgia.[44]

Third, our emotions are decidedly mixed. Going back to a place and time, prompted by memories of a particular cultural touchstone that we may have forgotten, is often both personally and collectively bittersweet. As the sociologist Fred Davis noted, "in English at least, there exists no antonym for [nostalgia], no word to describe feelings of rejection or revulsion toward one's past or some segment thereof."[45] Never mind that the past we mourn may never have existed in the first place. Nostalgia—an emotional state—is neither memory nor reminiscence.

The Past as a Resource for the Present

Nostalgia seems to be prompted by current stress. Logically, if one were living *in* a golden age, the past would have little appeal. Roger Aden, a professor of communications, set this insight in the context of his study of US attitudes toward baseball: "Nostalgic communication provides individuals with a means of symbolically escaping cultural conditions that they find depressing and/or disorientating. Using communication to move through time allows individuals to situate themselves in a sanctuary of meaning, a place where they feel safe from oppressive cultural conditions." Not only is nostalgia an escape, it can also signal a desire for empowerment: "nostalgia indicates individuals' desire to regain some control over their lives in an uncertain time."[46]

Nostalgia is a luxury in most countries. My colleague the Syracuse postdoctoral scholar Margaret Jack traced the use of social media by

Cambodians in a much more urgent mission. After the destruction of so many cultural artifacts in the political upheaval that followed US bombing of the country during the Vietnam War, Facebook and other platforms serve as a type of recovered cultural memory. Movies from 1969 and earlier, old postcards, and other records of a nation had been systematically sought out and destroyed in the fashion of other "cultural revolutions" in China and the Middle East. The remaining artifacts that were discovered could be digitally restored (sometimes at national libraries in other countries), and shared. Cambodians who were born after the Khmer Rouge left power can share a mixture of pride, sadness, and resourcefulness. Fragmentary scenes of a movie stopped in midproduction might be shown at a public gathering, for example, then live actors (in rare cases including the original stars) reenact missing scenes on stage.[47] The point here is that online video is a new kind of cultural repository for new kinds of artifacts, sometimes put to new and important uses.

How does nostalgia serve as this sanctuary and as a psychological resource? Fred Davis posits it does so by reinforcing our continuity of identity. Nostalgia cultivates "appreciative stances toward our former selves" which serve as benchmarks. It "locates in memory an earlier version of self with which to measure . . . some current condition of the self."[48] The fact that research indicates nostalgia is a response to "distressing or psychologically threatening experiences"[49] would suggest that this notion of continuity, or rootedness, makes sense.

YouTube and Nostalgia

Everybody experiences nostalgia, a great many people visit YouTube, and there are many indications that old content is heavily watched. Movies, cars, and television clips can all summon up nostalgic feelings, but many researchers point to music as having a particularly powerful triggering capability. Two factors stand out. First, in a study using a sample of subjects from age sixteen to age eighty-six, an overwhelming number gravitated to songs from their teenage years. This is remarkable considering the wide range of ages involved. Second, music with an autobiographical anchor continued to resonate emotionally for decades afterward. This has been experimentally validated in multiple settings.[50] The fact that YouTube hosts millennia worth of video, much of it a nostalgic trigger for someone (video gameplay, Soul Train dance moves, modem sounds, television commercials, Vines, etc.), means that it is unlikely that a YouTube visitor does not have a nostalgic moment now and then, whether intentionally or not.

Why does this matter? Let me posit three reasons. First, the lack of a gatekeeper allows millions of people to crowdsource collective memory. As opposed to Turner Classic Movies or Nick at Nite (US cable television channels devoted to retro content), YouTube lacks schedules, programming, and ratings pressure. Second, nobody makes judgments about what is "important" or "viable." If a random person uploads a random commercial or clip, it's likely that nobody will watch it—but one never knows. This surplus-based model of cultural inventory is something new, unlike any museum or retro channel ever before launched. Finally, YouTube's nostalgic content illustrates how far technology's impacts can ripple outward. The eclectic nature of that content is a distant side effect of videocassette technology launched forty years ago, not to mention LP record technology launched seventy years ago. Numerous videos consist of footage of a stylus tracking phonograph grooves, accompanying audio of a song that never made it to CD or streaming. Consider that mobile broadband, machine learning, mass storage on an unprecedented scale, and a powerful handheld device might be bringing that music to a listener's ear, and we have many strata of technological history to sort through as we assess that moment of recollection, reflection, and reliving.

Print

Only five years after YouTube launched in 2005, Chris Anderson of TED gave a remarkably insightful talk on—and about—his own online video platform. He pointed first to the primacy of print for more than five hundred years given its capability to move words, still pictures, and ideas to mass audiences. The scale of print eventually overwhelmed face-to-face communication. In a blink of historical time, he argued, that primacy was challenged by online video. As a medium, it conveys vocal inflection, body languages, and facial features, the cues we humans spent millennia learning to discern in order to survive. Even more importantly, online video conveys these nuances at often zero cost to massive audiences, nearly instantaneously but asynchronously.

Anderson spotted this transition a mere five years after YouTube launched—a historical blip relative to the long domination of print in the spread of knowledge. It's easy to talk about the power of print in cultural transformation as a hand-wave, but if in fact online video could matter much like print did, we owe it to ourselves to dig more deeply. What exactly did print change, and what do those changes suggest about what might be in store as online video transforms life in the twenty-first century?

The University of Michigan historian Elizabeth Eisenstein published a two-volume study of *The Printing Press as an Agent of Change* in 1979[51] (before embarking on a distinguished career as a masters-level tennis champion known as "the Assassin"[52]). The scope of the book is truly eye-opening, and hints at the vast number of institutions and practices that online video could change in the coming decades. We have already analyzed Khan Academy and other educational ventures and how streaming music has changed the recording and radio industries worldwide. How else can the history of print inform our understanding of online video?

First, "print" was not just related to the printing press. Rather, it took advances in metallurgy, chemistry, textiles and paper (materials science, as it were), and precision manufacturing to create and run the devices. Further, entrepreneurs had to invest in the infrastructure. A scribe was unlikely to buy a press, so publishers (a new job category) were both printers and speculators in public taste. Booksellers, librarians, censors, and other occupations followed. Technological and organizational innovations were both required.[53] We see parallels in the "mechanics" of online video from chapter 2. Bandwidth; compression; video capture and editing capabilities; browser- and app-based players; machine indexing, learning, and search; and mass storage all had to evolve for the volume of uploads and downloads to become practical. Furthermore, new job categories such as "influencer" and "vlogger" are emerging within online video economies. Both media spurred new entrepreneurial niches.

Second, the changes wrought by printing, paper/ink, and bookselling business models (to name a few) took decades and even centuries to emerge. The history of the automobile is instructive here. Look at suburbs, drive-through fast-food chains, or the near-death of US train service. None of these was easily projected from Daimler, Ford, or Sloan's innovations: the lightweight internal combustion engine, mass production, and the "ladder" of brands under the General Motors umbrella, respectively. Thinking of print more broadly than books, we can see how far-ranging its impact became:

- Paper money
- Legislative and judicial proceedings
- Calendars
- Maps
- Playing cards
- Dictionaries
- Anatomical and scientific illustrations

- Architectural prints
- Sewing patterns[54]

Tourism grew with maps, casinos with cards, medical care with anatomical guides, and so on. Apart from dictionaries, grammar guides went from idiosyncratic one-off volumes to standardized texts. It is important to see that the rise of literacy came both from more readers reading and from more writers writing in recognizable ways. From our vantage point, only fifteen years into the transition from print to online video, what besides the obvious—television clips, education, and how-to—will be transformed? What kinds of literacy (for both creators and viewers) will emerge by necessity? Who will vet specialized content? Tellingly, a study of thirty-seven reviews of medical videos by physicians and other experts revealed no set of metrics by which they could be evaluated.[55]

Eisenstein goes farther still, arguing that print created a new "public." That is, groups are constituted by what they hear (in oral cultures) versus what they read (in literate ones). Legislators spoke differently to each other after the development of printed transcripts. Sermons were reprinted and often redelivered, amplifying the original message. Significantly, listening typically occurred in groups whereas reading was solitary. The reading public took form one perusal at a time, asynchronously.[56] Libel laws had to emerge to protect individuals from the reputational damage of which print was newly capable. Online video is a new species of moving image, but it does break the synchronous nature of movie or television viewing, and this time-shifted landscape is one aspect online video and streaming video (e.g., TikTok, Netflix) share, however else they differ.

Finally, for our purposes, Eisenstein argues persuasively that literacy enhances the everyday world. Maps make new terrain navigable. Explanations make technical achievements easier to appreciate or replicate. Biographies enhance the enjoyment of a work of art. Histories set events in context. Birdwatching, to take but one example, is essentially impossible before one can collect research guides, maps, rosters of other birdwatchers, and so on. "All the creative arts," she asserts, "were, indeed, transformed by typography in ways that need to be taken into account."[57] Johann Sebastian Bach's relation to printed copies of his works remains historically contentious. The composer had to successfully notate the compositions, contract with printers, and ensure that composer and typographer were on the same page, literally. Printed scores constitute an important part of Bach's legacy. Keyboard suites are a poor candidate for either hand scribing or oral transmission.

Implications

It's a long way from Bach to Bieber, but they are in fact kin. Art, entertainment, and the media of their creation and distribution will always coevolve. Once we see online video, most conveniently but not exclusively via its YouTube and TikTok exemplars, as something decisively new and different, we can begin to understand what it might become and, more important, what might emerge as implications. It relies on video content, but few lessons of broadcast television seem to apply. It is built on crowd labor that shows the best, the crassest, and the most deplorable aspects of human existence. It can explain both physical techniques and abstract concepts better than print, and connects humans with vocal, body language, and facial cues that have never been "published" in a free, nearly global many-to-many format. It serves as a powerful repository for nostalgic triggers like television and movie clips, music, speeches, home movies, ambient sounds, all at a scale never before possible. In the end, while we recognize online video—"It's sort of like TV, but sort of like the web, and four companies own huge portions of it"—it is decisively new and unfathomably large. The possibilities for both good and, to use Google's word, "evil" are enormous, so I believe it is of pressing importance to understand and develop new literacies for navigating this new tool.

What do Eisenstein's insights into the broad impact of print tell us about what to expect from online video? First, "print" was much more involved than printing presses. Technology artifacts such as inks, type, and paper had to be present at the outset and coevolve with the technology, then business models and organizational and managerial innovations were both facilitated and required. Second, print was initially and primarily disruptive to existing institutions (the Catholic Church) and practices. Finally, the changes took decades or longer to percolate through social norms and institutions. The same tendency can be observed in the larger history of technology. The invention of the automobile led to innovations in roads and road building, in businesses premised on a supply of occupied automobiles (drive-through fast food at interstate highway interchanges), in consumer finance (the auto loan), and in urban geography (the prevalence of parking lots in younger cities such as Los Angeles compared to Vienna or Paris). These kinds of wide-ranging impacts do not emerge immediately.

The first place we should be watching is at the intersection of social norms and online content moderation. Because of the existential threat posed by copyright infringement litigation, YouTube got very good very fast at using machine learning to spot uploads of copyrighted material. Preventing child endangerment via online video is almost as urgent a priority, and the tools are getting better. In dozens of other areas, however, personal vendettas, misogyny, misinformation, and other forms of deception are rampant. How long can the big platforms maintain the hands-off stance that served their economic interests for the first fifteen years of their existence? Will we see the emergence of a climate-denial YouTube, a white supremacist YouTube,[58] parallel Palestinian and Israeli YouTubes, and an anti-vaccine YouTube? The historical alternative—elite gatekeepers at a few journals and newspapers controlling what counts as orthodoxy—appears no longer viable.

A second venue where long-term change will emerge is education. As the sudden shift to distance learning in 2020 proved, our bandwidth, cameras, and microphones are all almost good enough. But online pedagogy is a long way from adequate to the needs of multiple kinds of content, multiple kinds of learners, multiple kinds of home situations, and multiple educational objectives. Live sessions versus prerecorded materials, didactic versus interactive instruction, and pure-play versus multiple modalities ("hybrid") need to be sorted through. The educational institutions that for so long were built on assembly-line metaphors will be forced to examine higher-order questions. What is the cost of delivering instruction? What are the various outcomes of completing coursework: degrees, certifications, badges, intrinsic enjoyment? Who is allowed to (1) deliver instruction, (2) certify competence, and (3) charge for their services? What are the timelines of instruction versus viewing, of lecture versus homework, of "completion"? What are the times and places for hands-on versus video demonstrations versus virtual reality demos, for theory versus practice, for "finding oneself" versus being trained for one's first job, versus being trained to abstract, synthesize, and discover?

How we entertain ourselves and others is already in a period of upheaval that will almost certainly grow more chaotic before things settle out. Fame and stardom are already very different in the era of YouTube, Instagram, and TikTok compared to the Hollywood period epitomized by first movies then television. The timelines of YouTube versus NBC versus Netflix versus Columbia Pictures are illustrative. A YouTuber can react to a major event in minutes whereas a movie studio operates years ahead of the present day. Gatekeeping, both in what is taken down and what is algorithmically elevated, has changed and will change further. Will something like the Motion Picture Association's voluntary movie ratings keep online video clear of dismemberment, disinformation, or doxing? Will some variant of "freedom of the press" treat online video more like a newspaper and less like a television channel?

What will happen to the behavioral experiments the major platforms perform on their users? Now that the platforms have become so good at understanding and shaping behavior, is advertising the ultimate objective? The 2016 US election taught the world that people can be easily gamed for political gain, so where will the next frontier emerge? What guardrails will be erected to prevent perceived abuses?

Algorithmic *transparency* seems to be an impossibility from a practical standpoint. Given how few people can read and understand C++ or PHP, does showing the code behind the recommendation help matters? That said, algorithmic *accountability* will need to improve, and an early move was made by the Chinese government in 2021. As part of wide-ranging reforms aimed at the country's consumer Internet companies, new rules were posted for public review before presumably being implemented. The document establishes the need for their version of what the television networks called "standards and practices," one situated in China's sociopolitical milieu using phrases that most likely do not translate literally to English. "Algorithm recommendation service providers shall adhere to the mainstream value orientation, optimize the algorithm recommendation service mechanism, actively disseminate positive energy. . . . [These providers] shall not use algorithm recommendation service . . . [to disrupt] economic and social order." Article 8 of the document as it stood in 2021 seemingly prohibits the dopamine-pump model that currently powers Facebook and TikTok: "Algorithm recommendation service providers shall regularly review, evaluate and verify the algorithm mechanism model, data and application results, etc., and shall not set up algorithm models that induce users to indulge or consume in high amounts that violate public order and good customs." Article 14 appears to call for algorithmic transparency. "The provider of algorithm recommendation service shall inform the user of the situation of providing algorithm recommendation service in a significant way, and publicize the basic principle, purpose intention and operation mechanism of algorithm recommendation service in an appropriate way."[59]

However it is established, some variety of consumer protection will be applied to the platforms, and as with so many instances of regulation over technically complex phenomena, the unexpected side effects may well be the most important outcome. An example of this dynamic unfolded in 2021. Apple announced that it would screen users' uploads to cloud storage for images that matched existing images of child pornography. Another announcement stated that teens would be warned against sending explicit images via Apple Messages. The public reaction sent the team back to revise the plan, in part because the various aspects of the plan were confusing.[60]

For our purposes, that fact that Apple sought to perform content moderation on the client rather than in the cloud raises an interesting question. Might users be able to subscribe to fact-checkers and other curation tools to live on their devices? For the platforms to screen every upload and potentially every download for factuality, religious heresy (in some countries), emotional triggers of whatever sort, and other facets of personal taste and public welfare has proven to be impossible. Rethinking the architecture of content moderation could be viable in some situations.

What will we see as technical innovation in relation to online video? Deep fakes are getting very good very fast, and the tools of their creation outrun the tools of detection. Even more concerning, the platform owners seem reluctant to take down any content short of the most egregious violations. Will fact-checking, authentication, and other vetting fall to the user rather than the hosting platform? Will third-party private sector fact-checkers emerge on the *Consumer Reports* or Underwriters Laboratories model? A second area of innovation might be in the realm of virtual and augmented reality. Having user-uploaded tourism guides to London or Hong Kong that blend video with various forms of data overlay could be both popular and damaging to the local services that currently perform these functions.

The virtual and augmented reality issue raises the larger question of how people will interact with online video. Just as printing brought game boards and playing cards, what will happen to self-entertainment? Will learning a new language become a three-week process using some turbocharged version of Duolingo or Berlitz? That is, will the long-foretold "gamification" of everything be delivered less through a browser and more via YouTube or some future platform?

We already have cameras almost everywhere there are people. What is the next phase of information capture? What sensors will be combined with video capture—location data, social data, atmospheric or climate data—to enhance our enjoyment or understanding of the phenomenon? Most importantly, who do and who will the platforms answer to? What is and what should be the future of regulatory limits, of privacy, of the right to be forgotten by either the algorithms or the Internet more widely defined? How do people as persons, as consumers, as citizens relate to these platforms? What are the rights of the many viewers, of national governments, of the platforms, and of the algorithms themselves?[61] Along with rights, we must consider the responsibilities of each of these entities, but today, we lack even the language to begin to discuss this issue, let alone codify it.

Conclusion

As the entire planet responded to a virus, online video was shown under scrutiny to do what it always does: entertain and disgust, instruct and deceive, connect and divide. A long-standing laissez-faire approach to post-factual commentary was tested as false information literally got people killed. Instead, Google assertively shifted to promoting government dogma regarding masking, handwashing, staying home, and the like. Authoritative sources were given prime placement and misinformation was taken down more aggressively than in normal times. Videos linking 5G cellular service to the virus are just one example of misinformation. The externalities of social distancing—less air pollution, fewer traffic deaths, more domestic violence, ritual appreciation for medical front-liners, empty shelves for both toilet paper and bread flour—extended to online video as well. According to Alexa Internet, Google and YouTube ranked one and two in global web traffic for ninety days ending in April 2020. Information, explanation, and entertainment appear to have aced out social networking and FOMO in a crisis.

In those stressful times, creative YouTube uploaders attracted audiences with timely content. How to cut your hair, exercise inside, plant a garden, entertain your child, cook creatively, maintain mental health, reenact classic movie scenes, bake bread, fix the dishwasher (a staple well before the pandemic), remember what nature looks like. Late-night comedians and YouTubers stood on equal footing in regard to production value. Longtime *The Office* star John Krasinski launched a basic but uplifting show simply called *Some Good News* (*SGN*). It grew to upward of 5 million views a week before getting bought by CBS. YouTube highlighted educational resources for the millions of parents thrust into the world of home-classroom instruction.

Meanwhile, global teens led a charge to a new medium, one built from the ground up to be addictively entertaining, bite-sized rather than weighty, massively self-referential, and demographically narrow. The contrast between YouTube's efforts to put serious CDC (Centers for Disease Control) content high in viewers' recommendations and TikTok's most popular themes for 2020 tells us much about the moment. TikTok's rapid growth during the lockdown was fueled not with public health messaging or tips for parents learning to navigate Zoom elementary school. Instead, pranks, lip-syncs, dancing animals, and dancing people proved to be incredibly popular. Blowing off steam, trying to remain connected to friends you can't see, finding some way to laugh, and maintaining an identity distinct from the parents with whom you're in quarantine were pressing needs for these young adults, and TikTok was the perfect tool for the job.

How long these policy and audience shifts will persist remains to be seen. In 2025, how will vaccination-related material be treated relative to 2019 norms? How far will future conspiracy theories be allowed to speculate? How long will public appetite for authoritative sources (in this case, the World Health Organization, Dr. Anthony Fauci, and the CDC) continue to dominate fringe messages after the crisis eases? As the future of online video plays out, it appears that the pandemic will stand as a moment of demarcation, a time when both fact-checking was taken seriously and user-fueled creative mayhem hooked a billion people across the globe.

TikTok Emerges

Among the under-thirty demographic, TikTok was a new enthusiasm perfectly suited to the pandemic lockdown. The fifteen-second commitment was addicting, to the point that watch times soon approached those of streaming services like Netflix. The service's initial focal points—lip-syncs and dancing alone for the camera—were perfect fits for people suddenly stuck inside their apartments. Having tuned its recommendation algorithms first in newsfeeds then in dance-along videos for teens in the Music.ly years, ByteDance was perfectly poised for the surge of interest.

TikTok's parent company ByteDance paralleled Baidu, Alibaba, and Tencent as a successful Chinese Internet company, but of the four, it was the only one to achieve popularity among non-Chinese-speakers outside of China (WeChat, part of Tencent, is heavily used outside of China, often by Chinese family members connecting with their home country). As with Ant Group and Didi, ByteDance seemed to be growing in Western fashion, with substantial personal wealth awaiting the founders. This all changed in 2020–21 as the Chinese government suddenly took a much more activist position toward its consumer Internet companies.

Unlike YouTube, TikTok's traction with consumers could support a variety of adjacent launches. According to the tech analyst Turner Novak, ByteDance could leverage the TikTok success in short video into services in the following areas: longer video, music streaming, gaming, consumer finance, education (potentially including tutoring), messaging, enterprise software (a tool like Slack, potentially aimed at the Chinese home market), cloud hosting, and mobile handsets.[1]

ByteDance bears watching for several reasons. First, it grew to global prominence rapidly and without help from the Chinese state. Second, like drone maker DJI, this success allowed the company access to Western markets and, in some cases, capital. Both factors created a sense of independence from the state, at least for a time. Now that China is redefining its tech policy to spur development of sectors that matter more on the global stage—it's hard to win a war without a microprocessor industry no matter how viral your apps—the fate of consumer Internet companies is less clear. The contradictions of multi-billion-dollar fortunes in a communist society may also have become too visible to allow. Either way, the skills ByteDance and its peers require are potentially being redeployed to the tasks of military intelligence, machine learning for less frivolous purposes, and hardware development.[2]

Both YouTube and Facebook launched copycat services, Shorts (beta in 2020, full rollout in 2021) and Instagram Reels (2020), respectively. Neither seems to have slowed TikTok so far, but in the long term, Shorts may have a viable place in the ecosystem. For one thing, TikTok's reliance on machine-learning-driven "push" means that looking for something can be difficult: TikTok is extremely well tuned as a stream, not an archive. As teens age and they want to experience nostalgia, how will TikTok serve them? Second, YouTube pays better, most visibly with the announcement of a $100 million creator's fund in 2021. Third, TikTok's legal standing is still in question as of press time, in both China and the United States, as is its organizational ability to cope with hypergrowth under a unique set of regulatory constraints.

Further, as the pandemic passes, will people accustomed to making and watching dance videos amid quarantine's constraints stay with the service? Will TikTok flare out the way Words with Friends, DrawSomething, and other brief Internet sensations peaked but could not sustain their popularity? Amid so much other uncertainty after 2020–21, the future of online video is yet another development on which we can only wait and see.

YouTube and COVID-19

The COVID-19 pandemic put YouTube into the bright lights of public opinion for a number of reasons and drove a number of changes at the service. What had been a generally laissez-faire approach to "alternative" scientific theories changed as the consequences of misinformation—people drinking bleach, mass panic, or delegitimization of authority—grew in their impact. At press time, the long-term impact of these changes could not yet be fully judged, but it is clear that COVID-19 marked an inflection point in the history of online video.

Early in the pandemic, YouTube highlighted videos from authoritative sources such as the CDC and World Health Organization (WHO). In addition, takedown policies also evolved rapidly in the early months of the pandemic. On March 21, 2020, researchers at the University of Ottawa found that 27 percent of sampled videos that came up in searches for "Coronavirus" and "COVID-19" contained nonfactual information.[3] Google was clearly seeing the same tendency, so in that same month, the lockdown was classified as a "sensitive event" much like a natural disaster or mass shooting. As a result, content creators were not allowed to monetize COVID-themed videos. The policy was designed to protect audiences in a state of shock or confusion from being served clickbait capitalizing on their state. Soon after, YouTube CEO Susan Wojcicki reversed the ban, even as the service struggled to marginalize unofficial and often potentially harmful content. Given that the content moderation tools were looking for child endangerment, copyrighted material, and terrorist videos, finding conspiracy theories, quack cures, and similar material was difficult.

Making the task more difficult was previous YouTube policy. In the pursuit of a "moon shot" billion-hours-per-day aggregate watch time, Google's algorithmic engineers leaned away from clickbait (racy or deceiving thumbnails for example) and toward long watch times. It turns out that conspiracy theorists who tell long, complex stories can hold their audience, given the paucity of flat-earth, Pizzagate, and similarly bizarre theories in traditional broadcast media.[4] As a result of those past decisions, in the early months of COVID-19, YouTube was trying to undo years of policy and practice that had fueled one of the service's key growth metrics.[5]

Spurred in part by a flood of disinformation after the 2017 Las Vegas concert shooting, YouTube settled on a policy of three Rs: *remove* content that clearly violated terms of use, such as Infowars' claims denying the Sandy Hook school shooting; *raise up* authoritative sources; and *reduce* (downrank) material that flirted with the terms of use or otherwise promoted misinformation. It turned out that the third R was the most difficult. Training data for misinformation is extremely subtle and highly contextual. Intolerance and satire can be worded almost identically; much depends on tone of voice and other cues. Significantly, misinformation videos often can't be visually detected when the voiceover narration contains the problematic material, rather than the images, which often consist of stock photos.[6]

In addition, takedowns became more automated during the pandemic. As offices were closed and moderators had to work from home, algorithmic content policing was emphasized, with the acknowledgment that mistakes would be made. On March 16, the YouTube official blog stated that given the distributed workforce and safety issues, automated content takedowns would be emphasized. Buried in the announcement was this sentence: "In some cases, unreviewed content may not be available via search, on the homepage, or in recommendations."[7] In other words, absent official approval, some material that was not taken down was effectively invisible.

As the "Plandemic" video illustrated, conspiracy theorists coevolve with social media algorithms. The speaker established credibility by having published a book. Much like QAnon, she intermixed a range of theories that lead a viewer from gray area to falsehoods via a "slippery slope" argument. Here, assertions about reopening closed businesses (an extremely problematic matter for analysts and policymakers of any orientation) segued to outright fabrications about mask-wearing "triggering" the virus. Most importantly, cross-platform traffic of the sort we discussed in chapter 7 proved decisive in the absence of YouTube's previously gamed recommendations. Once conspiracy videos stopped getting promoted by the algorithms, the role of Facebook, Twitter, Reddit, and traditional social networks connected via text ("Watch this before it gets taken down" was how I was told about Plandemic) grows more important.[8] As early as 2019, Rebecca Lewis at Stanford was showing how "micro-celebrities" were adopting this outside-the-norms rhetoric as a deliberate positioning move for a certain kind of audience.[9]

As for the "raise up" prong of the anti-misinformation initiative, YouTube quickly began creating its own authoritative content. It focused on everything from mental health during lockdown to teaching one's school-aged children

Fig. 5 YouTube promoted its own content in an effort to steer viewership away from conspiracy theories and medical quackery during the 2020 global pandemic.

to public health updates. YouTube Originals addressed the following (see fig. 5): personal finance, including information about and recommendations regarding stimulus checks; personal fitness, including in-home dance classes; positive images of compliance with public health directives; story hours; celebrity virtual schoolteachers; and global celebrations of creativity and diversity amidst quarantines in many countries.[10]

Shortly after the initial North American spread of COVID-19 in March 2020, a round of police violence directed at US Black people spurred a heated national dialogue on matters of race. YouTube quickly adopted similar tactics very similar to what was done with coronavirus-related conspiracy theories. Once again, the service raised up authoritative sources, reduced traffic to fringe groups inside the content guardrails, and removed offensive videos as quickly and efficiently (including stopping reposts by other channels) as possible. YouTube Originals quickly began to produce its own content on the presumably "correct" side of a complex and heated debate. Banners began appearing (see fig. 6) and YouTube-branded content was prominently featured (see fig. 7).

Note that these editorial decisions were most decidedly not bot driven. Instead, content moderation by humans was made a priority in the campaign against dis- and misinformation. Medical doctors were brought in to vet health-related content, which meant changing advice as knowledge accumulated. For example, early in the pandemic when N-95 masks were scarce and needed by New York critical care and other hospital personnel, public masking was discouraged. Relatively soon thereafter, masking became highly politicized as red-state governors lifted quarantines and lockdowns. Some leaders insisted that the coronavirus was as harmless to the general population as the seasonal flu. In this phase of the disease, YouTube programmers consciously worked to use authoritative faces to explain the evolution of guidance in a fluid situation.

Fig. 6 YouTube promoted preferred content during the national Black Lives Matter debate in 2020.

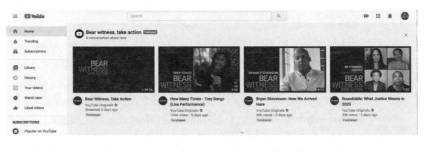

Fig. 7 YouTube created its own authoritative content during the Black Lives Matter debate in 2020.

These changes had implications for content creators on many social media platforms. As anyone running a channel has experienced, and about which many have written, being discovered by the promotion/recommendation algorithm can be just as random as being forgotten by it. This is not only an issue for conspiracy content. In the economic uncertainty of COVID-19, YouTube creators in many genres had to tweak their economic models. No longer content to rely on the capriciousness of ad revenue, creators diversified their revenue streams to include crowdfunding (often through Patreon, which has fewer experiences with content removal), merchandise such as hats and T-shirts, and subscriptions. In April 2020, 80,000 YouTube channels earned money from non-ad sources, up 20 percent from March but still a tiny minority of the more than 31 million channels onthe platform.[11]

This development highlights the importance of understanding platforms within the larger ecosystem. More people are on Facebook than Twitter, for example, but millions are on both. As the coronavirus drove traffic to social media even as the economic recession put a major dent in ad spending (particularly in the travel and entertainment sectors where many "influencers" had staked a claim), rethinking monetization became a survival strategy. YouTubers who rely on copyrighted content for their reaction videos, for example, saw videos from major stars such as Queen, Led Zeppelin, and Billy Joel not only

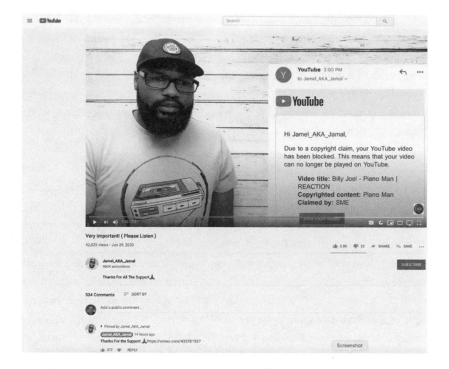

Fig. 8 YouTuber Jamel_AKA_Jamal tells his viewers that a Billy Joel reaction video has been taken down by YouTube, but the pinned comment announces it is available on Vimeo.

demonetized (in which the ad revenue flowed to the music copyright-holder rather than the video creator) but taken down completely (see fig. 8).

YouTube itself appears to support this move away from ad royalties as the sole economic stream, particularly in a recession. In 2017 the service followed Twitch's practice and introduced SuperChat, a feature in which viewers of a live chat can make a financial donation in return for having their comment highlighted in the feed. (Notably, the feature does not work on Apple's iOS YouTube app. This is presumably the case because Apple would charge a commission on the in-app purchase and Google conveniently does no such thing on its Android platform.) In addition, members of a creator's channel can pay up to $99 USD a year for insider benefits, including early access to new content drops, badges, stickers, and other identifying materials.

Beyond Human Scale to Relying on Algorithms

Making sense of online video is not fully possible. As with robotics, we have entered a domain of technology so broad, deep, and different that human attempts to comprehend it encounter cognitive limits. With robotics, one key issue is anthropomorphism: will a robot "take" my job? The implicit metaphor of artificial intelligence is of an electromechanical brain. Is it smarter than a mouse, a five-year-old, Stephen Hawking, me? Online video is hard to comprehend for different reasons. There are no ready metaphors. The platforms are building, variously, economies, multiple mediums, storehouses of memories, instruction manuals, classrooms, communities, and much else besides.

Online video is, finally, different from anything humanity has seen before. Let us examine this issue in more depth. The World Wide Web, while indexed by Google, is a network of independent content servers and thus differs significantly from YouTube or TikTok in its governance and economic model. The web's documents are indexed, making search highly but not exclusively dependent on the *content* of the webpage being offered as a search result. In contrast, as we have seen, YouTube's content is privately held and not yet publicly indexed. Search results are largely (but again not exclusively) a function of monitored responses to yet another series of huge and unregulated behavioral experiments. In this regard, YouTube is of a piece with Amazon, Facebook, and Google, along with a vast online advertising industry.

That said, YouTube—the largest example of an online video repository/ ecosystem—is distinct from the behavioral experiments in its video component. Broadcast-like forays such as Red aside, YouTube is not really related to BBC, NBC, NTT, or others, at least in their traditional schedule-bound incarnations. It has more overlap with on-demand cable, with Hulu, Netflix, and Amazon Prime Video, but even here, the vast majority of content on offer comes from uploads rather than from spending on content production. It's easier to see YouTube taking viewership from ABC or Netflix than to imagine Google leadership worrying about the Disney Channel stealing viewers of cat videos, music, or dishwasher repair instructions. As Jean Burgess and Joshua Green noted in one of the first scholarly investigations of YouTube, media portrayals of YouTube in its early years focused on its disruptive character without coming to terms with what it was becoming. Nobody—the founders, Google, the Federal Communications Commission—knew the trajectory.[12] The power of mass uploaded video distribution wasn't fully appreciated in 2009; it's not clear it was in 2023 either. Finally, its human interconnections—readily represented as a different social graph quickly contrasted to Facebook, Twitter, or WeChat—make online video a different kind of social network as well. YouTube and TikTok are at once similar to and not much like the World Wide Web, television, Instagram, and Facebook.

Returning to our earlier assertion—that making sense of the massive online video platforms is pretty much impossible—we see both the areas of overlap with and the many points of departure from our previous frames of reference. By making the human communication of gesture, performance, vocal inflection, and demonstration scale to—and past—the reach of print, Google and then ByteDance redefined communications, altering television in the process. But by having to rely on algorithms more correlated to viewers' behavioral inputs than to the videos' content, Google and ByteDance have also redefined the technologies of observation—building latter-day panopticons—and manipulation.

Put differently, online video makes possible important new interactions, including the new public spaces we noted in the book's opening. By being built at extrahuman scale and having to rely on algorithmic technologies of exclusion and promotion, online video platforms also raise urgent questions about how and why we see what we see. Because of its scale of participation and the power of its behavioral manipulation, online video has grown in less than two decades to become a factor in geopolitics. In the end, how Google and ByteDance walk this tightrope of communications and manipulation, under the increasingly watchful eye of the state, will determine the legacy of this breakthrough in how people can interact.

This upheaval at the juncture of media, technology, politics, and economics parallels the rise of print, insofar as the book both helped overthrow the Catholic Church as the dominant political actor in the West and introduced entirely new economic sectors and winners. How will social media, including online video, alter political participation and governance? How will the Internet platform companies displace, absorb, or lose ground to incumbents in publishing, broadcasting, education, and entertainment? The process is clearly underway. Where will it settle?

Where to from Here?

Given the incredible variety of uses to which online video has been put and the wide demographic variation in its users, projecting its future is highly speculative. Nevertheless, here are ten extrapolations and guesses.

Some Content Moderation Will Move to the Client
Smartphones are now capable of considerable feats of microprocessor performance. The platforms' user bases, measured as they are in the billions, are getting too large for one-size-fits-all content moderation. A joke in one

context is heresy in another. Irony reads badly in a flat medium. There are situations where the two sides of a story both have merit, but the video platform must present one at a time. Governments will insist on domain-specific content rules. For these and other reasons, moving some tasks of content moderation to the handset makes sense. Just as one can download an ad-blocker, so too might fact-checkers, statistics-testers, and other functions become available as add-ons.

Fakes Will Generate Some Large-Scale Catastrophe, Prompting Serious Regulation

Whether in the realm of health, politics, sports, or entertainment, a deep fake will cross a line and affect some major event or population. The breakthroughs in generative AI in 2022 accelerate the timetable for this prediction.

Watermarking Is Historically Proven but Difficult to Implement

If you were to make a color photocopy of a hundred-dollar bill and try to pass it as legitimate in the United States, you'd have Secret Service agents at your doorstep in a short while. Every color copier embeds microscopic signatures of the particular device in every image they create, making supposedly anonymous illegal uses easy to track. The lack of such technology in 3D printing has people concerned about fraudulent parts being created, and the same logic could apply to video. If every camera phone embeds a watermark in its videos, the cost of spreading libel, falsehoods, or other objectionable content should become more easily assigned.

YouTube Will Continue to Serve as a Video Storehouse

Whether for 1970s television or Vines, YouTube is the repository of choice. TikToks are ending up there as well. We saw how Cambodians are using online video and other social media to repair and recover their culture after the fall of the Khmer Rouge, and this pattern will be repeated in other cultures, demographics, and even languages that are going extinct.

TikTok's Future Depends on the Chinese Government as Much as on Product Innovation or Technical Execution

As Turner Novak suggested above, ByteDance could apply its algorithmic expertise to many adjacent markets, any of which could be sizable. The lack of clarity regarding the status of consumer Internet companies, however, limits the company's options in reassuring regulators elsewhere, accessing capital, and keeping momentum with an easily distracted user base.

Online Video Will Further Revolutionize Education

Much as Khan Academy started with one uncle tutoring his nieces and nephews, the technical capabilities of online video will be mobilized to reshape another educational segment. I don't think it's an accident that the rate of tuition inflation in US universities has slowed dramatically in the past ten years at the same moment that online video reaches audiences in the billions. The implicit question—how much does it cost to offer a college degree?—is being confronted more openly every year. If I can watch the lectures for free, what does that $50,000–$100,000 a year actually buy? What separates a traditional institution that moves online from a MasterClass, a Teaching Company, a Coursera, a Lynda?

Parasocial Relationships Will Continue to Be a Key Aspect of Online Video

As we saw, the US fascination with so-called reality TV dates back fifty years. As barriers to entry drop, more experiments in what YouTube used to call "broadcasting yourself" will take hold. Whether it's on YouTube, Twitch, or TikTok, the illusion that you "know" an online celebrity is powerful and widespread.

Cross-Platform Experimentation Will Continue to Proliferate

TikTok star Charli D'Amelio has a television series on Hulu. Amazon and YouTube stream NFL games. YouTube is creating original shows that look a lot like television series. Celebrity chefs distill hours of cooking time into an eye-grabbing TikTok, then teach the process on YouTube. How will creators further mash up multiple platforms into distinctive multimodal electronic personalities?

Globalization Will Inform the Next Fifteen Years

If the early history of online video was defined by Silicon Valley technologies, investors, and social norms, TikTok's ascendancy has shown innovators in most countries a different path. Seeing ByteDance build "global-first" rather than export a US-centric model raises the possibility of other innovators employing different aesthetics, algorithms, business models, and value systems.

Real-Time Streaming Will Expand Beyond Twitch's Gaming Model

Although YouTube already facilitates live streams, the form of these events is very much one-to-many, a broadcast with a chat panel alongside (usually with a virtual tip jar, which is one of the reasons for hosting the event in the first place). Can multiple video streams be more artfully and compellingly mashed up, maybe not for recording? (Think of the Snapchat model of impermanent content.) Can audio improve to simulate, variously, a nightclub, a worship service, or a walk in the park with a distant friend or relative with video playing a new kind of role in the experience? Will virtual reality appliances play a part in this innovation?

Maybe none of these will happen. The history of music may hold a clue. Between 1955 and 1990 or so, artists tapped the possibilities of new technologies such as the electric guitar, multitrack recording, and electronic synthesizers to create new genres of music. After 1990, musical innovation has largely stagnated while distribution has moved through many different waves: terrestrial radio to satellite, compact discs to streaming (and a vinyl renaissance), royalties from radio play, or the sale of physical media to merchandise and touring revenues. Maybe the general outlines of online video are relatively firmly established such that the coming years will see a flowering of artistic and educational forms. To take only one example, is the song the logical unit of musical transmission in the TikTok era? Maybe it will be the beat, the hook, the drop, or the rhyme.

One can hope for such creative flowering. Me? I'm betting on more stunts, more misogyny, more slavish imitation, more behavioral manipulation. As they say on Reddit, prove me wrong.

Notes

Introduction

1. Sorvino, "Could Mr. Beast."
2. Chun, "Enduring Ephemeral." See also Weltevrede, Helmond, and Gerlitz, "Politics of Real-Time." I learned of this concept from Margaret Jack when she did a postdoctoral fellowship at Syracuse.
3. Palmer, "TikTok Diplomatic Crisis."
4. Rizzo, "Sunday Ticket."
5. On Brand, see Turner, *Counterculture*.
6. Berners-Lee et al., "World-Wide Web," 461. See also Bush, "As We May Think."
7. Katz, "Struggle in Cyberspace," 194.
8. Andersen, "How America Lost Its Mind." Emphases in original.
9. Andersen, "How America Lost Its Mind."
10. Gillespie, "Content Moderation."
11. Dean, "TikTok User Statistics."
12. I am indebted to Amanda Lotz's scholarship for this formulation. See Lotz, *Portals*, 2.

Chapter 1

1. A useful introduction to the notion of design debt is Knight, "Design Debt."
2. See Newport, "TikTok and the Fall of the Social Media Giants."
3. Van Kessel, Toor, and Smith, "Week in the Life."
4. Zuboff, *Surveillance Capitalism*, 8. Emphasis in original.

5. For example, see Narayanan et al., "Polarization, Partisanship and Junk News."
6. Bak-Coleman et al., "Stewardship of Global Collective Behavior."
7. Aguiar et al., "Facebook Shadow Profiles."
8. Mozur, Mac, and Che, "TikTok Browser."

Chapter 2

1. Leskin, "YouTube Is 15 Years Old."
2. O'Reilly, "Web 2.0."
3. For contemporaneous views of the death of GeoCities in the face on the platforms, see Mackinnon, "Death of GeoCities."
4. O'Reilly, "Web 2.0." Emphasis mine.
5. Ibid. Emphasis in original.
6. Ibid. Emphasis in original.
7. Ibid. Emphasis in original.
8. "A/B Testing Statistics—2023," Truelist, January 7, 2023, https://truelist.co/blog/ab-testing-statistics/.
9. Kohavi and Thomke, "Surprising Power of Online Experiments."
10. O'Reilly, "Web 2.0." Emphasis in original.
11. Manpreet Singh, "These Are the Programming Languages TikTok Uses," *Medium* (blog), April 25, 2021, https://preet theman.medium.com/these-are-the-program ming-languages-tiktok-uses-491bfb796ebe.
12. O'Reilly, "Web 2.0." Emphasis in original.

13. Ibid. Emphasis in original.

14. Ibid.

15. Salam Aslam, "TikTok by the Numbers," Omnicore Marketing Agency, last accessed March 13, 2022, https://www .omnicoreagency.com/tiktok-statistics.

16. Leskin, "TikTok Has 18 Million Users Who Are 14 or Younger."

17. Ramli and Banjo, "Kids Use TikTok Now."

18. Baker-White, "Leaked Audio from 80 Internal TikTok Meetings."

19. Schellewald, "On Getting Carried Away."

20. Pamela Bump, "TikTok Brands That Are Winning at Marketing in 2022," *Hubspot* (blog), July 15, 2022, https://blog .hubspot.com/marketing/brands-on-tiktok.

21. CB insights, "World's Most Valuable Unicorn."

22. Turner Novak, "The Rise of TikTok and Understanding Its Parent Company ByteDance," *Split* (blog), May 21, 2020, https://turner.substack.com/p/the-rise -of-tiktok-and-understanding.

23. Gillespie, *Custodians of the Internet*, 18.

24. Gillespie, "Politics of 'Platforms.'"

25. Andreesen quoted in ibid., 352.

26. Gillespie, "Politics of 'Platforms,'" 351.

27. Cherney, "YouTube Creators Were Paid $30 Billion."

28. Montfort and Bogost, *Racing the Beam*.

29. Van Alstyne, Parker, and Choudary, *Platform Revolution*; and Van Alstyne, Parker, and Choudary, "Pipelines, Platforms."

30. See Metcalfe, "Metcalfe's Law After 40 Years"; and Hendler and Golbeck, "Metcalfe's Law."

31. For a sampling of dissenting opinions and their rebuttal, see Briscoe, Odlyzko, and Tilly, "Metcalfe's Law Is Wrong"; and see Van Hove, "Metcalfe's Law."

32. Saloner, "Automated Teller Machines"; Katz and Shapiro, "Network Externalities"; Besen and Farrell, "Choosing How to Compete."

33. See Zuboff, *Surveillance Capitalism*, 64–65.

34. Berry, *Critical Theory*, introduction.

35. Cheney-Lippold, *We Are Data*, 158.

36. Costa, "Fox Sports."

37. Albert Calamug, "Delivering on Our US Data Governance," TikTok, June 17, 2022, https://newsroom.tiktok.com/en-us /delivering-on-our-us-data-governance.

38. Bärtl, "YouTube Channels, Uploads and Views."

39. Brynjolfsson and McAfee, *Second Machine Age*, chapter 5.

40. Horrigan, "Home Broadband 2008."

41. Rodriguez, "TikTok Insiders."

42. The classic explanation of this concept is found in Watts and Strogatz, "Collective Dynamics of 'Small-World' Networks."

43. Stempel, "Google, Viacom Settle YouTube Lawsuit."

44. "Video Identification," Google corporate video posted to YouTube, February 4, 2008, https://www.youtube.com /watch?v=xWizsV5Le7s.

45. See Amadeo, "Cheaper Bandwidth."

46. Romm, Dwoskin, and Timberg, "YouTube Under Federal Investigation."

47. Snyder, "AT&T, Disney, Epic Games Drop YouTube Ads."

48. Carroll, "Is TikTok a Chinese Cambridge Analytica."

49. Lorenz, Browning, and Frenkel, "TikTok Teens."

50. See Chan, "When AI Is the Product."

51. Barnhart, "TikTok Challenges."

52. Clark, "TikTok 'Blackout Challenge.'"

53. For example, see Kriegel et al., "TikTok, Tide Pods and Tiger King."

54. Botella, "TikTok Admits It Suppressed Videos."

55. Simpson and Semaan, "For You."

56. Wells, Jie, and Kubota, "TikTok's Videos Are Goofy."

Chapter 3

1. Gillespie *Custodians*, 13. Emphasis in original.

2. Ibid., 30.

3. Ibid., 34.

4. See Marantz, "Why Facebook Can't Fix itself"; and Knowledge at Wharton Staff,

"How Can Social Media Firms Tackle Hate Speech?"

5. Solon and Levin, "Google's Search Algorithm Spreads False Information."

6. West, "Censored, Suspended, Shadowbanned." See also Vaccaro, Sandvig, and Karahalios, "Facebook Does What It Wants."

7. Harvey quoted in Gillespie, *Custodians*, 74. See also Hailey Reissman, "How to Keep 240 Million Twitter Users Safe: Del Harvey at TED2014," *TED* (blog), March 19, 2014, https://blog.ted.com/how-to-keep-240 -million-twitter-users-safe-del-harvey -at-ted2014/.

8. Gillespie, *Custodians*, 5. See also Roberts, *Behind the Screen*, 38.

9. Roberts, *Behind the Screen*, 39.

10. Sartariano and Isaac, "Silent Partner."

11. Newton, "Terror Queue."

12. Ibid.

13. As of 2022, there is no indication of a settlement in the Microsoft case. Facebook agreed in 2020 to pay current and former content moderators $52 million and to provide jobsite counseling services. Newton, "Facebook Will Pay $52 Million."

14. Newton, "Terror Queue."

15. Roberts, *Behind the Screen*, 178.

16. See Pilipets and Paasonen, "Nipples, Memes, and Algorithmic Failure."

17. Gehl, Moyer-Horner, and Yeo, "Training Computers to See Pornography."

18. Rika, "Content Moderation: B*obs, or No B*obs?," *Zoning Out* (blog), July 26, 2022, https://zoningout.substack.com/p /content-moderation-at-tiktok-bobs.

19. Ibid.

20. For a closer look at the Christchurch episode from a content moderation perspective, see Gorwa, Binns, and Katzenbach, "Algorithmic Content Moderation."

21. "Facebook Teams Up with Police to Stop Streaming of Terrorist Attacks," *Guardian*, September 17, 2019, https://www .theguardian.com/technology/2019/sep/17 /facebook-teams-up-with-police-to-stop-live -streaming-of-terror-attacks.

22. Cox, "Internal Google Email."

23. Hamilton, "YouTube's Human Moderators."

24. "YouTube Investigates 'Disturbing' Autofill Results," *BBC*,

November 27, 2017, https://www.bbc.com /news/technology-42137406.

25. Keller and Dance, "Child Abusers Run Rampant."

26. "Expanding Our Work Against Abuse of Our Platform," YouTube Official Blog, December 4, 2017, https://youtube .googleblog.com/2017/12/expanding-our -work-against-abuse-of-our.html.

27. Chotiner, "Underworld of Content Moderation."

28. Pierson, "YouTube's Balancing Act."

29. A quick introduction to the topic can be found at "Brand Safety: The Ultimate Guide," Bannerflow, accessed January 17, 2023, https://www.bannerflow.com/blog /the-ultimate-guide-to-brand-safety/.

30. See Targetoo, "Brand Safety: Tools and Solutions to Keep Your Brand Safe," https://www.targetoo.com/brand -safety.

31. Danielle Wolinski, "YouTube Receives Brand Safety Distinction for a Second Year," Google Ads and Commerce blog, May 12, 2022, https://blog.google/products/ads-com merce/youtube-brand-safety-second -accreditation/.

32. "How TikTok Recommends Videos #ForYou," June 18, 2020, https:// newsroom.tiktok.com/en-us/how-tiktok -recommends-videos-for-you.

33. See also Grandinetti, "Examining Embedded Apparatuses."

34. Paumgarten, "Looking for Someone."

35. In this section I rely heavily if indi- rectly on Eugene Wei's blog posts, "TikTok and the Sorting Hat," August 3, 2020, https:// www.eugenewei.com/blog/2020/8/3/tiktok -and-the-sorting-hat; and Wei, "Seeing Like An Algorithm," September 18, 2020, https:// www.eugenewei.com/blog/2020/9/18 /seeing-like-an-algorithm.

36. Madrigal, "Netflix Reverse-Engineered Hollywood."

37. Ibid.

38. TikTok Transparency Report January 1, 2020, through June 30, 2020, released September 22, 2020, https://www .tiktok.com/safety/resources/transparency -report-20201?lang=en.

39. "YouTube U-Turn over Red Dead Redemption 2 Suffragette Clips," *BBC*,

195

November 8, 2018, https://www.bbc.com
/news/technology-46137186.

40. Dwoskin, "YouTube's Arbitrary
Standards."

41. Carroll, "Is TikTok a Chinese
Cambridge Analytica."

42. Keller and Dance, "Child Abusers
Run Rampant."

43. Harwell, "Face-Scanning
Algorithm."

44. Harwell, "AI Researchers Race to
Detect 'Deepfake' Videos."

45. Ghaffary, "Facebook Is Banning
Deepfake Videos."

46. "How Google Fights Disinformation,"
February 2019, https://www.blog.google
/documents/37/How_Google_Fights
_Disinformation.pdf?hl=en.

47. Leslie Miller, "How YouTube Supports
Elections," YouTube Official Blog, February
3, 2020, https://blog.youtube/news-and
-events/how-youtube-supports-elections?m
=1.

48. Phillips, *This Is Why We Can't
Have Nice Things*.

49. For example, see Martineau,
"Facebook's New Content Moderation
Tools."

50. Twitch, "Terms of Service,"
last modified November 9, 2022, https://
www.twitch.tv/p/legal/terms-of-service/;
and Twitch, "Community Guidelines:
Introduction to Safety on Twitch," accessed
January 13, 2023, https://www.twitch.tv/p
/legal/community-guidelines/.

51. "Watching 'Made for Kids' Content,"
YouTube Help, accessed January 13, 2023,
https://support.google.com/youtube/answer
/9632097.

52. "YouTube Community Guidelines" as
of February 9, 2010, accessed via Internet
Archive Wayback Machine, https://web
.archive.org/web/20100209183437/http:
//www.youtube.com/t/community
_guidelines.

53. YouTube Community Guidelines,
accessed January 20, 2020, https://
www.youtube.com/about/policies
/#community-guidelines.

54. Ibid.

55. Ibid.

56. See Gillespie, *Custodians*, 116.

57. See TikTok, "Terms of Service," last
updated February 2019, https://www.tiktok
.com/legal/terms-of-service?lang=en; and

TikTok, "Community Guidelines," last
updated October 2022, https://www.tiktok
.com/community-guidelines?lang=en.

58. For example, see Jones, "What
Teenagers Are Learning from Online Porn."

59. Pornhub Insights, "The 2019 Year
in Review," December 11, 2019, https://www
.pornhub.com/insights/2019-year-in-review,
graphed alongside prior years' data.

Chapter 4

1. Given TikTok's and Twitch's primary
focus on entertainment-centric content,
this chapter will focus more narrowly on
YouTube.

2. Van Kessel, Toor, and Smith, "Week in
the Life."

3. Adams, "YouTube Is My Father."

4. Ken Wheaton, "How 'Normal People'
Are Taking over the Product Review," Think
with Google, March 2018, https://www.think
withgoogle.com/consumer-insights/con
sumer-purchase-product-reviews/.

5. Neate, "Ryan Kaji, 9, earns $29.5m."

6. Vanderbilt, "Why We Love
How-to Videos." Vanderbilt gets this
insight from Luc Proteau, Department of
Kinesiology, University of Montreal.

7. Alice Waters, "Changing America's
Palate," Talks at Google, YouTube,
September 16, 2009, https://www.youtube
.com/watch?v=ue2U90VJJ3I.

8. Julia Child, "Omelette via Beans,"
YouTube, accessed January 16, 2023, https://
www.youtube.com/watch?v=AySmkqTlrVA.

9. "The French Chef—SNL,"
YouTube, accessed January 16, 2023, https://
www.youtube.com/watch?v=eSxv6IGBgFQ.

10. "Vincent Scully | Frank Lloyd
Wright 1914–1959 (Modern Architecture
Course)," YouTube, accessed January 16,
2023, https://www.youtube.com/watch?v=
Xp6pZQSn7gI.

11. Jeanette Wing, "Computational
Thinking and Thinking About Computing,"
YouTube, September 2, 2009, https://www
.youtube.com/watch?v=C2Pq4N-iE4I.

12. "Latanya Sweeney: When Anonymized
Data Is Anything but Anonymous," YouTube,
accessed January 16, 2023, https://www
.youtube.com/watch?v=tivCK_fBBf0.

13. "Richard Feynman Messenger Lectures
at Cornell: The Character of Physical Law

Part: 1 The Law of Gravitation," YouTube, accessed January 16, 2023, https://www.youtube.com/watch?v=-kFOXP026eE&list=PLS3_1JNX8dEh5YcO-Yo5stUou_T9nqIlF.

14. "Elinor Ostrom Nobel Prize in Economics Lecture," YouTube, February 16, 2010, https://www.youtube.com/watch?v=T6OgRki5SgM.

15. "Toni Morrison Nobel Lecture (1993)," YouTube, accessed January 16, 2023, https://www.youtube.com/watch?v=ticXzFEpN90.

16. "This Is Water David Foster Wallace Commencement Speech," YouTube, accessed January 16, 2023, https://www.youtube.com/watch?v=DCbGM4mqEVw.

17. The OpenCourseWare catalog can be found at https://ocw.mit.edu/courses/.

18. Salman Khan, "Let's Use Video to Reinvent Education," TED talk, March 2011, https://www.ted.com/talks/salman_khan_let_s_use_video_to_reinvent_education?language=en.

19. Noer, "One Man, One Computer, 10 million Students."

20. Khan, "Let's Use Video to Reinvent Education."

21. Khan Academy, "Impact," accessed January 16, 2023, https://www.khanacademy.org/about/impact.

22. Khan, *One World Schoolhouse*, 221.

23. Coe, "TED's Chris Anderson."

24. "The Best Stats You've Ever Seen | Hans Rosling," YouTube, February 2006, https://www.youtube.com/watch?v=hVimVzgtD6w.

25. See https://www.gapminder.org.

26. Bindel, "Why I'd Never Do a TED talk."

27. Harouni, "Sound of TED."

28. Robbins, "Trouble with TED Talks."

29. All summary data from https://www.exhibitedge.com/ted-talk-trends/.

30. Bratton, "We Need to Talk About TED."

31. Ibid.

32. Ibid.

33. The Chautauqua movement was a movement in the United States in the late nineteenth and early twentieth centuries, originating in upstate New York but expanding widely, that combined moral uplift, wholesome entertainment, and intellectual edification via camps and traveling troupes. See University of Iowa Libraries Special Collections and Archives, "What Was Chautauqua?," accessed January 16, 2023, https://www.lib.uiowa.edu/sc/tc/.

34. Hudders, De Jans, and De Veirman, "Commercialization of Social Media Stars."

35. Cotter, "Playing the Visibility Game."

36. Van Driel and Dumitrica, "Selling Brands While Staying 'Authentic.'"

37. Abidin, "Communicative Intimacies."

38. Brown and Freeman, "Top-Earning TikTok-ers 2022."

39. Phillips, "Charli D'Amelio's Top 10."

40. Grothaus, "Hotels Are Sick of Instagram 'Influencers.'"

41. "Armed Extremism in Buffalo," Everytown Gun Safety Support Network, August 12, 2022, https://everytownresearch.org/report/armed-extremism-buffalo-shooting/.

42. And there is a scholarly article on the topic: Landrum, Olshansky, and Richards, "Differential Susceptibility to Misleading Flat Earth Arguments on YouTube."

43. Karic et al., "Evaluation of Surgical Educational Videos."

Chapter 5

1. "OK Go—Here It Goes Again (Official Music Video)," YouTube, February 26, 2009, https://www.youtube.com/watch?v=dTAAsCNK7RA.

2. "Info," OK Go, accessed January 16, 2023, http://okgo.net/info/.

3. As of early 2023, more than 250,000 online creators had Patreon accounts. Patreon homepage, accessed January 16, 2023, https://www.patreon.com.

4. "Snarky Puppy—Lingus (We Like It Here)," YouTube, March 31, 2014, https://www.youtube.com/watch?v=L_XJ_s5IsQc.

5. Poerio et al., "More Than a Feeling."

6. Keiles, "How A.S.M.R. Became a Sensation."

7. Ebert, *New Media Invasion*, 43.

8. For more on *National Lampoon*, see the 2015 documentary *Drunk Stoned Brilliant Dead* (https://www.imdb.com/title/tt1674785).

9. For one set of 2021 figures, see Hoang Nguyen, "The Most Popular

Music Streaming Platforms in Key Markets Globally," YouGov, March 19, 2021, https://yougov.co.uk/topics/entertainment/articles-reports/2021/03/18/services-used-stream-music-poll.

10. Kavoori, *Reading YouTube*, 75.

11. For a representative sample of this vein of reporting, see Chmielewski, "Spotify Profit Margins." For 2021 user counts, see David Curry, "Music Streaming App Revenue and Usage Statistics," Business of Apps, last updated January 10, 2023, https://www.businessofapps.com/data/music-streaming-market/.

12. Marcus, "Beverly Hills Police."

13. Shirky, *Here Comes Everybody*.

14. Neelie Andreeva, "'Kennedy Center Honors' Slips in Ratings From 2014, Helps CBS Win Night," *Deadline*, December 30, 2015, https://deadline.com/2015/12/kennedy-center-honors-ratings-cbs-1201674128/.

15. All Beato information is from his YouTube channel and from an interview conducted September 5, 2019.

16. O'Dell, "Musical.ly Speaking."

17. Sleiman, "Surprising Legacy."

18. Goble's homepage is preserved at the Internet Archive: https://web.archive.org/web/20010208101450/http://ghg.ecn.purdue.edu/~ghg/; "Lighting a Charcoal Grill with Liquid Oxygen," YouTube, December 2, 2007, https://www.youtube.com/watch?v=UjPxDOEdsX8.

19. Hale, "Social Media Stardom."

20. Gina Shalavi and Stéphanie Thomson, "How Online Video Has Transformed the World of Sports," Think with Google, Consumer Insights, last updated January 2019, https://www.thinkwithgoogle.com/advertising-channels/video/sports-fan-video-consumption/.

21. "The Ancient Combat Sport Revived by YouTube," *BBC*, December 3, 2019, https://www.bbc.com/sport/av/africa/50565773.

22. Shalavi and Thomson, "How Online Video Has Transformed the World of Sports."

23. Marshall, "Football on YouTube."

24. Television: "Traditional TV Industry Revenue Worldwide from 2019 to 2024," Statista, accessed January 16, 2023, https://www.statista.com/statistics/265983/global-tv-industry-revenue; video games: "Gaming Revenue of Leading Public Companies Worldwide in 2021," Statista, accessed January 16, 2023, https://www.statista.com/statistics/983227/global-video-games-revenue-companies/; recorded music: "Global Recorded Music Revenue from 1999 to 2021," Statista, accessed January 16, 2023, https://www.statista.com/statistics/272305/global-revenue-of-the-music-industry; streaming video: Erik Gruenwedel, "U.S. Leads Global OTT Video Revenue Increases at $8.3 Billion," MediaPlay News, August 10, 2020, https://www.mediaplaynews.com/u-s-leads-global-ott-video-revenue-increases-at-8-3-billion/; box office: Jesse Rifkin, "Global Box Office Reaches Record $42.5 Billion in 2019," Boxoffice Pro, January 10, 2020, https://www.boxofficepro.com/global-box-office-2019-record-42-5-billion.

25. For example, see Bakos and Brynjolfsson, "Aggregation and Disaggregation of Information Goods."

26. Cveticanin, "Twitch Stats."

27. Wulf, Schneider, and Beckert, "Watching Players," 340.

28. Taylor, *Watch Me Play*, 55.

29. Ibid., 9.

30. Ibid., 26.

31. Ibid., 39–41.

32. Michael Wesch, "An Anthropological Introduction to YouTube," Library of Congress lecture, YouTube, June 23, 2008, https://www.youtube.com/watch?v=TPAO-lZ4_hU.

33. Horton and Wohl, "Mass Communication and Para-social Interaction."

34. Boerman and van Reijmersdal, "Disclosing Influencer Marketing."

35. Ault, "YouTube Stars More Popular Than Mainstream Celebs."

36. Hoggins, "How YouTube Changed the World: Video Games."

37. See Teng, "Logan Paul Boxing."

38. Parker, "Cult of PewDiePie."

39. Ohlheiser and Park, "Forever War of PewDiePie."

40. Padilla quoted in Alexander, "Golden Age of YouTube Is Over."

41. Kjellberg quoted in Alexander, "YouTubers, Twitch Streamers Are Opening Up."

42. Klein quoted in Alexander, "YouTubers, Twitch Streamers Are Opening Up."

43. Paul quoted in Teng, "Logan Paul Boxing."

44. Ibid.

45. "A Defining Question in an iPhone Age: Live for the Moment or Record It?," *New York Times*, September 26, 2014.

46. Dickson, "David Dobrik Was the King of YouTube."

47. Ibid.

Chapter 6

1. I'm relying heavily on the Homestar Runner wiki (http://www.hrwiki.org/wiki/Main_Page), a vast compendium of transcriptions, chronologies, trivia, and other information. Some information on the brothers' pre-Homestar years derives from their guest appearance on "Lost in the Stacks," a podcast from the Archives and Manuscripts division of the Georgia Tech library on December 15, 2017, https://content.libsyn.com/p/c/b/5/cb5c0e85f700b06c/LITS_Episode_366.mp3.

2. "Strong Bad Email #203—Independent," YouTube, accessed January 16, 2023, https://www.youtube.com/watch?v=kjwlrvcKcfI.

3. "Record Store Day b/w B-est of B-sides," YouTube, accessed January 16, 2023, https://www.youtube.com/watch?v=XecNSd_lOYs.

4. Dessem, "New Fisher-Price Record." For more on 3D printing, see Jordan, *3D Printing*.

5. Eric Ravenscraft, "Homestar Runner: How to Master a Dying Art Form," YouTube, accessed January 16, 2023, https://www.youtube.com/watch?v=Wbh9-mNmviE.

6. Squires, "Incredible Treasure Chest."

7. Watson, "What Makes Flash So Insecure."

8. Harrison and Navas, "Mashup," 188–90.

9. Browne, "Danger Mouse's 'Grey Album.'"

10. Future Music, "Brief History of Ableton Live."

11. "Michael Jackson and Eric Clapton—'Billie Cocaine,'" YouTube, February 8, 2018, https://www.youtube.com/watch?v=SE0bQ7WQF9c; "MASHUP—Beat It, Trooper! [Iron Maiden vs. Michael Jackson]," YouTube, May 25, 2015, https://www.youtube.com/watch?v=dU2Pbm9wtnw; "Bob Marley and Billy Idol—'With a Rebel Yell, She Cried, "Don't Give Up the Fight,"'" YouTube, July 20, 2018, https://www.youtube.com/watch?v=yayq3W-Mayk; "Daft Punk vs The Doobie Brothers—Get Lucky The Long Train Running (Mash Up)," YouTube, August 15, 2013, https://www.youtube.com/watch?v=udjV1Udvrl4; "MASHUP—Mariah Manson—'All I Want For Christmas Is the Beautiful People,'" YouTube, December 8, 2019, https://www.youtube.com/watch?v=A1X3d2zWx94; "Stayin' in Black (Bee Gees + AC/DC Mashup) by Wax Audio," YouTube, April 29, 2014, https://www.youtube.com/watch?v=OrlWWrSwaB8.

12. "Miss You, The Happiest Days of Our Lives, Another Brick in the Wall—Stones + Pink Floyd (cover)," YouTube, March 3, 2017, https://www.youtube.com/watch?v=ErHo_oCkspc; "The Thrill is Gone + Summertime (BB king + George Gershwin cover)," YouTube, May 26, 2017, https://www.youtube.com/watch?v=pFEIJSXLmFs.

13. See "History of Rock," YouTube, March 8, 2016, https://www.youtube.com/watch?v=_zflDkNJ990; "The Mixtape," YouTube, December 14, 2012, https://www.youtube.com/watch?v=c9JV-eK1PQg; and "Brighton Dome Projection Mapping Mashup," YouTube, September 26, 2012, https://www.youtube.com/watch?v=OjiyClswRlQ.

14. Ithaca Studio homepage, "Work," accessed January 16, 2023, https://ithaca.studio/#work.

15. "VULFPECK /// Live at Madison Square Garden," YouTube, December 9, 2019, https://www.youtube.com/watch?v=rv4wf7bzfFE; "SOUND OF TWO // Bernard Purdie & Cory Henry," YouTube, January 31, 2016, https://www.youtube.com/watch?v=ptKn85LoD2Y; "SOUND OF TWO /// Bernard Purdie & Herbie Hancock," YouTube, July 26, 2012, https://www.youtube.com/watch?v=IUhaTEpTC9g; "VULFPECK x KATY PERRY /// Disco Ulysses' Teenage Dream (Mashup)," December 24, 2020, https://www.youtube.com/watch?v=3nM6eg5kFfw.

16. Two brilliant examples are: "Ain't No Mountain High Enough," YouTube, July 26, 2014 https://www.youtube.com/watch?v=kAT3aVj-A_E; and "I Was Made to Love

Her," YouTube, February 4, 2015 https://www
.youtube.com/watch?v=KKBmkxFm7-U.

17. "Jamiroquai Bee Gees Mashup—
Pomplamoose," YouTube, May 24, 2018,
https://www.youtube.com/watch?v=ooZ
R4LSuppk; "Sweet Dreams + White Stripes
Mashup | Pomplamoose ft. Sarah Dugas,"
YouTube, September 19, 2019, https://www
.youtube.com/watch?v=hmLBSCiEoas.

18. FAROFF, "PSY vs Ghostbusters—
Gangnam Busters—Mashup by FAROFF,"
YouTube, October 10, 2012, https://www
.youtube.com/watch?v=82LCKBdjywQ;
FAROFF, "Britney Spears vs Metallica—
Enter Toxman—Mashup by FAROFF,"
YouTube, March 9, 2009, https://www.you
tube.com/watch?v=sAlDqw7eOUw; FAROFF,
"MC Hammer vs Eurythmics vs New Order
vs Talking Heads vs Donna Summer—
Mashup by FAROFF," YouTube, September
16, 2011, https://www.youtube.com/watch?v=
W2eeB44rZU0; DJs From Mars, "Beethoven
Vs Chemical Brothers—Symphony No. 5 Vs
Galvanize," YouTube, June 16, 2015, https://
www.youtube.com/watch?v=6aZzVnOmGtY.

19. "September Train—Mashup of
September and Crazy Train," YouTube,
August 29, 2022, https://www.youtube.com
/watch?v=YTQS43Hm8lo; "DJ
Cummerbund—Play That Funky Music
Rammstein," YouTube, April 26, 2019,
https://www.youtube.com/watch?v=
tcUB-3lud60.

20. Anderson, "Watching People."

21. For one history of the genre, see
"Know Your Meme: Reaction Videos," last
updated October 24, 2019, https://knowyour
meme.com/memes/reaction-videos.

22. "Best Reaction Videos (& Why
They're So Popular)," Riverside blog, July 3,
2022, https://riverside.fm/blog/best-reaction
-videos.

23. The Australian columnist Anson
Cameron wrote "I'm hooked on YouTube
reaction videos. Why are they so addictive?"
in the *Sydney Morning Herald* (June 16, 2022)
and all these positions emerged, either in
the column or the comments, https://www
.smh.com.au/culture/music/i-m-hooked-on
-youtube-reaction-videos-why-are-they
-so-addictive-20220613-p5ata5.html.

24. Blatt, "How Reaction Videos
Took Over the Content Universe."

25. For example, see Bliss, "'Would
You Rather?"; and McDaniel, "Popular Music
Reaction Videos."

Chapter 7

1. Vogels, Gelles-Watnick, and Massarat,
"Teens, Social Media and Technology 2022."

2. Brennan, *Attention Factory*, 210–11.

3. Light, "Country Changed Its Mind."

4. See Plantin et al., "Infrastructure
Studies Meet Platform Studies."

5. Fiesler and Dym, "Moving Across
Lands."

6. Hatmaker, "Twitch Sues Two
Users."

7. Brice-Saddler, Selk, and Rosenberg,
"Prankster Sentenced to 20 Years." The
episode was included in a Netflix true crime
series entitled "Web of Make-Believe" in
2022. See "Death By Swat," IMDb, https://
www.imdb.com/title/tt20857842/.

8. Grayson, "Twitch Streamers
Traumatized."

9. Anti-Swatting Act of 2018, H.R.
6003, 115th Cong. (2017–18).

10. "Early Heads-Up: Abbreviated
Public Subscriber Counts Across YouTube,"
YouTube Help page, May 21, 2019, https://
support.google.com/youtube/thread/6543166
?msgid=13119244.

11. "Most Popular YouTube Brand
Channels as of March 2021, Ranked by Total
Number of Video Views," Statista, August 23,
2021, https://www.statista.com/statis
tics/277765/most-popular-youtube-brand
-channels-ranked-by-views/.

12. Werner Geyser, "Top 64 TikTok Stats
You Need to Know in 2023," Influencer
Marketing Hub, last updated January 2, 2023,
https://influencermarketinghub.com
/tiktok-stats/.

13. "3 Ways Digital Video Has Upended
Shopping as We Know It," Think with
Google, Marketing Strategies, July 2018,
https://www.thinkwithgoogle.com/con
sumer-insights/online-video-shopping/.

14. Perez, "Kids Now Spend Nearly as
Much Time."

15. My understanding of beauty vloggers on YouTube was heavily influenced
by the Penn State undergraduate honors
thesis written by Qingyi (Sally) Wang who
I supervised in academic year 2018–19. See

also Rasmussen, "Parasocial Interaction in the Digital Age."

16. Lora Jones and Hannah Gelbart, "Make-Up: Have YouTube Stars Boosted Beauty Sales?," *BBC*, June 7, 2018, https://www.bbc.com/news/business-43966384.

17. Geyser, "Top 64 TikTok Stats."

18. Teitell, "$600 Hair Dryer."

19. Derek Blasberg, "When Brands Become Creators: How Beauty Brands Can Use YouTube to Look Their Best," Think with Google, March 2019, https://www.thinkwithgoogle.com/advertising-channels/video/beauty-videos-on-youtube/.

20. Bishop, "YouTube Algorithmic Gossip."

21. See Klug et al., "Trick and Please"; and Karizat et al., "Algorithmic Folk Theories."

22. For a far more complete discussion of this and related issues, see Manne, *Down Girl*.

23. "BitChute Reveals How YouTube Is Shadowbanning Me?," August 8, 2018. Video removed by YouTube.

24. Brennan, "Bitchute Claims to Be a Decentralized Platform."

25. Grind et al., "How Google Interferes."

26. Kron, "Mission from God."

27. Ibid.

28. Internet Archive Wayback Machine, Invisible Children, "Frequently Asked Questions," March 25, 2006, http://web.archive.org/web/20060325043957/http:/www.invisiblechildren.com/theMission/faq/#3.

29. Sanders, "'Kony 2012' Effect."

30. Rainie et al., "Viral Kony 2012 Video."

31. Ethan Zuckerman, "Useful Reads on Kony 2012," *My Heart's in Accra* (blog), March 14, 2012, http://www.ethanzuckerman.com/blog/2012/03/14/useful-reads-on-kony-2012.

32. Kron, "Mission from God."

33. Rainie et al.

34. Wark, *Telesthesia*, 208.

35. Sanders, "'Kony 2012' Effect."

36. Parenthetical citations in this section refer to Stuart, *Bullet*.

37. Whack, "Black Teens Most Active."

38. See also Johnson and Schell-Busey, "Old Message in a New Bottle."

39. Cairncross, *Death of Distance*.

40. Lopez, Gonzalez-Barrera, and Patten, "Closing the Digital Divide."

Chapter 8

1. See Plantin et al., "Infrastructure Studies Meet Platform Studies."

2. Cockerell, "Inside China's Massive Surveillance Operation."

3. Paul Adams, "Strong, Weak, & Temporary Ties," *Bokardo* (blog), April 15, 2010, http://bokardo.com/archives/strong-weak-temporary-ties/.

4. Vizcaíno-Verdú and Abidin, "Music Challenge Memes," 26.

5. Lin, "TikTok CEO Quits."

6. On ByteDance's management of parallel platforms, see Kaye, Chen, and Zeng, "Co-evolution of Two Chinese Mobile Short Video Apps."

7. Perrin and Anderson, "Share of U.S. Adults Using Social Media."

8. McIntyre, "Despite Gains with Streaming."

9. Salman Aslam, "TikTok by the Numbers," Omnicore Digital Marketing, January 6, 2023, https://www.omnicoreagency.com/tiktok-statistics/.

10. "Average Daily Activation Count: 43 Times a Day," App Ape Lab, July 26, 2018, https://en.lab.appa.pe/2018-07/addicted-to-tiktok.html.

11. Mansoor Iqbal, "TikTok Revenue and Usage Statistics (2023)," Business of Apps, last updated January 9, 2023, https://www.businessofapps.com/data/tik-tok-statistics/.

12. Data.ai, "The State of Mobile 2021," accessed January 16, 2023, https://www.appannie.com/en/go/state-of-mobile-2021/.

13. Solsman, "YouTube's AI."

14. Fishman, "Rethinking Marshall McLuhan," 571.

15. Herbert, Lotz, and Marshall, "Approaching Media Industries Comparatively."

16. Meyer, "Why Twitter May Be Ruinous."

17. Berg, "Highest-Paid YouTube Stars."

18. For example, see Jenkins, Ito, and boyd, *Participatory Culture*; and Burgess and Green, *YouTube*.

19. Burnett, "Interview with David Hollinger."

20. Hollinger, "Historians and the Discourse of Intellectuals," 42.

21. Harris, "TikTok Became a Bestseller Machine."

22. Lave and Wenger, *Situated Learning*.

23. Orr, *Talking About Machines*.

24. Thomas, Kellogg, and Erickson, "Knowledge Management Puzzle."

25. Albarrak, Alnefaie, and Almasoud, "Randomized Controlled Trial."

26. Sawyer and Jarrahi, "Sociotechnical Perspective."

27. Jenkins, Ito, and boyd, *Participatory Culture*, 129.

28. Customer reviews for Tuscan Dairy Whole Vitamin D Milk, Amazon.com, accessed January 17, 2023, https://www.amazon.com/Tuscan-Whole-Milk-Gallon-128/dp/B00032G1SO/ref=pd_sbs_k_3#customerReviews.

29. Customer reviews for Mizuno Women's Wave Rider 16 Running shoe, Amazon.com, accessed January 17, 2023, https://www.amazon.com/Mizuno-Womens-Running-Blazing-Orange/dp/B00AHND77S/ref=cm_cr_arp_d_product_top?ie,=UTF8.

30. Customer reviews for AudioQuest Diamond HDMI 2 Black Cable at Amazon.com, accessed January 17, 2023, https://www.amazon.com/AudioQuest-Diamond-6-56-Braided-Cable/product-reviews/B003CT2A2M.

31. Adams, "Designing for Social Interaction."

32. Hamilton et al., "Understanding the Effects of Algorithm Awareness."

33. For example, see Matt Gielen and Jeremy Rosen, "Reverse Engineering the YouTube Algorithm: Part I," Tubefilter, June 23, 2016, https://www.tubefilter.com/2016/06/23/reverse-engineering-youtube-algorithm/. Sophie Bishop, whose study of "algorithmic gossip" was noted in chapter 7, also studied these consultants. See Bishop, "Algorithmic Experts."

34. Jarboe, "Why You Must Unlearn."

35. "YouTube Help: Discovery and Performance FAQs," accessed January 17, 2023, https://support.google.com/youtube/answer/141805?hl=en.

36. "5 Tips for TikTok Creators," TikTok blog, July 30, 2020, https://newsroom.tiktok.com/en-us/5-tips-for-tiktok-creators.

37. Munger and Phillips, "Supply and Demand Framework," 7.

38. Ibid., 27.

39. Wilson, *Nostalgia: Sanctuary of Meaning*.

40. Routledge, *Nostalgia: A Psychological Resource*.

41. For example, see Cross, *Consumed Nostalgia*.

42. See Sterne, "Preservation Paradox in Digital Audio," 55.

43. "Miles Davis—So What—The Robert Herridge Theater, New York—April 2, 1959," YouTube, December 2, 2012, https://www.youtube.com/watch?v=diHFEapOr_E; "Mary Lou Retton Makes History | Gold Medal Moments Presented by HERSHEY'S," YouTube, June 28, 2018, https://www.youtube.com/watch?v=cD0IBGFwCNU; "Euell Gibbons For Grape Nuts (fixed sound)," YouTube, July 6, 2006, https://www.youtube.com/watch?v=_XJMIu18I8Y; "Sesame Street: Grover Stars in 'Smell Like a Monster,'" YouTube, October 7, 2010, https://www.youtube.com/watch?v=zkd5dJIVjgM; "The Farbers Meet the Coneheads—SNL," YouTube, June 15, 2019, https://www.youtube.com/watch?v=qrUOFs-hZ-M.

44. Boym quoted in Wilson, *Nostalgia: Sanctuary of Meaning*, 22.

45. Davis quoted in Wilson, *Nostalgia: Sanctuary of Meaning*, 21.

46. Aden, "Nostalgic Communication as Temporal Escape," 35, 21.

47. Jack, "Infrastructural Restitution," especially 213–50.

48. Davis quoted in Wilson, *Nostalgia: Sanctuary of Meaning*, 34–35.

49. Routledge, *Nostalgia: A Psychological Resource*, 37.

50. Ibid., 40–41.

51. Eisenstein, *Printing Press*.

52. Elizabeth Eisenstein obituary, *Washington Post*, February 24, 2016, https://www.washingtonpost.com/national/elizabeth-eisenstein-printing-press-historian-and-tennis-star-dies-at-92/2016/02/23/5a6342a6-da47-11e5-925f-1d10062cc82d_story.html.

53. Eisenstein, *Printing Press*, 21–22.

54. Ibid., 81–82.

55. Drozd, Couvillon, and Suarez, "Medical YouTube Videos."

56. Eisenstein, *Printing Press*, 128–29.

57. Ibid., 152.

202

58. A Reuters report contends that BitChute and Odysee already perform this function. See "SkewTube," August 22, 2022, https://www.reuters.com/investigates /special-report/usa-media-misinformation/.

59. "National Internet Information Office on the Regulations on the Recommended Management of Internet Information Service Algorithms (Draft for Comments)," Cyberspace Administration of China, August 27, 2021, http://www.cac.gov .cn/2021-08/27/c_1631652502874117.htm#.

60. Gurman, "Apple Races to Temper Outcry."

61. On the potential rights of algo- rithms, see Bayern, "Implications of Modern Business–Entity Law."

Conclusion

1. Turner Novak, "The Rise of TikTok and Understanding Its Parent Company ByteDance," *Split* (blog), May 21, 2020, https://turner.substack.com/p/the-rise -of-tiktok-and-understanding.

2. For a fuller and more expert discussion of these issues, see Wang, "China's Sputnik Moment?"; and Noah Smith, "Why Is China Smashing Its Tech Industry?," *Noahpinion* (blog), July 24, 2021, https://noahpinion .substack.com/p/why-is-china-smashing -its-tech-industry.

3. Li et al., "YouTube as a Source of Information on COVID-19."

4. For more on Pizzagate, see "The Saga of 'Pizzagate': The Fake Story That Shows How Conspiracy Theories Spread," *BBC* trending, December 2, 2016, https://www.bbc .com/news/blogs-trending-38156985.

5. Thompson, "YouTube's Plot to Silence Conspiracy Theories."

6. Ibid.

7. "Protecting Our Extended Workforce and the Community," YouTube Official Blog, March 16, 2020, https://blog.youtube/news -and-events/protecting-our-extended-work force-and/.

8. Newton, "How the 'Plandemic' Video Hoax Went Viral."

9. Lewis, "This Is What the News Won't Show You."

10. YouTube Official Blog, "YouTube Originals Announces Slate of New Content Amidst COVID-19 #WithMe Initiatives," April 22, 2020, https://blog .youtube/news-and-events/youtube-originals -announces-slate-of/.

11. Shaw and Bergen, "YouTubers Turn to Subscriptions."

12. Burgess and Green, *YouTube*, 25.

203

Bibliography

Abidin, Crystal. "Communicative Intimacies: Influencers and Perceived Interconnectedness." *Ada: A Journal of Gender, New Media, and Technology*, no. 8 (2015). https://scholarsbank .uoregon.edu/xm lui/handle/1794 /26365.

Adams, Michael Anthony. "YouTube Is My Father." *Atlantic*, June 13, 2013. https://www.theatlantic.com/sexes /archive/2013/06/youtube-is-my -father/276823.

Aden, Roger C. "Nostalgic Communication as Temporal Escape: *When It Was a Game*'s Re-construction of a Baseball/ Work Community." *Western Journal of Communication* 59 (Winter 1995): 20–38.

Aguiar, Luis, Christian Peukert, Maximilian Schäfer, and Hannes Ullrich. "Facebook Shadow Profiles." *ArXiv* (May 2022): 1–21.

Albarrak, Abdullah Ahmed S., Faisal A. Alnefaie, and Riyadh Almasoud. "Randomized Controlled Trial on the Effect of YouTube Surgical Videos on Procedural Knowledge and Perceived Self-Efficacy of Surgery Residents." Preprint, submitted September 16, 2019. https://doi.org/10.21203/rs.2 .13906/v1.

Alexander, Julia. "The Golden Age of YouTube Is Over." *Verge*, April 5, 2019. https://www.theverge .com/2019/4/5/18287318/you

tube-logan-paul-pewdiepie -demonetization-adpocalypse -premium-influencers-creators.

———. "YouTubers, Twitch Streamers Are Opening Up About Serious Burnout, Personal Struggles." *Polygon*, January 18, 2018. https://www.polygon.com /2018/1/18/16899532/youtube-twitch -burnout-h3h3-pewdiepie-lirik.

Amadeo, Ron. "Cheaper Bandwidth or Bust: How Google Saved YouTube." *Ars Technica*, April 23, 2015. https:// arstechnica.com/gadgets/2015 /04/cheaper-bandwidth-or-bust -how-google-saved-youtube.

Andersen, Kurt. "How America Lost Its Mind." *Atlantic*, September 2017. https://www.theatlantic.com/maga zine/archive/2017/09/how-america -lost-its-mind/534231.

Anderson, Sam. "Watching People Watching People Watching." *New York Times*, November 25, 2011.

Ault, Suzanne. "Survey: YouTube Stars More Popular Than Mainstream Celebs Among U.S. Teens." *Variety*, August 5, 2014. https://variety.com/2014/digital /news/survey-youtube-stars-more -popular-than-mainstream-celebs -among-u-s-teens-1201275245/.

Bak-Coleman, Joseph B., Mark Alfano, Wolfram Barfuss, Carl T. Bergstrom, Miguel A. Centeno, Iain D. Couzin, Jonathan F. Donges et al. "Stewardship of Global Collective

Behavior." *Proceedings of the National Academy of Sciences* 118, no. 27 (2021): e2025764118.

Baker-White, Emily. "Leaked Audio from 80 Internal TikTok Meetings Shows That US User Data Has Been Repeatedly Accessed from China." *BuzzFeed*, June 17, 2022. https://www.buzzfeednews.com/article/emily bakerwhite/tiktok-tapes-us-user -data-china-bytedance-access.

Bakos, Yannos, and Erik Brynjolfsson. "Aggregation and Disaggregation of Information Goods: Implications for Bundling, Site Licensing, and Micropayment Systems." In *Lectures in E-Commerce*, edited by Hannes Werthner and Martin Bichler, 103–22. Vienna: Springer, 2001.

Barnhart, Brent. "TikTok Challenges: What They Are and Why They're Great for Brands." Sprout Social, May 4, 2022. https://sproutsocial.com/insights /tiktok-challenges.

Bärtl, Matthias. "YouTube Channels, Uploads and Views: A Statistical Analysis of the Past 10 Years." *Convergence* 24, no. 1 (2018): 16–32.

Bayern, Shawn. "The Implications of Modern Business-Entity Law for the Regulation of Autonomous Systems." *European Journal of Risk Regulation* 7, no. 2 (2016): 297–309.

Berg, Madeline. "The Highest-Paid YouTube Stars of 2019: The Kids Are Killing It." *Forbes*, December 18, 2019. https://www.forbes.com/sites /maddieberg/2019/12/18/the-highest -paid-youtube-stars-of-2019-the -kids-are-killing-it/#5fde7c3838cd.

Berners-Lee, Tim, Robert Cailliau, Jean-François Groff, and Bernd Pollermann. "World-Wide Web: The Information Universe." *Internet Research* 2, no. 1 (1992): 52–58.

Berry, David M. *Critical Theory and the Digital*. London: Bloomsbury Academic, 2014.

Besen, Stanley M., and Joseph Farrell. "Choosing How to Compete: Strategies and Tactics in Standardization." *Journal of Economic Perspectives* 8, no. 2 (1994): 117–31.

Bindel, Julie. "Why I'd Never Do a TED Talk." *Guardian*, July 23, 2018.

https://www.theguardian.com /commentisfree/2018/jul/23/ted-talk -smugness-presenters-embarrassing.

Bishop, Sophie. "Algorithmic Experts: Selling Algorithmic Lore on YouTube." *Social Media and Society* 6, no. 1 (2020). https://journals.sagepub.com/doi/full /10.1177/2056305119897323.

———. "Managing Visibility on YouTube Through Algorithmic Gossip." *New Media and Society* 21 (2019): 2595–98.

Blatt, Shephali. "How Reaction Videos Took Over the Content Universe amid the Pandemic." *Economic Times (India)*, January 25, 2021. https:// economictimes.indiatimes.com/tech /technology/the-phenomenon-that-is -reaction-videos-on-youtube-and-in -india/articleshow/80144051.cms.

Bliss, Lauren. "'Would You Rather?' Weirdness and Affect in Reaction Videos to Porn." *First Monday*, April 13, 2022. https://journals.uic.edu /ojs/index.php/fm/article/view/12580 /10656.

Boerman, Sophie C., and Eva A. Van Reijmersdal. "Disclosing Influencer Marketing on YouTube to Children: The Moderating Role of Para-social Relationship." *Frontiers in Psychology* 10 (2020): 3042.

Botella, Elena. "TikTok Admits It Suppressed Videos by Disabled, Queer, and Fat Creators." *Slate*, December 4, 2019. https://slate.com /technology/2019/12/tiktok-disabled -users-videos-suppressed.html.

Bratton, Benjamin. "We Need to Talk About TED." *Guardian*, December 30, 2013. https://www.theguardian.com /commentisfree/2013/dec/30/we-need -to-talk-about-ted.

Brennan, Frederick. "Bitchute Claims to Be a Decentralized Platform—That's Not True." *Daily Dot*, November 27, 2019. https://www.dailydot.com/layer8 /bitchute-decentralization-claims.

Brennan, Matthew. *Attention Factory: The Story of TikTok and China's ByteDance*. China Channel, 2020.

Brice-Saddler, Michael, Avi Selk, and Eli Rosenberg. "Prankster Sentenced to 20 Years for Fake 911 Call That Led Police to Kill an Innocent Man." *Washington Post*, March 29, 2019.

Briscoe, Bob, Andrew Odlyzko, and Benjamin Tilly. "Metcalfe's Law Is Wrong: Communications Networks Increase in Value as They Add Members—but by How Much?" *IEEE Spectrum* 43, no. 7 (2006): 34–39.

Brown, Abram, and Abigail Freeman. "Top-Earning TikTok-ers 2022." *Forbes*, January 7, 2022. https://www.forbes.com/sites/abrambrown/2022/01/07/top-earning-tiktokers-charli-dixie-damelio-addison-rae-bella-poarch-josh-richards/?sh=57da476e3afa.

Browne, David. "'Danger Mouse's 'Grey Album' Could Never Happen Today. Here's Why That's a Shame." *Rolling Stone*, February 26, 2020. https://www.rollingstone.com/music/music-features/danger-mouse-grey-album-jay-z-beatles-history-957198.

Brynjolfsson, Erik, and Andrew McAfee. *The Second Machine Age: Work, Progress, and Prosperity in a Time of Brilliant Technologies*. New York: W. W. Norton, 2014.

Burgess, Jean, and Joshua Green. *YouTube: Online Video and Participatory Culture*. 2nd ed. Cambridge: Polity, 2018.

Burnett, L. D. "An Interview with David Hollinger." *Society for U.S. Intellectual History* (blog), November 2, 2012. https://s-usih.org/2012/11/an-interview-with-david-hollinger.

Bush, Vannevar. "As We May Think." *Atlantic*, July 1945. https://www.theatlantic.com/magazine/archive/1945/07/as-we-may-think/303881.

Cairncross, Frances. *The Death of Distance: How the Communications Revolution Is Changing Our Lives*. Boston: Harvard Business Review Press, 2001.

Carroll, David. "Is TikTok a Chinese Cambridge Analytica Data Bomb Waiting to Explode?" *Quartz*, May 7, 2019. https://qz.com/1613020/tiktok-might-be-a-chinese-cambridge-analytica-scale-privacy-threat.

Chan, Connie. "When AI Is the Product: The Rise of AI-Based Consumer Apps." Andreesen Horowitz, December 3, 2018. https://a16z.com/2018/12/03/when-ai-is-the-product-the-rise-of-ai-based-consumer-apps.

Cheney-Lippold, John. *We Are Data*. New York: New York University Press, 2017.

Cheng, Xu, Cameron Dale, and Jiangchuan Liu. "Statistics and Social Network of YouTube Videos." In *2008 16th International Workshop on Quality of Service*, IEEE (2008): 229–38.

Cherney, Max A. "YouTube Creators were Paid $30 billion by Alphabet." *Barrons*, August 23, 2021. https://www.barrons.com/articles/youtube-creators-30-billion-51629751124.

Chmielewski, Dawn. "Spotify Profit Margins Squeezed by Slow Ad Growth; Stock Sinks." Reuters, October 25, 2022. https://www.reuters.com/technology/spotify-beats-revenue-forecasts-ad-growth-slow-2022-10-25.

Chotiner, Isaac. "The Underworld of Online Content Moderation." *New Yorker*, July 5, 2019. https://www.newyorker.com/news/q-and-a/the-underworld-of-online-content-moderation.

Chun, Wendy Hui Kyong. "The Enduring Ephemeral, or the Future Is a Memory." *Critical Inquiry* 35, no. 1 (2008): 148–71.

Clark, Marshall. "The Tiktok 'Blackout Challenge' Has Now Allegedly Killed Seven Kids." *Verge*, July 7, 2022. https://www.theverge.com/2022/7/7/23199058/tiktok-lawsuits-blackout-challenge-children-death.

Cockerell, Isobel. "Inside China's Massive Surveillance Operation." *Wired*, May 9, 2019. https://www.wired.com/story/inside-chinas-massive-surveillance-operation.

Coe, Julie. "TED's Chris Anderson." *Departures*, March 1, 2012. https://www.departures.com/lifestyle/technology-gadgets/ted%E2%80%99s-chris-anderson.

Costa, Brandon. "Fox Sports Worked a Live Mirrorless Camera into an NFL Broadcast—And It Caught Viewers' Attention." Sportsvideo.org, December 22, 2020. https://www.sportsvideo.org/2020/12/22/fox-sports-worked-a-live-mirrorless-camera-into-an-nfl-broadcast-and-it-caught-viewers-attention.

Cotter, Kelley. "Playing the Visibility Game: How Digital Influencers and

Algorithms Negotiate Influence on Instagram." *New Media and Society* 21, no. 4 (2019): 895–913.

Cox, Joseph. "Internal Google Email Says Moderating Christchurch Manifesto 'Particularly Challenging.'" *Vice Motherboard*, March 19, 2019. https://www.vice.com/en_us/article/eve9ke/internal-google-email-christchurch-content-moderation-manifesto.

Cross, Gary. *Consumed Nostalgia: Memory in the Age of Fast Capitalism.* New York: Columbia University Press, 2015.

Cveticanin, Nikolina. "Twitch Stats and Demographics for 2022." DataProf, last updated August 24, 2022. https://dataprot.net/statistics/twitch-stats.

Dean, Brian. "TikTok User Statistics." Backlink, January 5, 2022. https://backlinko.com/tiktok-users.

Dessem, Matthew. "The Homestar Runner Guys Celebrated Record Store Day by Making a New Fisher-Price Record." *Slate*, April 22, 2018. https://slate.com/culture/2018/04/the-homestar-runner-guys-celebrated-record-store-day-by-making-a-new-fisher-price-record.html.

Dickson, E. J. "David Dobrik Was the King of YouTube. Then He Went Too Far." *Rolling Stone*, June 23, 2021. https://www.rollingstone.com/culture/culture-features/david-dobrik-youtube-vlog-squad-profile-1185706.

Drozd, Brandy, Emily Couvillon, and Andrea Suarez. "Medical YouTube Videos and Methods of Evaluation: Literature Review." *JMIR Medical Education* 4, no. 1 (2018): e8527.

Dwoskin, Elizabeth. "YouTube's Arbitrary Standards: Stars Keep Making Money Even After Breaking the Rules." *Washington Post*, August 9, 2019. https://www.washingtonpost.com/technology/2019/08/09/youtubes-arbitrary-standards-stars-keep-making-money-even-after-breaking-rules.

Ebert, John David. *The New Media Invasion: Digital Technologies and the World They Unmake.* Jefferson, NC: McFarland, 2011.

Economist. "A Brief History of Wi-Fi." June 12, 2004. https://www.economist.com/technology-quarterly/2004/06/12/a-brief-history-of-wi-fi.

Eisenstein, Elizabeth. *The Printing Press as an Agent of Change.* Vol. 1. Cambridge: Cambridge University Press, 1979.

Fiesler, Casey, and Brianna Dym. "Moving Across Lands: Online Platform Migration in Fandom Communities." *Proceedings of the ACM on Human-Computer Interaction* 4, no. CSCW1 (2020): 1–25.

Fishman, Donald A. "Review and Criticism: Research Pioneer Tribute— Rethinking Marshall McLuhan: Reflections on a Media Theorist." *Journal of Broadcasting and Electronic Media* 50, no. 3 (2006): 567–74.

Fortney, Lucas. "How Amazon's Twitch Platform Makes Money." *Investopedia*, October 20, 2019. https://www.investopedia.com/investing/how-does-twitch-amazons-video-game-streaming-platform-make-money.

Future Music. "A Brief History of Ableton Live." Musicradar, January 13, 2011. https://www.musicradar.com/tuition/tech/a-brief-history-of-ableton-live-357837.

Gehl, Robert W. Lucas Moyer-Horner, and Sara K. Yeo. "Training Computers to See Internet Pornography: Gender and Sexual Discrimination in Computer Vision Science." *Television and New Media* 18, no. 6 (2017): 529–47.

Ghaffary, Ahirin. "Facebook Is Banning Deepfake Videos." *Vox*, January 7, 2020. https://www.vox.com/recode/2020/1/7/21055024/facebook-ban-deepfake-video.

Gillespie, Tarleton. "Content Moderation, AI, and the Question of Scale." *Big Data and Society* 7, no. 2 (2020).

———. *Custodians of the Internet: Platforms, Content Moderation, and the Hidden Decisions That Shape Social Media.* New Haven: Yale University Press, 2018.

———. "The Politics of 'Platforms.'" *New Media and Society* 12, no. 3 (2010): 347–64.

Gorwa, Robert, Reuben Binns, and Christian Katzenbach. "Algorithmic Content Moderation: Technical and Political

208

Challenges in the Automation of Platform Governance." *Big Data and Society* 7, no. 1 (2020).

Grandinetti, Justin. "Examining Embedded Apparatuses of AI in Facebook and TikTok." *AI and Society* 30, no. 4 (2021): 1–14.

Grayson, Nathan. "Twitch Streamers Traumatized After Four 'Swattings' in a Week." *Washington Post*, August 12, 2022.

Grind, Kirsten, Sam Schechner, Robert McMillan, and John West. "How Google Interferes with Its Search Algorithms and Changes Your Results: The Internet Giant Uses Blacklists, Algorithm Tweaks and an Army of Contractors to Shape What You See." *Wall Street Journal*, November 15, 2019.

Grothaus, Michael. "Hotels Are Sick of Instagram 'Influencers' Pestering for Free Stays." *Fast Company*, June 18, 2018. https://www.fastcompany .com/40586222/hotels-are-sick-of -instagram-influencers-pestering-for -free-stays.

Gurman, Mark. "Apple Races to Temper Outcry Over Child-Porn Tracking System." *Bloomberg*, August 13, 2021. https://www.bloomberg.com/news /articles/2021-08-13/apple-warns -staff-to-be-ready-for-questions -on-child-porn-issue.

Hale, David M. "Social Media Stardom: How Changes to NIL Will Benefit Athlete-Influencers Across the NCAA." *ESPN*, March 8, 2021. https: //www.espn.com/womens-college -basketball/story/_/id/30945653/ social-media-stardom-how-changes-nil -benefit-athlete-influencers-ncaa.

Hamilton, Isobel Asher. "YouTube's Human Moderators Couldn't Stem the Deluge of Christchurch Massacre Videos, so YouTube Benched Them." *Business Insider*, March 18, 2019. https://www.businessinsider.com /youtube-benched-humans-and -used-ai-to-deal-with-christchurch -massacre-2019-3.

Hamilton, Kevin, Christian Sandvig, Karrie Karahalios, and Motahhare Eslami. "A Path to Understanding the Effects of Algorithm Awareness." *CHI EA '14*: 631–42.

Harouni, Houman. "The Sound of TED: A Case for Distaste." *American Reader*, accessed January 10, 2023. https:// theamericanreader.com/the-sound -of-ted-a-case-for-distaste.

Harris, Elizabeth A. "How TikTok Became a Bestseller Machine." *New York Times*, July 1, 2022. https://www.nytimes .com/2022/07/01/books/tiktok-books -booktok.html.

Harrison, Nate, and Eduardo Navas. "Mashup." In *Keywords in Remix Studies*, edited by Eduardo Navas, Owen Gallagher, and xtine burrough, 188–90. New York: Routledge, 2017.

Harwell, Drew. "A Face-Scanning Algorithm Increasingly Decides Whether You Deserve the Job." *Washington Post*, November 6, 2019. https://www .washingtonpost.com/technology /2019/10/22/ai-hiring-face-scanning -algorithm-increasingly-decides -whether-you-deserve-job.

———. "Top AI Researchers Race to Detect 'Deepfake' Videos: 'We Are Outgunned.'" *Washington Post*, June 12, 2019. https://www.washingtonpost .com/technology/2019/06/12/top-ai -researchers-race-detect-deepfake -videos-we-are-outgunned.

Hatmaker, Taylor. "Twitch Sues Two Users for Harassing Streamers with Hate Raids." *TechCrunch*, September 13, 2021. https://techcrunch.com/2021/09 /13/twitch-hate-raids-lawsuits.

Hendler, James, and Jennifer Golbeck. "Metcalfe's Law, Web 2.0, and the Semantic Web." *Journal of Web Semantics* 6, no. 1 (2008): 14–20.

Herbert, Daniel, Amanda D. Lotz, and Lee Marshall. "Approaching Media Industries Comparatively: A Case Study of Streaming." *International Journal of Cultural Studies* 22, no. 3 (2019): 349–66.

Hoggins, Tom. "How YouTube Changed the World: Video Games." *Telegraph*, February 9, 2015. https://s.telegraph .co.uk/graphics/projects/youtube.

Hollinger, David A. "Historians and the Discourse of Intellectuals." In *New Directions in American Intellectual History*, edited by John Higham and

Paul K. Conklin, 42–63. Baltimore: Johns Hopkins University Press, 1979.

Horrigan, John B. "Home Broadband 2008." Pew Research Center, last modified July 2, 2008. https://www.pewinter net.org/2008/07/02/home-broadband -2008.

Horton, Donald, and R. Richard Wohl. "Mass Communication and Para-social Interaction: Observations on Intimacy at a Distance." *Psychiatry* 19, no. 3 (1956): 215–29.

"How TikTok's Owner Became the World's Most Valuable Unicorn." CB Insights report, June 18, 2020. https://www .cbinsights.com/research/report/byte dance-tiktok-unicorn/.

Hudders, Liselot, Steffi De Jans, and Marijke De Veirman. "The Commercialization of Social Media Stars: A Literature Review and Conceptual Framework on the Strategic Use of Social Media Influencers." *International Journal of Advertising: The Review of Marketing Communications* 40, no. 3 (2021): 24–67.

Jack, Margaret. "Infrastructural Restitution: Cambodian Postwar Media Reconstruction and the Geopolitics of Technology." PhD diss., Cornell University, 2020.

Jarboe, Greg. "Why You Must Unlearn What You Know About the YouTube Algorithm." *Search Engine Journal*, March 13, 2019. https://www.search enginejournal.com/youtube -algorithm-findings/296291/#close.

Jenkins, Henry, Mizuko Ito, and danah boyd. *Participatory Culture in a Networked Era*. Cambridge: Polity, 2016.

Johnson, Joseph, and Natalie Schell-Busey. "Old Message in a New Bottle: Taking Gang Rivalries Online Through Rap Battle Music Videos on YouTube." *Journal of Qualitative Criminal Justice and Criminology* 4, no. 1 (2016): 42–81.

Jones, Lora, and Hannah Gelbart. "Make-Up: Have YouTube Stars Boosted Beauty Sales?" *BBC*, June 7, 2018. https:// www.bbc.com/news/business -43966384.

Jones, Maggie. "What Teenagers Are Learning from Online Porn." *New York Times*, February 7, 2018. https:// www.nytimes.com/2018/02/07/maga zine/teenagers-learning-online-porn -literacy-sex-education.html.

Jordan, John M. *3D Printing*. MIT Press Essential Knowledge. Cambridge, MA: MIT Press, 2019.

Karic, Berina, Veronica Moino, Andrew Nolin, Ashley Andrews, and Paul Brisson. "Evaluation of Surgical Educational Videos Available for Third Year Medical Students." *Medical Education Online* 25, no. 1 (2020).

Karizat, Nadia, Dan Delmonaco, Motahhare Eslami, and Nazanin Andalibi. "Algorithmic Folk Theories and Identity: How TikTok Users Co-produce Knowledge of Identity and Engage in Algorithmic Resistance." *Proceedings of the ACM on Human-Computer Interaction* 5, no. CSCW2 (2021): 1–44.

Katz, James E. "Struggle in Cyberspace: Fact and Friction on the World Wide Web." *Annals of the American Academy of Political and Social Science* 560, no. 1 (1998): 194–99.

Katz, Michael L., and Carl Shapiro. "Network Externalities, Competition, and Compatibility." *American Economic Review* 75, no. 3 (1985): 424–40.

Kavoori, Anandam. *Reading YouTube: The Critical Viewers Guide*. New York: Peter Lang, 2011.

Kaye, D. Bondy Valdovinos, Xu Chen, and Jing Zeng. "The Co-Evolution of Two Chinese Mobile Short Video Apps: Parallel Platformization of Douyin and TikTok." *Mobile Media and Communication* 9, no. 2 (2021): 229–53.

Keiles, Jamie Lauren. "How A.S.M.R. Became a Sensation." *New York Times*, April 4, 2019. https://www.nytimes.com /2019/04/04/magazine/how-asmr -videos-became-a-sensation-youtube .html.

Keller, Michael H., and Gabrielle J. X. Dance. "Child Abusers Run Rampant as Tech Companies Look the Other Way." *New York Times*, November 9, 2019. https://www.nytimes.com/interac tive/2019/11/09/us/internet-child -sex-abuse.html.

Khan, Salman. *The One World Schoolhouse.* New York: Twelve, 2012.

Klug, Daniel, Yiluo Qin, Morgan Evans, and Geoff Kaufman. "Trick and Please: A Mixed-Method Study on User Assumptions About the Tiktok Algorithm." In *WebSci '21: Proceedings of the 13th ACM Web Science Conference 2021*, 84–92. New York: Association for Computing Machinery, 2021.

Knight, Austin. "Design Debt." *Invision*, November 3, 2016. https://www .invisionapp.com/inside-design /design-debt.

Knowledge at Wharton Staff. "How Can Social Media Firms Tackle Hate Speech?" *Knowledge at Wharton*, September 22, 2018. https://knowl edge.wharton.upenn.edu/article /can-social-media-firms-tackle-hate -speech.

Kohavi, Ron, and Stefan Thomke. "The Surprising Power of Online Experiments." *Harvard Business Review* 95, no. 5 (2017): 74–82.

Kriegel, Elana R., Bojan Lazarevic, Christian E. Athanasian, and Ruth L. Milanaik. "TikTok, Tide Pods and Tiger King: Health Implications of Trends Taking over Pediatric Populations." *Current Opinion in Pediatrics* 33, no. 1 (2021): 170–77.

Kron, Josh. "Mission from God: The Upstart Christian Sect Driving Invisible Children and Changing Africa." *Atlantic*, April 10, 2012. https://www.theatlantic.com /international/archive/2012 /04/mission-from-god-the -upstart-christian-sect-driving -invisible-children-and-changing -africa/255626.

Landrum, Asheley R., Alex Olshansky, and Othello Richards. "Differential Susceptibility to Misleading Flat Earth Arguments on YouTube." *Media Psychology* 24, no. 1 (2021): 136–65.

Lave, Jean, and Etienne Wenger. *Situated Learning: Legitimate Peripheral Participation*. Cambridge: Cambridge University Press, 1991.

Leskin, Paige. "TikTok Reportedly has 18 Million Users Who Are 14 or Younger, Renewing Concerns for Children's Safety." *Business Insider*, August 14, 2020. https://www.businessinsider .com/tiktok-children-users-data -privacy-safety-concerns-coppa -ftc-report-2020-8.

———. "YouTube Is 15 Years Old. Here's a Timeline of How YouTube Was Founded, Its Rise to Video Behemoth, and Its Biggest Controversies Along Way." *Business Insider*, May 30, 2020. https://www .businessinsider.com/history-of -youtube-in-photos-2015-10.

Lewis, Rebecca. "'This Is What the News Won't Show You': YouTube Creators and the Reactionary Politics of Micro-Celebrity." *Television and New Media* 21, no. 2 (2020): 201–17. https://journals.sagepub.com/doi/abs /10.1177/1527476419879919?journalC ode=tvna.

Li, Heidi Oi-Yee, Adrian Bailey, David Huynh, and James Chan. "YouTube as a Source of Information on COVID-19: A Pandemic of Misinformation?" *BMJ Global Health* 5, no. 5 (2020): e002604.

Light, Elias. "Lil Nas X's 'Old Town Road' Was a Country Hit. Then Country Changed Its Mind." *Rolling Stone*, March 29, 2019. https://www.rolling stone.com/music/music-features/ lil-nas-x-old-town-road-810844.

Lin, Liza. "TikTok CEO Kevin Mayer Quits as Trump Pushes Chinese App to Sell U.S. Business." *Wall Street Journal*, August 27, 2020. https://www.wsj .com/articles/tiktok-ceo-kevin-mayer -quits-as-trump-pushes-chinese-app -to-sell-u-s-business-11598505535.

Lopez, Mark Hugo, Ana Gonzalez-Barrera, and Eileen Patten. "Closing the Digital Divide: Latinos and Technology Adoption." Pew Research Center, last modified March 7, 2013. https://www.pewresearch.org /hispanic/2013/03/07/closing-the -digital-divide-latinos-and -technology-adoption.

Lorenz, Taylor, Kellen Browning, and Sheera Frenkel. "TikTok Teens and K-Pop Stans Say They Sank Trump Rally." *New York Times*, June 21, 2020. https://www.nytimes.com/2020/06/21 /style/tiktok-trump-rally-tulsa.html.

Lotz, Amanda. *Portals: A Treatise on Internet-Distributed Television.* Ann Arbor: Michigan Publishing, University of Michigan Library, 2017.

Mackinnon, Katie. "The Death of Geocities: Seeking Destruction and Platform Eulogies in Web Archives." *Internet Histories* 6, no. 1–2 (2022): 237–52.

Madrigal, Alexis. "How Netflix Reverse-Engineered Hollywood." *Atlantic*, January 2, 2014. https://www .theatlantic.com/technology/archive /2014/01/how-netflix-reverse -engineered-hollywood/282679/.

Manne, Kate. *Down Girl: The Logic of Misogyny.* New York: Oxford University Press, 2017.

Marantz, Andrew. "Why Facebook Can't Fix Itself." *New Yorker*, October 12, 2020. https://www.newyorker.com /magazine/2020/10/19/why-facebook -cant-fix-itself.

Marcus, Josh. "Beverly Hills Police Are Playing Beatles Songs to Avoid Being Filmed on Instagram, Activist Claims." *Independent*, February 12, 2021. https://www.independent.co.uk /news/world/americas/beverly-hills -police-beatles-instagram-b1801643 .html.

Marshall, Carla. "Football on YouTube." Tubular Insights, October 12, 2015. https://tubularinsights.com/you tube-football.

Martineau, Paris. "Facebook's New Content Moderation Tools Put Posts in Context." *Wired*, July 3, 2019. https:// www.wired.com/story/facebooks-new -content-moderation-tools-put -posts-in-context.

McDaniel, Byrd. "Popular Music Reaction Videos: Reactivity, Creator Labor, and the Performance of Listening Online." *New Media and Society* 23, no. 6 (June 2021): 1624–41.

McIntyre, Hugh. "Despite Gains with Streaming, YouTube Is Still How the World Listens to Music." *Forbes*, April 14, 2017. https://www.forbes .com/sites/hughmcintyre/2017/04 /14/despite-gains-with-streaming -youtube-is-still-how-the-world -listens-to-music/#28a5f9f67a8f.

Metcalfe, Bob. "Metcalfe's Law After 40 Years of Ethernet." *Computer* 46, no. 12 (2013): 26–31.

Meyer, Robinson. "Why Twitter May Be Ruinous for the Left." *Atlantic*, January 17, 2020. https://www .theatlantic.com/technology/archive /2020/01/how-twitter-harms-left /605098/.

Montfort, Nick, and Ian Bogost. *Racing the Beam: The Atari Video Computer System.* Cambridge, MA: MIT Press, 2009.

Mozur, Paul, Ryan Mac, and Chang Che. "TikTok Browser Could Track Users' Keystrokes, According to New Research." *New York Times*, August 19, 2022. https://www.nytimes.com /2022/08/19/technology/tiktok -browser-tracking.html.

Munger, Kevin, and Joseph Phillips. "A Supply and Demand Framework for YouTube Politics." Penn State Political Science, Working Paper, October 1, 2019. https://osf.io/73jys.

Narayanan, Vidya, Vlad Barash, John Kelly, Bence Kollanyi, Lisa-Maria Neudert, and Philip N. Howard. "Polarization, Partisanship and Junk News Consumption over Social Media in the US." *ArXiv* (February 6, 2018): 1–9.

Neate, Rupert. "Ryan Kaji, 9, Earns $29.5m as This Year's Highest-Paid YouTuber." *Guardian*, December 18, 2020. https:// www.theguardian.com/technology /2020/dec/18/ryan-kaji-9-earns -30m-as-this-years-highest-paid -youtuber.

Newport, Cal. "TikTok and the Fall of the Social Media Giants." *New Yorker*, July 28, 2022. https://www.newyorker .com/culture/cultural-comment /tiktok-and-the-fall-of-the -social-media-giants.

Newton, Casey. "Facebook Will Pay $52 Million in Settlement with Moderators Who Developed PTSD on the Job." *Verge*, May 12, 2020. https://www.theverge.com/2020 /5/12/21255870/facebook-content -moderator-settlement-scola-ptsd -mental-health.

———. "How the 'Plandemic' Video Hoax Went Viral." *Verge*, May 12, 2020.

https://www.theverge.com/2020/5/12
/21254184/how-plandemic-went-viral
-facebook-youtube.

———. "The Terror Queue." *Verge*,
December 16, 2019. https://www
.theverge.com/2019/12/16/2102
1005/google-youtube-moderators
-ptsd-accenture-violent-disturbing
-content-interviews-video.

Noer, Michael. "One Man, One Computer,
10 Million Students: How Khan
Academy Is Reinventing Education."
Forbes, November 2, 2012. https://
www.forbes.com/sites/michaelnoer
/2012/11/02/one-man-one-computer
-10-million-students-how-khan
-academy-is-reinventing-education
/#3fa520f644e0.

O'Dell, Liam. "Musical.ly Speaking: How
TikTok Is Keeping On-Track with
Music and Copyright." *Teneighty*,
April 13, 2020. https://teneighty
magazine.com/2020/04/13/musical-ly
-speaking-how-tiktok-is-keeping-on
-track-with-music-and-copyright.

Ohlheiser, Abby, and Gene Park. "The
Forever War of PewDiePie,
YouTube's Biggest Creator."
Washington Post, December 20, 2018.
https://www.washingtonpost.com
/technology/2018/12/20/forever-war
-pewdiepie-youtubes-biggest-creator.

O'Reilly, Tim. "What Is Web 2.0: Design
Patterns and Business Models for
the Next Generation of Software."
O'Reilly, September 30, 2005. https://
www.oreilly.com/lpt/a/1.

Orr, Julien. *Talking About Machines: An
Ethnography of a Modern Job*. Ithaca:
Cornell University Press, 1996.

Palmer, Alex W. "How TikTok Became a
Diplomatic Crisis." *New York Times*,
December 20, 2022.

Parker, Laura A. "The Cult of PewDiePie:
How a Swedish Gamer Became
YouTube's Biggest Star." *Rolling
Stone*, December 16, 2015.
https://www.rollingstone.com
/culture/culture-news/the-cult
-of-pewdiepie-how-a-swedish-gamer
-became-youtubes-biggest-star
-228730.

Paumgarten, Nick. "Looking for Someone."
New Yorker, June 27, 2011. https://

www.newyorker.com/magazine/2011
/07/04/looking-for-someone.

Perez, Sarah. "Kids Now Spend Nearly as
Much Time Watching TikTok as
YouTube in US, UK and Spain."
TechCrunch, June 4, 2020. https://
techcrunch.com/2020/06/04
/kids-now-spend-nearly-as-much
-time-watching-tiktok-as-youtube-in
-u-s-u-k-and-spain.

Perrin, Andrew, and Monica Anderson.
"Share of U.S. Adults Using Social
Media, Including Facebook, Is
Mostly Unchanged Since 2018."
Pew Research Center, last modified April 10, 2019. https://www
.pewresearch.org/fact-tank/2019
/04/10/share-of-u-s-adults-using
-social-media-including-facebook
-is-mostly-unchanged-since-2018.

Phillips, Grant. "Charli D'Amelio's Top 10
Brand Deals and Endorsements."
Richest, March 29, 2021. https://
www.therichest.com/rich-powerful
/charli-damelio-brand-deals
-endorsements.

Phillips, Whitney. *This Is Why We Can't
Have Nice Things: Mapping the
Relationship Between Online Trolling
and Mainstream Culture*. Cambridge,
MA: MIT Press, 2015.

Pierson, David. "Youtube's Balancing Act:
Stars vs. Advertisers; The Platform
Changed Its Ad Policies After
Controversial Videos Bruised Its
Image. Now Its Creators Are Upset."
Los Angeles Times, January 30, 2018.

Pilipets, Elena, and Susanna Paasonen.
"Nipples, Memes, and Algorithmic
Failure: NSFW Critique of Tumblr
Censorship." *New Media and Society*
24, no. 6 (2022): 1459–80.

Plantin, Jean-Christophe, Carl Lagoze,
Paul N. Edwards, and Christian
Sandvig. "Infrastructure Studies
Meet Platform Studies in the Age of
Google and Facebook." *New Media
and Society* 20, no. 1 (2018): 293–310.

Poerio, Giulia Lara, Emma Blakey, Thomas
J. Hostler, and Theresa Veltri. "More
Than a Feeling: Autonomous Sensory
Meridian Response (ASMR) Is
Characterized by Reliable Changes in
Affect and Physiology." *PLOS ONE* 13,
no. 6 (2018): e0196645.

Rainie, Lee, Mark Jurkowitz, Michael Dimock, and Shawn Neidorf. "The Viral Kony 2012 Video." Pew Research Center: Internet and Technology, last modified March 15, 2012. https://www.pewresearch.org/internet/2012/03/15/the-viral-kony-2012-video.

Ramli, David, and Shelly Banjo. "The Kids Use TikTok Now Because Data-Mined Videos Are So Much Fun." *Bloomberg Businessweek*, April 17, 2019. https://www.bloomberg.com/news/features/2019-04-18/tiktok-brings-chinese-style-censorship-to-america-s-tweens.

Rasmussen, Leslie. "Parasocial Interaction in the Digital Age: An Examination of Relationship Building and the Effectiveness of YouTube Celebrities." *Journal of Social Media in Society* 7 (2018): 280–94. https://www.thejsms.org/index.php/JSMS/article/view/364.

Rizzo, Lillian. "NFL 'Sunday Ticket' Goes to Youtube in Seven-Year, $2 Billion Annual Deal." CNBC, December 22, 2022. https://www.cnbc.com/2022/12/22/nfl-sunday-ticket-youtube-tv.html.

Robbins, Martin. "The Trouble with TED Talks." *New Statesman*, September 10, 2012. https://www.newstatesman.com/martin-robbins/2012/09/trouble-ted-talks.

Roberts, Sarah T. *Behind the Screen: Content Moderation in the Shadows of Social Media*. New Haven: Yale University Press, 2019.

Rodriguez, Salvador. "Tiktok Insiders Say Social Media Company Is Tightly Controlled by Chinese Parent Bytedance." CNBC, June 25, 2021. https://www.cnbc.com/2021/06/25/tiktok-insiders-say-chinese-parent-bytedance-in-control.html.

Romm, Tony, Elizabeth Dwoskin, and Craig Timberg. "Youtube Under Federal Investigation over Allegations It Violates Children's Privacy." *Washington Post*, June 19, 2019. https://www.washingtonpost.com/technology/2019/06/19/facing-federal-investigation-youtube-is-considering-broad-changes-childrens-content.

Routledge, Clay. *Nostalgia: A Psychological Resource*. New York: Routledge, 2016.

Saloner, Garth, and Andrea Shepard. "Adoption of Technologies with Network Effects: An Empirical Examination of the Adoption of Automated Teller Machines." National Bureau of Economic Research, Working Paper 4048, April 1992.

Sanders, Sam. "The 'Kony 2012' Effect: Recovering from A Viral Sensation." NPR, June 14, 2014. https://www.npr.org/2014/06/14/321853244/the-kony-2012-effect-recovering-from-a-viral-sensation.

Sartariano, Adam, and Mike Isaac. "The Silent Partner Cleaning Up Facebook for $500 Million a Year." *New York Times*, August 31, 2021. https://www.nytimes.com/2021/08/31/technology/facebook-accenture-content-moderation.html.

Sawyer, Steve, and Mohammad Jarrahi. "The Sociotechnical Perspective." *Information Systems and Information Technology* 2 (2014): 1–39.

Schellewald, Andreas. "On Getting Carried Away by the TikTok Algorithm." *AoIR Selected Papers of Internet Research* (2021).

Shalavi, Ginan, and Stephanie Thomson. "How Online Video Has Transformed the World of Sports." Think with Google, January 2019. https://www.thinkwithgoogle.com/advertising-channels/video/sports-fan-video-consumption.

Shaw, Lucas, and Mark Bergen. "With Covid Crushing Advertising, YouTubers Turn to Subscriptions." *Bloomberg*, August 3, 2020. https://www.bloomberg.com/news/articles/2020-08-03/youtube-influencers-charge-for-subscriptions-after-coronavirus-hits-ads.

Shirky, Clay. *Here Comes Everybody: The Power of Organizing Without Organizations*. New York: Penguin, 2008.

Simpson, Ellen, and Bryan Semaan. "For You, or For 'You'? Everyday LGBTQ+ Encounters with TikTok." *Proceedings of the ACM on Human-Computer Interaction* 4, no. CSCW3 (2021): 1–34.

Sleiman, Jad. "The Surprising Legacy of the ALS Ice Bucket Challenge." *WHYY* podcast, August 22, 2022. https://whyy.org/segments/the-surprising-legacy-of-the-als-ice-bucket-challenge.

Snyder, Mike. "AT&T, Disney, Epic Games Drop YouTube Ads Over Concerns of Pedophile Comments on Videos." *USA Today*, February 22, 2019. https://www.usatoday.com/story/tech/news/2019/02/22/at-t-disney-epic-games-pull-youtube-ads-child-exploitation-concerns-pedophiles/2948825002.

Solon, Olivia, and Sam Levin. "How Google's Search Algorithm Spreads False Information with a Rightwing Bias." *Guardian*, December 16, 2016. https://www.theguardian.com/technology/2016/dec/16/google-autocomplete-rightwing-bias-algorithm-political-propaganda.

Solsman, Joan E. "YouTube's AI Is the Puppet Master over Most of What You Watch." *CNet*, January 10, 2018. https://www.cnet.com/news/youtube-ces-2018-neal-mohan.

Sorvino, Chloe. "Could Mr. Beast Be the First YouTuber Billionaire?" *Forbes*, November 30, 2022. https://www.forbes.com/sites/chloesorvino/2022/11/30/could-mrbeast-be-the-first-youtuber-billionaire/?sh=495a4f04191a.

Squires, Bethy. "The 'Incredible Treasure Chest' of Homestar Runner." *Vulture*, March 2, 2022. https://www.vulture.com/article/homestar-runner-krister-johnson.html.

Stempel, Jonathan. "Google, Viacom Settle Landmark YouTube Lawsuit." *Reuters*, March 18, 2014. https://www.reuters.com/article/us-google-viacom-lawsuit/google-viacom-settle-landmark-youtube-lawsuit-idUSBREA2H11220140318.

Sterne, Jonathan. "The Preservation Paradox in Digital Audio." In *Sound Souvenirs: Audio Technologies, Memory and Cultural Practices*, edited by Karin Bijsterveld and Jose van Dijck, 55–65. Amsterdam: Amsterdam University Press, 2009.

Stuart, Forrest. *Ballad of the Bullet: Gangs, Drill Music, and the Power of Online Infamy*. Princeton, NJ: Princeton University Press, 2020.

Taylor, T. L. *Watch Me Play: Twitch and the Rise of Game Live Streaming*. Princeton: Princeton University Press, 2018.

Teitell, Beth. "Who Would Spend $600 for a Hair Dryer? You'd Be Surprised." *Boston Globe*, January 8, 2023. https://www.bostonglobe.com/2023/01/08/metro/who-would-spend-600-hair-dryer-youd-be-surprised.

Teng, Elaine. "Can YouTube Star Logan Paul Find Redemption in Boxing?" *ESPN*, November 6, 2019. https://www.espn.com/boxing/story/_/id/28008560/can-youtube-star-logan-paul-find-redemption-boxing.

Thomas, John C., Wendy A. Kellogg, and Thomas Erickson. "The Knowledge Management Puzzle: Human and Social Factors in Knowledge Management." *IBM Systems Journal* 40, no. 4 (2001): 863–84.

Thompson, Clive. "YouTube's Plot to Silence Conspiracy Theories." *Wired*, September 18, 2020. https://www.wired.com/story/youtube-algorithm-silence-conspiracy-theories.

Turner, Fred. *From Counterculture to Cyberculture: Stewart Brand, the Whole Earth Network, and the Rise of Digital Utopianism*. Chicago: University of Chicago Press, 2006.

Vaccaro, Kristin, Christian Sandvig, and Karrie Karahalios. "'At the End of the Day Facebook Does What It Wants': How Users Experience Contesting Algorithmic Content Moderation." *Proceedings of the ACM on Human-Computer Interaction* 4 CSCW2 (2020): 1–22.

Van Alstyne, Marshall W., Geoffrey G. Parker, and Sangeet Paul Choudary. "Pipelines, Platforms, and the New Rules of Strategy." *Harvard Business Review* 94, no. 4 (2016): 54–62.

———. *Platform Revolution: How Networked Markets Are Transforming the Economy and How to Make Them Work for You*. New York: Norton, 2016.

Vanderbilt, Tom. "Why We Love How-to Videos." *Nautilus*, September 8, 2016.

215

http://nautil.us/issue/40/learning /why-we-love-how_to-videos.

Van Driel, Loes, and Delia Dumitrica. "Selling Brands While Staying 'Authentic': The Professionalization of Instagram Influencers." *Convergence* 27, no. 1 (2021): 66–84.

Van Hove, Leo. "Metcalfe's Law: Not So Wrong After All." *Netnomics: Economic Research and Electronic Networking* 15, no. 1 (June 2014): 1–8.

van Kessel, Patrick, Skye Toor, and Aaron Smith. "A Week in the Life of Popular YouTube Channels." Pew Research Center, last modified July 25, 2019. https://www.pewinternet .org/2019/07/25/a-week-in-the-life-of -popular-youtube-channels.

Vizcaíno-Verdú, Arantxa, and Crystal Abidin. "Music Challenge Memes on TikTok: Understanding In-Group Storytelling Videos." *International Journal of Communication* 16 (2022): 26.

Vogels, Emily A., Risa Gelles-Watnick, and Navid Massarat. "Teens, Social Media and Technology 2022." Pew Research Center, last modified August 10, 2022. https://www.pewresearch.org /internet/2022/08/10/teens-social -media-and-technology-2022.

Wang, Dan. "China's Sputnik Moment?" *Foreign Affairs*, July 29, 2021. https:// www.foreignaffairs.com/articles /united-states/2021-07-29/chinas -sputnik-moment.

Wark, McKensie. *Telesthesia: Communication, Culture and Class*. Cambridge: Polity, 2012.

Watson, Jon. "What Makes Flash So Insecure and What Are the Alternatives?" Comparitech, June 8, 2017. https:// www.comparitech.com/blog/inform ation-security/flash-vulnerabilities -security.

Watts, Duncan, and Steve Strogatz. "Collective Dynamics of 'Small-World' Networks." *Nature* 393 (1998): 440–42.

Wells, Georgia, Yang Jie, and Yoko Kubota. "TikTok's Videos Are Goofy. Its Strategy to Dominate Social Media Is Serious." *Wall Street Journal*, June 29, 2019. https://www.wsj.com/articles /tiktoks-videos-are-goofy-its-strategy -to-dominate-social-media-is-serious -11561780861.

Weltevrede, Esther, Anne Helmond, and Carolin Gerlitz. "The Politics of Real-Time: A Device Perspective on Social Media Platforms and Search Engines." *Theory, Culture, and Society* 31, no. 2 (2014): 125–50.

West, Sarah Myers. "Censored, Suspended, Shadowbanned: User Interpretations of Content Moderation on Social Media Platforms." *New Media and Society* 20, no. 11 (2018): 4366–83.

Whack, Errin Haynes. "AP-NORC Poll: Black Teens Most Active on Social Media Apps." *AP News*, April 20, 2017. https://apnews.com/7897c2f3b 1954da5a15f32cb5a6632fc/AP-NORC -Poll:-Black-teens-most-active -on-social-media-apps.

Wilson, Janelle L. *Nostalgia: Sanctuary of Meaning*. Lewisburg, PA: Bucknell University Press, 2005.

Wulf, Tim, Frank M. Schneider, and Stefan Beckert. "Watching Players: An Exploration of Media Enjoyment on Twitch." *Games and Culture* 15, no. 3 (May 2020): 328–46.

Zuboff, Shoshana. *The Age of Surveillance Capitalism: The Fight for a Human Future at the New Frontier of Power*. New York: Public Affairs, 2019.

Index